Penguin Education

Penguin Critical Anthologies
General Editor: Christopher Ricks

Geoffrey Chaucer
Edited by J. A. Burrow

Geoffrey Chaucer

A critical anthology

edited by J. A. Burrow

Penguin Books   Baltimore · Maryland

Penguin Books Ltd, Harmondsworth,
Middlesex, England
Penguin Books Inc., 7110 Ambassador Road,
Baltimore, Md 21207, U.S.A.
Penguin Books Australia Ltd, Ringwood,
Victoria, Australia

First published 1969
This selection copyright © J. A. Burrow, 1969
Introduction and notes copyright © J. A. Burrow, 1969

Made and printed in Great Britain by
Hazell Watson & Viney Ltd,
Aylesbury, Bucks
Set in Monotype Bembo

Contents

Preface   13

List of Plates   15

Table of Dates   17

Part One Contemporaneous Criticism

Introduction   19

Geoffrey Chaucer   25
from *House of Fame* (?1380)

Geoffrey Chaucer   25
from *Troilus and Criseyde* (?1385)

Eustache Deschamps   26
Ballade addressed to Chaucer (?1386)

Geoffrey Chaucer   28
from *Legend of Good Women* (?1386)

Thomas Usk   29
from *Testament of Love* (?1387)

Geoffrey Chaucer   30
from *Canterbury Tales* (?1387)

John Gower   30
from *Confessio Amantis* (?1390)

Geoffrey Chaucer   31
from *Complaint of Venus* (?after 1390)

Part Two The Developing Debate

Introduction   33

Thomas Hoccleve   41
from *Regement of Princes* (1412)

6 Contents

John Lydgate 42
from *Siege of Thebes* (1420–22)

Anonymous 44
from *Book of Courtesy* (1477)

William Caxton 44
from the Proem to his Second Edition of the *Canterbury Tales* (1484)

William Dunbar 45
from *The Golden Targe* (1503)

John Skelton 46
from *Philip Sparrow* (before 1509)

Gavin Douglas 47
from his translation of Virgil's *Aeneid* (1513)

Sir Brian Tuke 48
from the Preface to *Works of Geoffrey Chaucer* edited by W. Thynne (1532)

Gabriel Harvey 48
from his manuscript notes (after 1574)

George Puttenham 49
from *The Art of English Poesy* (1589)

Sir Philip Sidney 51
from *Apology for Poetry* (1595, but written about 1581)

Edmund Spenser 51
from *The Faerie Queene* (1596)

Sir Francis Beaumont 51
from a letter to Thomas Speght (1597)

Thomas Speght 54
from his edition, *Works of our Ancient and Learned English Poet Geoffrey Chaucer* (1598)

7   Contents

Richard Brathwait   55
from *A Comment upon . . . the 'Miller's Tale' and the
Wife of Bath* (1665, but begun before 1617)

Alexander Pope   58
from *The Wife of Bath her Prologue* (1714)

Edward Phillips   59
from *Theatrum Poetarum* (1675)

Joseph Addison   60
from *Account of the Greatest English Poets* (1694)

John Dryden   60
from the Preface to *Fables* (1700)

Alexander Pope   73
in conversation (1730)

Elizabeth Cooper   73
from *The Muses' Library* (1737)

Samuel Johnson   73
from 'The History of the English Language',
Dictionary of the English Language (1755)

Richard Hurd   74
from *Letters on Chivalry and Romance* (1762)

Thomas Warton   75
from *History of English Poetry* (1774)

Joseph Warton   76
from *Essay on the Genius and Writings of Pope* (1782)

William Blake   77
from *A Descriptive Catalogue* (1809)

George Crabbe   84
from the Preface to *Tales* (1812)

William Hazlitt   85
from 'On Chaucer and Spenser', *Lectures on the English
Poets* (1818)

S. T. Coleridge   88
in conversation (1834)

Francis Jeffrey, Lord Jeffrey   88
from a review of Sir James Mackintosh's *Memoirs* (1835)

Walter Savage Landor   89
from a letter to R. H. Horne (before 1841)

Leigh Hunt   89
from *Imagination and Fancy* (1844)

Leigh Hunt   90
from *Wit and Humour* (1846)

Leigh Hunt   90
from the Preface to *Stories in Verse* (1855)

John Ruskin   94
from *Lectures on Art* (1870)

James Russell Lowell   94
from 'Chaucer' 1870, *My Study Windows* (1871)

Walter Bagehot   95
from 'Charles Dickens' 1858, *Literary Studies* (1879)

Matthew Arnold   96
from 'The Study of Poetry' (1880)

A. C. Swinburne   101
from 'Short Notes on English Poets' 1880, *Miscellanies* (1886)

T. R. Lounsbury   103
from *Studies in Chaucer: His Life and Writings* (1892)

W. P. Ker   104
from 'Chaucer and the Renaissance', Clark Lecture (1912)

9   Contents

Part Three Modern Views

Introduction   113

G. L. Kittredge   119
from *Chaucer and his Poetry* (1915)

Virginia Woolf   125
from 'The Pastons and Chaucer', *The Common Reader*
(1925)

J. M. Manly   126
from *Chaucer and the Rhetoricians* (1926)

Walter Raleigh   131
from 'On Chaucer', *On Writing and Writers* (1926)

G. K. Chesterton   134
from *Chaucer* (1932)

A. E. Housman   136
from *The Name and Nature of Poetry* (1933)

John Livingston Lowes   138
from *Geoffrey Chaucer* (1934)

Ezra Pound   141
from *ABC of Reading* (1934)

C. S. Lewis   142
from 'Chaucer', *The Allegory of Love* (1936)

Ezra Pound   155
from *A Guide to Kulchur* (1938)

Nevill Coghill   156
from *The Poet Chaucer* (1949)

William Empson   159
from *The Structure of Complex Words* (1951)

Kemp Malone   160
from 'The *Legend of Good Women*', *Chapters on
Chaucer* (1951)

John Speirs   165
from *Chaucer the Maker* (1951)

10 Contents

Raymond Preston 166
from 'The *Nun's Priest's Tale*', *Chaucer* (1952)

W. K. Wimsatt 169
from 'One Relation of Rhyme to Reason', *The Verbal Icon* (1954)

J. A. W. Bennett 175
from *The 'Parlement of Foules': An Interpretation* (1957)

Charles Muscatine 176
from 'The Mixed Style', *Chaucer and the French Tradition* (1957)

Erich Auerbach 186
from *The Literary Language and its Public* (1958)

Paull F. Baum 188
from *Chaucer, A Critical Appreciation* (1958)

E. T. Donaldson 190
'*Troilus and Criseyde*', *Chaucer's Poetry: An Anthology for the Modern Reader* (1958)

Rosemary Woolf 206
'Chaucer as a Satirist in the *General Prologue* to the *Canterbury Tales*' (1959)

Bertrand H. Bronson 214
from *In Search of Chaucer* (1960)

J. V. Cunningham 218
'Convention as Structure: The *Prologue* to the *Canterbury Tales*', *Tradition and Poetic Structure* (1960)

R. E. Kaske 233
from 'Patristic Exegesis: The Defence' (1960)

John Stevens 239
from 'The "Game of Love"', *Music and Poetry in the Early Tudor Court* (1961)

R. Neuse 242
'The Knight: The First Mover in Chaucer's Human
Comedy' (1962)

Wolfgang Clemen 263
from *Chaucer's Early Poetry* (1963)

A. C. Spearing 265
'Criseyde's Dream', *Criticism and Medieval Poetry*
(1964)

F. W. Bateson 273
from *A Guide to English Literature* (1965)

P. G. Ruggiers 276
'The *Franklin's Tale*', *The Art of the Canterbury
Tales* (1967)

Gervase Mathew 285
from 'The International Court Culture', *The Court of
Richard II* (1968)

Acknowledgements 291

Select Bibliography 293

Index 297

Preface

Supplementary information on the source of various extracts in this collection is cited in the index, under the name of the author. Page- and line-references at the end of an extract refer to this source. All extracts dated before 1500 are given in their original spelling, according to the source; the spelling of all later extracts is modernized (except in the cases of Spenser and Blake) and Anglicized (except in the cases of Dunbar and Douglas). All quotations from Chaucer are corrected according to the Second Edition (1957) of F. N. Robinson's *Complete Works of Geoffrey Chaucer*, except in three places (pp. 92, 99 and 160). All footnotes to extracts dated before 1700 are the work of the present editor; all footnotes to later extracts are the individual authors' unless otherwise stated.

I am much indebted to the collection of material in Caroline Spurgeon's *Five Hundred Years of Chaucer Criticism and Allusion, 1357–1900*. I should like also to acknowledge the help and suggestions of Andrew Kimmens, Martin Lightfoot and Christopher Ricks, the General Editor of this series.

Jesus College, Oxford   J.A.B.

List of Plates

1 *Chaucer reading to the Court of Richard II.*
Anonymous illumination in a manuscript in the
possession of Corpus Christi College, Cambridge.
Early fifteenth century.

2 *The Pilgrimage to Canterbury.* A painting by
Thomas Stothard. Exhibited 1807. Stirling
Maxwell Collection, Pollok House.

3 *The Canterbury Pilgrims.* A painting by William
Blake. Exhibited 1809. Tate Gallery.

4 *Chaucer at the Court of Edward III.* A painting
by Ford Madox Brown. This is a second,
slightly altered version of an earlier painting
by Ford Madox Brown, exhibited in 1851.
The second version was begun in 1856 and
finished in 1868. Tate Gallery.

Table of Dates

1343 or 4	Geoffrey born, son of John Chaucer, wealthy London wine merchant.
?1357–?9	Page in household of Elizabeth, Countess of Ulster.
1360	Captured by French and ransomed by Edward III. In service of Edward's son, Lionel, Earl of Ulster.
1361–6	In Ireland with Lionel? Studying at Inner Temple? In household of King Edward?
1366	In Spain.
?1366	Marriage to Philippa (?daughter of Paon de Roet of Hainault).
1367–?73	In household of Edward III, as 'valet' and esquire.
1369 or 70	*Book of the Duchess*.
1372–3	In Italy, negotiating with Genoese. Also in Florence.
1374–86	Residence above the gate of Aldgate.
1374–86	Controller of wool custom and subsidy and petty custom in port of London.
1378	In Italy, negotiating with Barnabò Visconti, lord of Milan.
?1380	*House of Fame* (unfinished).
?1382	*Parliament of Fowls*.
1385–9	Justice of the Peace for Kent. Probably resident there until 1399. Represented the county in Parliament, 1386.
?1385	Completion of *Troilus and Criseyde*.
?1386	*Legend of Good Women* (unfinished).
?1387	Begins work on the *Canterbury Tales*.
1389–91	Clerk of the King's Works.
?1390–?1400	Substitute forester of the royal forest at North Petherton, Somerset.
1399–1400	Resident in house adjoining Lady Chapel of Westminster Abbey.
1400	Death and burial (with other courtiers and royal officials) in Westminster Abbey.

Part One **Contemporaneous Criticism**

Introduction

Nearly all the evidences for Chaucer's early reputation –
manuscript copies, complimentary references, literary borrowings –
belong to the years after his death in 1400. From his own life-time
there survive just three compliments, a handful of imitations and
borrowings, and no manuscripts of his poetry whatever. His name
occurs frequently in official records; but he is never spoken of there
as a poet. Yet what evidence there is suggests that he was already
famous. The French writer Eustache Deschamps knew him as
translator of the *Romance of the Rose* and sent him a gift of his own
poetry accompanied by a flattering ballade addressed to the 'great
translator, noble Geoffrey Chaucer' (p. 26). John Gower,
Chaucer's contemporary and friend, says that England is 'filled full
everywhere' with the songs of love which he composed in his
youth (p. 31). Another Londoner, the unfortunate Thomas Usk
who was beheaded in 1388, speaks of Chaucer as 'the noble
philosophical poet in English', and borrows freely from him in his
Testament of Love (p. 29). And even Chaucer himself, in his
Canterbury Tales, allows the Man of Law to suggest that his creator
was well-known as a prolific, if not very expert, story-teller:

'I kan right now no thrifty tale seyn
That Chaucer, thogh he kan but lewedly
On metres and on rymyng craftily,
Hath seyd hem in swich Englissh as he kan
Of olde tyme, as knoweth many a man;
And if he have noght seyd hem, leve brother,
In o book, he hath seyd hem in another.'

(II 46–52)

It is safe to assume, then, that Chaucer was widely read and
admired by his contemporaries in the city, the court, and no doubt
the provinces too. But what was he admired for? What did they
make of him? One can guess plenty of answers to this question;
but the only direct evidence is provided by Deschamps, Gower and

Usk. This evidence is not very satisfactory, since the author of a compliment does not write upon oath; but it deserves to be examined, since it is all we have.

The three authors agree most obviously in associating Chaucer with Love. Deschamps calls him 'an earthly God of Love in Albion', an English Cupid, and goes on to praise him for introducing that great handbook of courtly love-behaviour, the *Romance of the Rose*, to English readers. In Gower's poem, Venus describes Chaucer as her disciple, her poet and her own clerk. Chaucer, she says, has flooded England with poems composed for her sake, and she is obliged to him 'above all other'; but it is now time, perhaps, for him to take leave of such subjects – as Gower himself is doing at this point in the *Confessio Amantis*. In Usk's *Testament of Love* the speaker is Love, a personification whose multiple significance includes both human love (true love of a lady) and the love of God. She calls Chaucer 'her own true servant . . . which evermore him busieth and travaileth right sore her name to increase'. No one, she says, is equal to him 'in school of my rules'. These comments do not mean that Chaucer's contemporaries thought of him as a 'love-poet' in the modern sense. His poems served, not his own cause as a lover, but the cause of Love itself. He was the 'clerk of Venus', who sang the praises of his goddess and taught men how to serve her according to the 'rules'.

Deschamps and Usk also agree in speaking of Chaucer as a 'philosophical' poet. In the *Testament*, Usk cites him as an authority on the problem of the relationship between events and God's knowledge of them (see *Troilus and Criseyde*, IV 958–1078); and this suggests that he thought Chaucer 'philosophical' in something like the modern sense of that word. It is less clear what Deschamps had in mind. The point of the first part of his ballade is perhaps simply that Chaucer is an all-round man, both a man of affairs and a master of many branches of knowledge. The image of the 'lofty eagle', however, does suggest that Chaucer was adept in natural and metaphysical sciences and in the contemplation of exalted truths – such being the significance of the eagle in medieval symbolism. This view of Chaucer, as a lofty, contemplative poet and an authority in many branches of knowledge, is quite strange to modern readers; but it was held not only by Deschamps and Usk but also, two hundred years later, by men such as Edmund Spenser and his friend Gabriel Harvey, as we shall see in the next section.

Usk, Gower and Deschamps all agree, finally, in praising Chaucer's skill and facility as a writer. Usk's phrase, 'goodness of gentil manly speech', suggests that he appreciated Chaucer's sweet new style, an easy and well-bred ('gentil') manner which had little precedent in the English vernacular. Deschamps goes so far as to imply that Chaucer was the very first to civilize English poetry, by sowing 'flowers' (of rhetoric), planting a 'rose tree' (the *Romance of the Rose* translated), and generally establishing an 'orchard' of literary cultivation in the Isle of Giants. He speaks of Chaucer's 'sweet music', his 'good English', his conciseness of expression, and his skill in the arts of rhetoric. Chaucer, for him, is one of the great ones, an 'authority' whose command of the art of poetry entitles him to rank with Ovid.

The commendatory extravagances of Usk and Deschamps meet their match, in Chaucer's own work, in an equally conventional and impenetrable humility. Here, instead of the 'earthly God of Love in Albion', we meet the servant of the servants of Love, one whom the God of Love himself regards as lower than a worm. Instead of the 'lofty eagle' and master of all sciences, we meet the 'lewed', or unlearned, Geoffrey who, in the *House of Fame*, lies helpless in the claws of his eagle-guide and confesses himself ignorant of sound-waves and constellations. The 'great Ovid', again, disclaims all 'art poetical' and represents himself as an unskilled rhymer doing his poor best to please. Chaucer was a natural ironist, and he never tires of such gestures of self-depreciation. It is impossible to extract from his formal writings any straight statement of what his Art meant to him; and there is, of course, no informal evidence – nothing in the way of anecdote or notebook.

Perhaps the nearest we come to catching Chaucer in serious mood, so far as his own poetry is concerned, is on those occasions where he speaks of technical matters. We may discover something, for example, of his preoccupation with rhymes. In the so-called *Complaint of Venus* (p. 31), he says that it is difficult to match in English the virtuoso rhyming of the French poet Graunson; but this is in an Envoy which itself, despite the 'scarcity of rhyme' in English, uses only two rhyme sounds in ten lines. Chaucer's parody of popular English romances in his *Tale of Sir Thopas* – a parody which represents his nearest approach to literary criticism – suggests that he was displeased, among other things, by what the Host calls their 'drasty rhyming'. He himself cultivated subtleties after the French fashion, such as 'equivocal rhyme', where two words of identical form but different meaning rhyme together. There is an example at the end of that most carefully worked paragraph which opens the *Canterbury Tales*:

The hooly blisful martir for to seke,
That hem hath holpen whan that they were seeke.
                    (I 17–18)

So we are not to believe the Man of Law when he says that Chaucer knows little about 'rhyming craftily'. He was clearly a connoisseur of rhymes and rhyme-schemes; and we may guess that such topics bulked large in any talk about poetry he may have had with colleagues such as Deschamps. What Deschamps understood by the art of 'poëterie' may be discovered from his little treatise on the subject, the *Art de Dictier*; and this is a work very largely concerned with technicalities of form, and especially rhyme.

Chaucer's verse, with the 'sweet music' of its rhymes, was well fitted to win the admiration of such men.

Chaucer shows a similar concern about metre. In the *House of Fame* (p. 25) he admits that some lines in the poem may be defective in a single syllable; but this admission itself reflects a care for the small technical detail which is not easy to parallel among his Middle English predecessors. It is in this spirit that he prays at the end of his *Troilus* that the poem should be correctly copied (p. 26). He is anxious that the text should be stable, down to those smallest details where the diversity of English dialects and spelling introduces, in the Middle Ages, greatest instability, and where the metre and movement of the poem is still very much at stake. Such anxiety is the mark of those who write, as Deschamps puts it, 'pour eulx auctorisier' – in order to win a place for themselves among the 'authorities', or canonical poets.

It is precisely because matters of rhyme and rhythm are – or appear to a lay audience to be – of minor importance that Chaucer felt free to speak of them fairly seriously in public. Weightier matters – of theme, structure, characterization, etc. – he waves aside. He reports, he says, what he finds either in old books or in the world about him, in a somewhat recalcitrant vernacular and without any special personal aptitude. The most he can hope for is that his work may prove intelligible and, perhaps, 'somewhat agreeable'. Such gestures belong rather to the history of rhetoric and manners than to the history of criticism; but I have included one or two examples in the collection which follows.

Geoffrey Chaucer

from *House of Fame* ?1380

O God of science and of lyght,
Appollo, thurgh thy grete myght,
This lytel laste bok thou gye![1]
Nat that I wilne, for maistrye,
Here art poetical be shewed;
But for the rym ys lyght and lewed,[2]
Yit make hyt sumwhat agreable,
Though som vers fayle in a sillable;
And that I do no diligence
To shewe craft, but o sentence.[3]
And yif, devyne vertu, thow
Wilt helpe me to shewe now
That in myn hed ymarked ys[4] –
Loo, that is for to menen this,
The Hous of Fame for to descryve –
Thou shalt se me go as blyve[5]
Unto the nexte laure y see,
And kysse yt, for hyt is thy tree.
Now entre in my brest anoon!

(1091–1109)

Geoffrey Chaucer

from *Troilus and Criseyde* ?1385

Go, litel bok, go, litel myn tragedye,
Ther God thi makere yet, er that he dye,
So sende myght to make in som comedye!
But litel book, no makyng[6] thow n'envie,
But subgit be to alle poesye;

1 direct   2 ignorant, unskilful   3 but only my meaning   4 what is
planned in my mind   5 straight away   6 poetry

And kis the steppes, where as thow seest pace
Virgile, Ovide, Omer, Lucan, and Stace.[1]

And for ther is so gret diversite
In Englissh and in writyng of oure tonge,
So prey I God that non myswrite the,
Ne the mysmetre for defaute of tonge.[2]
And red wherso thow be, or elles songe,
That thow be understonde, God I biseche!
                              (v 1786–98)

Eustache Deschamps

Ballade addressed to Chaucer ?1386

O Socratès plains de philosophie,
Seneque en meurs et Auglus en pratique,
Ovides grans en ta poëterie,
Briés en parler, saiges en rethorique,
Aigles treshaulz, qui par ta theorique
Enlumines le regne d'Eneas –
L'Isle aux Geans, ceuls de Bruth – et qui as
Semé les fleurs et planté le rosier
Aux ignorans de la langue Pandras,
Grant translateur, noble Geffroy Chaucier.

Tu es d'Amours mondains Dieux en Albie;
Et de la Rose, en la terre Angelique
Qui d'Angela saxonne est puis flourie
Angleterre – d'elle ce nom s'applique
Le derrenier en l'ethimologique –,
En bon anglès le Livre translatas;
Et un vergier, où du plant demandas
De ceuls qui font pour eulx auctorisier,
A ja longtemps que tu edifias,
Grant translateur, noble Geffroy Chaucier.

1 Statius   2 through failure of language

A toy pour ce de la fontaine Helye
Requier avoir un buvraige autentique
Dont la doys est du tout en ta baillie,
Pour rafrener d'elle ma soif ethique,
Qui en Gaule seray paralitique
Jusques a ce que tu m'abuveras.
Eustaces sui; quite mon plant aras;
Mais pran en gré les euvres d'escolier
Que par Clifford de moy avoir pourras,
Grant translateur, noble Gieffroy Chaucier.

L'Envoy
Poëte hault, loënge d'escurye,
En ton jardin ne seroie qu'ortie:
Considere ce que j'ay dit premier,
Ton noble plant, ta douce melodie.
Mais pour sçavoir, de rescripre te prie,
Grant translateur, noble Geffroy Chaucier.

O Socrates full of philosophy, Seneca in morals and Aulus Gellius in practical affairs[1], a mighty Ovid in your poetic skill, concise in expression and artful in rhetoric. O lofty eagle who by your theoretical knowledge light up the kingdom of Aeneas – the Isle of Giants, the people of Brutus[2] – and have sown the flowers and planted the rose tree for the benefit of those ignorant of the language of Pandras,[3] O great translator, noble Geoffrey Chaucer.

You are an earthly God of Love in Albion; and you have translated the Book of the Rose[4] into good English in that Angelic land which from the Saxon Angela has since flourished as England – for it is

1 Aulus Gellius, author of *Noctes Atticae*, was also a judge.
2 According to Geoffrey of Monmouth's *History of the Kings of Britain*, the descendants of Aeneas, under the leadership of Brutus, conquered Albion, the Isle of Giants, and renamed it Britain.
3 Pandrasus, according to Geoffrey of Monmouth, was a Greek king whom Brutus and his Trojans defeated. If the 'people of Brutus' are the English, then the 'language of Pandras' must be French – a graceful reference to the hostility between English and French and to the superiority of the latter's language.
4 An incomplete English translation of the *Romance of the Rose* survives, and part of it is thought to be Chaucer's.

from her that this name comes, the last in a series of names[1]; and long since you established an orchard, and asked for plants from those who write poetry for posterity, O great translator, noble Geoffrey Chaucer.

And so I ask that I may have from you an authentic draught from the spring of Helicon whose stream is altogether in your keeping, so that I may check my feverish thirst for it. Here in Gaul I shall be paralytic until you give me drink. I am Eustache; you are welcome to my plants; but look kindly on the schoolboy work which you will receive from me through Clifford,[2] O great translator, noble Geoffrey Chaucer.

High poet, glory of all squires,[3] I could only be a nettle in your garden. Consider what I said before about your noble plants, your sweet music. Yet I beg you to reply and let me know, O great translator, noble Geoffrey Chaucer.

Geoffrey Chaucer

from *Legend of Good Women* ?1386

Allas, that I ne had Englyssh, ryme or prose,
Suffisant this flour[4] to preyse aryght!
But helpeth, ye that han konnyng and myght,
Ye lovers that kan make of sentement;[5]
In this cas oghte ye be diligent
To forthren me somwhat in my labour,
Whethir ye ben with the leef or with the flour.
For wel I wot that ye han her-biforn
Of makyng ropen,[6] and lad awey the corn,
And I come after, glenyng here and there,
And am ful glad yf I may fynde an ere

---

1 According to one medieval tradition, England got its final name, 'Anglia', from a Saxon princess called Angela. See Spenser's *Faerie Queene*, III iii 55–6.
2 Sir Lewis Clifford, who carried Deschamps' gift of poems, was a courtier of Richard II and a friend of Chaucer.
3 Both Deschamps and Chaucer were squires.   4 the daisy   5 who can write from experience   6 reaped the harvest of poetry

Of any goodly word that ye han left.
And thogh it happen me rehercen eft
That ye han in your fresshe songes sayd,
Forbereth me, and beth nat evele apayd,[1]
Syn that ye see I do yt in the honour
Of love, and eke in service of the flour
Whom that I serve as I have wit or myght.

(Prologue, F 66–83)

Thomas Usk

from *Testament of Love* ?1387

'I wolde now,' quod I, 'a litel understande, sithen[2] that God al thing
thus beforn wot,[3] whether thilke wetinge[4] be of tho thinges, or els
thilke thinges ben to ben of Goddes weting . . . and if every thing be
thorow Goddes weting, and thereof take his being, than shulde God be
maker and auctour of badde werkes, and so he shulde not rightfully
punisshe yvel doinges of mankynde.'

Quod Love, 'I shal telle thee, this lesson to lerne. Myne owne
trewe servaunt, the noble philosophical poete in Englissh, whiche
evermore him besieth and travayleth right sore my name to encrese –
wherfore al that willen me good owe to do him worship and reverence
bothe, trewly his better ne his pere in scole of my rules coude I never
fynde – he,' quod she, 'in a tretis that he made of my servant Troilus,
hath this mater touched, and at the ful this question assoyled.[5] Cer-
taynly, his noble sayinges can I not amende. In goodnes of gentil
manliche speche, without any maner of nycete of storiers imagina-
cion,[6] in witte and in good reson of sentence he passeth al other
makers. In the boke of Troilus, the answere to thy question mayst
thou lerne.'

(Book III, Chapter 4)

---

1 displeased   2 since   3 knows in advance   4 knowledge   5 unravelled
6 foolishness of a storyteller's imagining

Geoffrey Chaucer

from *Canterbury Tales* ?1387

But first I pray yow, of youre curteisye,
That ye n'arette it nat my vileynye,[1]
Thogh that I pleynly speke in this mateere,
To telle yow hir wordes and hir cheere,
Ne thogh I speke hir wordes proprely.
For this ye knowen al so wel as I,
Whoso shal telle a tale after a man,
He moot reherce[2] as ny as evere he kan
Everich a word, if it be in his charge,
Al speke he never so rudeliche and large,
Or ellis he moot telle his tale untrewe,
Or feyne thyng, or fynde wordes newe.
He may nat spare, althogh he were his brother;
He moot as wel seye o word as another.
Crist spak hymself ful brode in hooly writ,
And wel ye woot no vileynye is it.
Eek Plato seith, whoso that kan hym rede,
The wordes moote be cosyn to the dede.
Also I prey yow to foryeve it me,
Al have I nat set folk in hir degree
Heere in this tale, as that they sholde stonde.
My wit is short, ye may wel understonde.

(General Prologue, 1725–46)

John Gower

from *Confessio Amantis* ?1390

(*Venus addresses Gower*)

'And gret wel Chaucer whan ye mete,
  As mi disciple and mi poete:

1 do not ascribe it to any coarseness in me   2 must repeat

For in the floures of his youthe
In sondri wise, as he wel couthe,
Of ditees and of songes glade,
The whiche he for mi sake made,
The lond fulfild is overal:
Wherof to him in special
Above alle othre I am most holde.[1]
For thi[2] now in hise daies olde
Thow schalt him telle this message,
That he upon his latere age,
To sette an ende of alle his werk,
As he which is myn owne clerk,
Do make his testament of love,
As thou hast do thi schrifte above,
So that mi court it mai recorde.'

(VIII 2941–57)

Geoffrey Chaucer

from *Complaint of Venus* ? after 1390

Princesse, receyveth this compleynt in gre,[3]
Unto your excelent benignite
Direct after my litel suffisaunce.
For elde, that in my spirit dulleth me,
Hath of endyting[4] al the subtilte
Wel nygh bereft out of my remembraunce;
And eke to me it ys a gret penaunce,
Syth rym in Englissh hath such skarsete,
To folowe word by word the curiosite[5]
Of Graunson,[6] flour of hem that make in Fraunce.

(73–82)

1 obliged   2 wherefore   3 with favour   4 poetical composition   5 fine
workmanship   6 Oton de Granson, a knight of Savoy, who wrote courtly
poetry in French

Part Two The Developing Debate

Introduction

The immediate heirs of Chaucer and his court audience were those circles which, in the fifteenth and sixteenth centuries, continued to read him as a polite author, 'friend of women' and, above all, poet of love. Puttenham, in 1589, describes the history of English poetry as a succession of 'companies of courtly makers': the first, in the time of Richard II, including Chaucer and Gower ('both of them, as I suppose, knights'); the second, in the time of Henry VIII, including Wyatt and Surrey; and the third, in the time of Elizabeth I, including Sidney and Raleigh (p. 49). Chaucer is not out of place in such company. Up to the time of Wyatt, at least, poets drew on his works – and especially his *Troilus* – for the language and lore of Venus. Yet this aspect of Chaucer's work was disappearing from view already in Puttenham's day; and it has been left for modern historical critics such as C. S. Lewis to rediscover Chaucer as the poet of 'Courtly Love'. When Dryden observed in passing that Chaucer, like Ovid, was 'well-bred, well-natured, amorous, and libertine', he came as near as anyone in his age to recognizing what Wyatt could have taken for granted; and in the nineteenth century we find one William Cyples, writing in the *Cornhill Magazine* of 1877, forced to remind his readers that Chaucer is not all humour, pathos, realism and indecency: 'two-thirds of his life-long labours were about love, having no other motive or inspiration whatsoever.' Contrary, he says, to common belief.

Chaucer the learned and philosophical poet fared better, at least until the time of the Restoration. In the century after his death, Hoccleve lamented the 'universal father in science' who rivalled Aristotle in philosophy; while Stephen Surigo, in a Latin epitaph which was hung by Chaucer's tomb in Westminster Abbey, went so far as to compare him with Socrates. When William Thynne published the first *Complete Works* in 1532, he prefixed a Dedication to Henry VIII in which the author (Sir Brian Tuke) gave pride of place to Chaucer's 'excellent learning in all kinds of doctrines and sciences' (p. 48). This letter was reprinted by subsequent editors for more than two hundred years; and no doubt it helped to form the opinions of readers such as Spenser and Milton, both of whom use 'learned' as a stock epithet when speaking of Chaucer. We can get an idea of what 'doctrines and sciences' such men actually found in their Chaucer from the marginal observations written by Gabriel Harvey in his copy of the 1598 Speght edition: he notes the alchemy in the *Canon's Yeoman's Tale*, 'cunning compositions by natural magic' in the *Squire's Tale*, and 'fine optics' in the *Romance of the Rose*. Harvey sums up his own view and that of many of his contemporaries when he writes in another book: 'Other commend Chaucer and Lydgate for their wit, pleasant vein, variety of poetical discourse, and all humanity. I specially note their astronomy, philosophy, and other parts of profound or cunning art' (p. 49). As late as 1700, Dryden speaks of Chaucer's 'deep and various' learning in philosophy, philology, astronomy and astrology; but he no longer suggests that one might go to Chaucer *for* such things.

One particular branch of Chaucer's learning deserves further mention. Deschamps addressed Chaucer as a 'Seneca in morals', and the author of the *Kingis Quair*, found him 'superlative' in morality. In the sixteenth century, this view of Chaucer as a source of moral doctrine appears, if anything, to have gained strength; and it may be considered characteristic of the Elizabethan age. Thus William Webbe, in his *Discourse of English Poetry*, refers to Chaucer as above all a satirist and moralist who, in Horace's phrase, mingled profit with delight: 'For who could with more delight prescribe such wholesome counsel and sage advice, where he seemeth only to respect the profit of his lessons and instructions?' Those who find Webbe's view strange might recall that Elizabethan 'Chaucers' contained – besides *Melibee*, the *Parson's Tale*, and other genuine Chaucerian moral pieces nowadays often ignored – a substantial number of works not now accepted as Chaucer's, some of which (and especially the anti-papist *Plowman's Tale*) appealed strongly to the Elizabethan taste for 'wholesome counsel and sage advice'.

Chaucer's contemporaries admired him as much for his eloquence and poetic skill as for his wisdom; but here, as we might expect, the chorus of praise grows fainter as Chaucer's language becomes more and more remote and rebarbative. From Hoccleve to Douglas and Skelton, English and Scots writers agree in praising the 'first finder of our fair language' for his rhetorical artifice and his ornate, or 'aureate', diction. The praise has a strong element of convention in it; but what to us is just a traditional English poetic manner – indeed, *the* English poetic manner – was to earlier readers a sweet new style, a 'fresh douce English', and an unprecedented achievement in the vernacular; and words which to us seem commonplace (like 'creature', for example) had, when first borrowed from Latin or French, a glamour and brilliance about them – a brilliance caught in Dunbar's outrageous phrase, 'thy fresch anamalit termes celicall' (p. 46). Chaucer created a new high style in English poetry; and writing such as the opening of John Lydgate's *Siege of Thebes* – however little we may like it (p. 42) – is evidence of the enormous impact which this 'rethorike and eloquence' had on his successors.

Yet most readers nowadays will feel more at ease when these early followers of Chaucer praise – as they also do – the 'brevity' or 'compendiousness' and the directness of his style. Deschamps called Chaucer 'briés en parler' (brief in expression); and similar observations are to be found in the *Book of Courtesy*, Caxton's Proem to the *Canterbury Tales*, and Skelton's *Philip Sparrow*. As the *Book of Courtesy* puts it:

Briefly to wryte suche was his suffysance
Whatever to saye he toke in his entente
His langage was so fayr and pertynente
It semeth unto mannys heerynge

Not only the worde, but verely the thynge (see p. 44).

The anonymous writer is still within the conventions of rhetorical analysis here, since brevity was itself an ideal of style in the medieval academies; but he succeeds in identifying what for many twentieth-century readers is a cardinal point in Chaucer's manner:

It semeth unto mannys heerynge
Not only the worde, but verely the thynge.

The old criticism of Chaucer has its monuments in the editions of Speght (1598) and Urry (1721). Speght's edition, which remained without a rival throughout the seventeenth century, concludes its 'Life of the Poet' with a collection of 'judgements and reports of some learned men of this worthy and famous poet'; and Urry devoted eleven folio pages to 'testimonies of learned men concerning Chaucer and his works'. The authorities gathered together in these collections – Hoccleve, Lydgate, Surigo, Gavin Douglas, Tuke, Spenser, and the rest – represent what one might call the 'black-letter' Chaucer (Urry's edition was the first in which modern, roman type was used). They commend the learning, the morality, and the eloquence of 'this worthy and famous poet'; and their tone is correspondingly formal and eulogistic. It is therefore something of a shock when we come to the very last of Urry's Testimonies: extracts from John Dryden's Preface to his *Fables* (1700).

In Dryden's essay we see for the first time Chaucer's poetry submitted to the considered judgement of a man who is not predisposed only to praise it. Chaucer the Poet of Love and Chaucer the Philosopher meant little more to Dryden than they do to us; courtly love, alchemy and Boethius were all things of the past. So Dryden judges Chaucer afresh and for himself (though not without reference to the invaluable Speght). His is an essay in the manner of 'honest Montaigne': informal, rambling, frank and

(as W. P. Ker said) 'disengaged'. He sets out to assess Chaucer's
worth, not by local standards, but by the universal standards of
Nature and Good Sense; and he concludes that Chaucer's poetry,
despite defects of style and language, deserves high praise. It is
vivid: 'I see . . . all the Pilgrims in the *Canterbury Tales*, their
humours, their features, and the very dress, as distinctly as if I had
supped with them at the Tabard.' It is comprehensive: 'here is
God's plenty'. It is natural: 'Chaucer followed Nature everywhere,
but was never so bold to go beyond her'. This last point is
especially interesting and important. Developing the remarks of
Elizabethan critics such as Sir Francis Beaumont, who had praised
Chaucer for his 'due observation of decorum', Dryden emphasizes
the natural propriety, the unostentatious rightness in the way
Chaucer's people feel, think and speak, as against the clever
'boyisms' of Ovid. Such observations cannot stand without
qualification (one recalls Dorigen's complaint in the *Franklin's Tale*);
but they point, certainly, to one of the hiding-places of Chaucer's
power. And in this matter of naturalness, Dryden and his followers
are expert guides.

The general standard of eighteenth-century criticism of Chaucer
is, however, rather low. The well-bred frankness of the Augustans,
which we can already see in Dryden, allowed many people, like
the young Addison (p. 60), to treat Chaucer as a merry and
somewhat improper poet who nevertheless somehow failed to
raise a laugh – unless one read him in a modernized and polished
version, such as Pope's brilliant *Wife of Bath*, published in 1714
(see p. 58). This idea of Chaucer as a jovial, even a coarse, poet
can be traced in the Elizabethan age; but it is in the age of Pope
that the modern popular image has its origins. And round about
this time, significantly, the *Canterbury Tales* begin to assume the
position of chief work in the Chaucer canon – a position occupied
in previous centuries by *Troilus and Criseyde*.

The best criticism of Chaucer in the eighteenth century stems

from Dryden, stressing the poet's good sense and propriety.
Richard Hurd's observations, in his *Letters on Chivalry and
Romance* (1762), on Chaucer's handling of romance in the
Canterbury Tales, may stand as an example (p. 74). Dryden's true
heir, however, is not the worthy Bishop Hurd, but William Blake.
The *Descriptive Catalogue* which Blake issued in 1809 in connexion
with an exhibition of his pictures, an exhibition which included
his painting of the Canterbury pilgrims (Plate 3), contains an
account of the pilgrims which deserves to stand with Dryden's
Preface as a classic of Chaucer criticism. Blake's judgement is not
always to be trusted. His theories about medieval monastic life,
for example, led him to take too friendly a view of the Monk.
But because he, like Dryden, sees in the pilgrims 'the physiognomies
or lineaments of universal human life, beyond which Nature never
steps', as he puts it, he responds to these pilgrims as if to
contemporaries. Above all, he has a sense of their magnitude. His
account of the Host – 'a first rate character, and his jokes are no
trifles' – stands as a corrective to the easy superiorities of some
modern academic criticism.

Many other nineteenth-century critics, in Blake's day and after,
followed with him in Dryden's footsteps. William Hazlitt's lecture,
published in 1818, stresses the vividness and 'matter-of-fact'
realism of Chaucer's poetry (p. 85); and Leigh Hunt – whose
discussions of Chaucer deserve more respect than they have
received – analyses with great finesse that vein of unaffected
simplicity in Chaucer's style which Dryden also appreciated (p. 90).
But the readers of this age saw new qualities in Chaucer, too; and
we find them praising his sublimity, his pathos, and his humour.
These new responses are represented already in the work of the
brothers Warton (Joseph and Thomas) in the 1770s and 80s; and
in Romantic and Victorian times, Chaucer's blend of pathos and
humour ('inseparable twin-born gifts', as Swinburne called them)
became a critical commonplace. This tender view of Chaucer,

shared by Coleridge, Leigh Hunt and Swinburne, finds its
justification chiefly in pieces such as the tales of the Man of Law,
the Clerk and (especially) the Prioress, where children or ladies
suffer extremes of distress. It is evident that Chaucer did cultivate
such pathetic effects, and probably in his last period.

The *Prioress's Tale* occupies a position of some prominence also
in Matthew Arnold's well-known discussion of Chaucer (p. 96),
first published in 1880, but as an example of the poet's 'liquid
diction' and 'fluid movement'. So far as the 'substance' of
Chaucer's poetry is concerned, Arnold is content to invoke Dryden
and praise the poet's 'central, truly human point of view', his
'largeness, freedom, shrewdness, benignity'. The distinctive
Victorian note is struck in what follows. Arnold denies Chaucer a
place in the first rank of poets: he lacks 'high seriousness', and
hence, though he can give 'joy and strength', he cannot console
or sustain. It is noteworthy that Arnold's 'touchstones' of high
seriousness – taken from Homer, Dante, Shakespeare and Milton –
all concern pain, or release from pain in death or sleep, or
immunity from pain in the peace of immortality. His Aristotelian
phrase 'high seriousness', in fact, disguises preoccupations which,
though not peculiar to himself or to the Victorians, are less
universal than they look. But this does not diminish the importance
of his criticism. There are many, mostly romantic, preoccupations
(pain and peace among them) which Chaucer's poetry does not
respond to; and Arnold's is the classic statement of this genuinely
regrettable (*pace* some tough-minded modern critics) fact. In his
criticism, as in Dryden's, the representative force is inseparable from
the individuality – if not the idiosyncrasy – of the judgement.
Arnold, because he is honest and disapproves of 'charlatanism',
speaks for many modern readers to whom Chaucer means less
than they like to admit.

Thomas Hoccleve

from *Regement of Princes* 1412

O maister deere and fadir reverent!
Mi maister Chaucer, flour of eloquence,
Mirour of fructuous entendement,[1]
O universel fadir in science!
Allas! that thou thyn excellent prudence
In thi bed mortel mightist naght byqwethe;
What eiled Deth? allas! whi wolde he sle the?

O Deth! thou didest naght harme singuleer
In slaghtere of him, but al this land it smertith;
But nathelees, yit hast thou no power
His name sle; his hy vertu astertith
Unslayn fro the, which ay us lyfly hertyth
With bookes of his ornat endytyng,[2]
That is to al this land enlumynyng. . . .

Allas! my worthi maister honorable,
This landes verray tresor and richesse,
Deth, by thi deth, hath harme irreparable
Unto us doon; hir vengeable duresse
Despoiled hath this land of the swetnesse
Of rethorik; for unto Tullius
Was never man so lyk amonges us.

Also, who was hier in philosophie
To Aristotle, in our tonge, but thow?
The steppes of Virgile in poesie
Thow filwedist eeke, men wot wel ynow. . . .

The firste fyndere of our faire langage
Hath seyde in caas semblable, and othir moo,
So hyly wel, that it is my dotage
For to expresse or touche any of thoo.
Alasse! my fadir fro the worlde is goo,

1 profitable significance   2 ornate composition

My worthi maister Chaucer, hym I mene.
Be thou advoket for hym, hevenes quene!

(1961–74, 2080–90, 4978–84)

John Lydgate

from *Siege of Thebes* 1420–22

Whan brighte Phebus passed was the Ram,[1]
Myd of Aprille, and into Bole cam,
And Satourn old with his frosty face
In Virgyne taken had his place,
Malencolik and slowgh of mocioun,
And was also in th'oposicioun
Of Lucina, the mone moyst and pale,
That many shour fro hevene made avale;[2]
Whan Aurora was in the morowe red,
And Iubiter in the Crabbes hed
Hath take his paleys and his mansioun;
The lusty tyme and ioly fressh sesoun
Whan that Flora, the noble myghty quene,
The soyl hath clad in newe tendre grene,
With her floures craftyly ymeynt,[3]
Braunch and bough with red and whit depeynt,
Fletinge the bawme[4] on hillis and on valys;
The tyme in soth whan Canterbury talys
Complet and told at many sondry stage
Of estatis in the pilgrimage,
Everich man lik to his degre,
Some of desport, some of moralite,
Some of knyghthode, love and gentillesse,
And some also of parfit holynesse,
And some also in soth of ribaudye
To make laughter in the companye
(Ech admitted, for non wold other greve),

1 Lydgate imitates, and outdoes, the opening of the *Canterbury Tales*, with zodiacal references, sustained syntax, etc.   2 fall   3 mingled   4 balm

Lich as the Cook, the Millere and the Reve
Aquytte hemsilf, shortly to conclude,
Boystously[1] in her teermes rude,
Whan thei hadde wel dronken of the bolle,
And ek also with his pylled nolle
The Pardowner, beerdlees al his chyn,[2]
Glasy-eyed and face of cherubyn,[3]
Tellyng a tale to angre with the Frere,[4]
As opynly the storie kan yow lere
Word for word with every circumstaunce,
Echon ywrite and put in remembraunce
By hym that was, yif I shal not feyne,
Floure of poetes thorghout al Breteyne,
Which sothly hadde most of excellence
In rethorike and in eloquence –
Rede his making, who list the trouthe fynde –
Which never shal appallen[5] in my mynde,
But alwey fressh ben in my memorye:
To whom be yove pris, honure and glorye,
Of wel-seyinge first in oure language,
Chief registrer of this pilgrimage,
Al that was tolde foryeting noght at al,
Feyned talis, nor thing historial,
With many proverbe divers and unkouth,[6]
Be rehersaile of his sugrid mouth,
Of eche thyng keping in substaunce
The sentence[7] hool, withoute variance,
Voyding the chaf,[8] sothly for to seyn,
Enlumynyng the trewe piked greyn[9]
Be crafty writinge of his sawes swete,
Fro the tyme that thei deden mete
First the pylgrimes sothly everichon,
At the Tabbard assembled on be on,

1 roughly   2 Chaucer's Pardoner is beardless, but not bald ('pylled nolle').
3 The Pardoner has 'glarynge eyen', but the 'fyr-reed cherubynnes face' is
the Summoner's.   4 Lydgate again confuses Pardoner and Summoner.
5 grow dim   6 various and unfamiliar   7 meaning   8 getting rid of the
chaff ('of superfluity', according to Caxton, who recalls this passage
below, p. 45)   9 choice grain

And fro Suthwerk, shortly for to seye,
To Canterbury ridyng on her weie,
Tellynge a tale, as I reherce can,
Lich as the Hoste assigned every man,
None so hardy his biddyng disobeye.

(1–65)

Anonymous

from *Book of Courtesy* 1477

O fader and founder of ornate eloquence,
That enlumened hast alle our Bretayne,
To soone we loste thy laureate scyence.
O lusty lyquour of that fulsom fontayne!
O cursid Deth, why hast thow that poete slayne,
I mene fader Chaucer, maister Galfryde?
Alas the whyle, that ever he from us dyde!

Redith his werkis, ful of plesaunce,
Clere in sentence,[1] in langage excellent,
Briefly to wryte suche was his suffysance
Whatever to saye he toke in his entente[2]
His langage was so fayr and pertynente
It semeth unto mannys heerynge
Not only the worde, but verely the thynge.

(330–43)

William Caxton

from the Proem to his Second Edition of the *Canterbury Tales* 1484

Grete thankes, laude and honour ought to be gyven unto the clerkes, poetes and historiographs that have wreton many noble bokes of

1 clear in meaning   2 whatever he took it into his head to say

wysedom, of the lyves, passions and myracles of holy sayntes, of hystoryes of noble and famous actes and faittes,[1] and of the cronycles sith the begynnyng of the creacion of the world unto thys present tyme, by whyche we ben dayly enformed and have knowleche of many thynges of whom we shold not have knowen yf they had not left to us theyr monumentis wreton; emong whom and in especial tofore alle other we ought to gyve a synguler laude unto that noble and grete philosopher Gefferey Chaucer, the whiche for his ornate wrytyng in our tongue may wel have the name of a laureate poete. For tofore that he by hys labour enbelysshyd, ornated and made faire our Englisshe, in thys royame was had rude speche and incongrue,[2] as yet it appiereth by olde bookes whyche at thys day ought not to have place ne be compared emong ne to hys beautevous volumes and aournate writynges; of whom he made many bokes and treatyces of many a noble historye, as wel in metre as in ryme and prose, and them so craftyly made that he comprehended hys maters in short, quyck and hye sentences,[3] eschewyng prolyxyte, castyng away the chaf of superfluyte, and shewyng the pyked grayn of sentence[4] utteryd by crafty and sugred eloquence; of whom emonge all other of hys bokes I purpose t'emprynte, by the grace of God, the *Book of the Tales of Cauntyrburye*, in whiche I fynde many a noble hystorye of every astate and degre, fyrst rehercyng the condicions and th'arraye of eche of them as properly as possyble is to be sayd, and after theyr tales, whyche ben of noblesse, wysedom, gentylesse, myrthe, and also of veray holynesse and vertue, wherin he fynysshyth thys sayd booke, whyche book I have dylygently oversen and duly examyned to th'ende that it be made acordyng unto his owen makyng.

William Dunbar

from *The Golden Targe* 1503

O reverend Chaucere, rose of rethoris all,
As in oure tong ane flour imperiall,

1 deeds 2 unpolished and incorrect speech 3 concise, vigorous and dignified expressions 4 the choice 'grain' (as against 'chaff') of meaning

That raise in Britane evir, quho redis rycht,
Thou beris of makaris the tryumph riall;
Thy fresch anamalit termes celicall[1]
This mater coud illumynit have full brycht:
Was thou noucht of oure Inglisch all the lycht,
Surmounting eviry tong terrestriall
Alls fer as Mayis morow dois mydnycht?

                              (253–61)

John Skelton

from *Philip Sparrow* before 1509

In Chaucer I am sped,[2]
His tales I have read:
His matter is delectable,
Solacious and commendable;
His English well allowed,[3]
So as it is enprowed,[4]
For as it is employed
There is no English void –
At those days much commended.
And now men would have amended
His English, whereat they bark,
And mar all they wark.
Chaucer, that famous clerk,
His terms were not dark,
But pleasant, easy and plain.
No word he wrote in vain.

                              (788–803)

1 your fresh, enamelled (i.e. adorned), heavenly diction   2 versed
3 approved of   4 well employed

Gavin Douglas

from his translation of Virgil's *Aeneid* 1513

And netheless into sum place, quha kend it,
My mastir Chauser gretly Virgill offendit.
All thoch I be to bald hym to repreif,
He was fer baldar, certis, by hys leif,
Sayand he followit Virgillis lantern toforn,
Quhou Eneas to Dydo was forsworn.[1]
Was he forsworn? Than Eneas was fals:
That he admittis, and callys hym traytour als.
Thus, wenyng allane Ene[2] to have reprevit,
He hass gretly the prynce of poetis grevit;
For, as said is, Virgill dyd diligens
But[3] spot of cryme, reproch or ony offens
Eneas for to loif[4] and magnyfy;
And gif he grantis hym maynsworn fowlely,
Than all hys cuyr and crafty engyne gais quyte,[5]
Hys twelf yheris laubouris war nocht worth a myte. . . .
Bot sikkyrly of resson me behufis
Excuss Chauser fra all maner repruffis:
In lovyng of thir ladeis lylly-quhite
He set on Virgill and Eneas this wyte,[6]
For he was evir (God wait) all womanis frend.

(*Prologue*, 409–24, 445–9)

1 Douglas alludes to the opening lines of the Legend of Dido, in Chaucer's
Legend of Good Women: 'Glorye and honour, Virgil Mantoan,|Be to thy
name! and I shal, as I can,|Folwe thy lanterne, as thow gost byforn,|How
Eneas to Dido was forsworn.' 2 Aeneas 3 without 4 praise 5 then all
his (Virgil's) care and skill goes for nothing 6 he attributed this fault to
Virgil and Aeneas

Sir Brian Tuke

from the Preface to *Works of Geoffrey Chaucer* edited by W. Thynne
1532

I, your most humble vassal, subject and servant William Thynne,[1]
chief clerk of your kitchen, moved by a certain inclination and zeal
which I have to hear of any thing sounding to the laud and honour
of this your noble realm, have taken great delectation, as the times
and leisures might suffer, to read and hear the books of that noble and
famous clerk Geoffrey Chaucer, in whose works is so manifest
comprobation of his excellent learning in all kinds of doctrines and
sciences, such fruitfulness in words well according to the matter and
purpose, so sweet and pleasant sentences,[2] such perfection in metre,
the composition[3] so adapted, such freshness of invention, compendiousness in narration, such sensible[4] and open style, lacking neither
majesty ne mediocrity covenable in disposition,[5] and such sharpness
or quickness in conclusion,[6] that it is much to be marvelled how in
his time, when doubtless all good letters were laid asleep throughout
the world, as the thing which either by the disposition and influence
of the bodies above or by other ordinance of God seemed like and
was in danger to have utterly perished, such an excellent poet in our
tongue should as it were (nature repugning) spring and arise.

Gabriel Harvey

from his manuscript notes after 1574

Notable astronomical descriptions in Chaucer and Lydgate; fine
artists[7] in many kinds, and much better learned than our modern
poets.
    Chaucer's conclusions of the astrolabe[8] still excellent, unim-

1 Editor Thynne, on whose behalf Tuke wrote this letter, served in the
household of Henry VIII. 2 maxims 3 sentence construction 4 easily
understood 5 suitable in context 6 in expression of opinion
7 men learned in the liberal arts 8 problems propounded in Chaucer's
Treatise on the Astrolabe

peachable; especially for the horizon of Oxford. A worthy man, that initiated his little son Lewis with such cunning and subtle conclusions, as sensibly and plainly expressed as he could devise. . . .

The description of the hour of the day: in the Man of Law's prologue, in the tale of the Nun's Priest, in the Parson's prologue.

Notable descriptions, and not any so artificial[1] in Latin or Greek. . . .

Other commend Chaucer and Lydgate for their wit, pleasant vein, variety of poetical discourse, and all humanity. I specially note their astronomy, philosophy, and other parts of profound or cunning art, wherein few of their time were more exactly learned. It is not sufficient for poets to be superficial humanists; but they must be exquisite artists[2] and curious[3] universal scholars.

(159–61)

George Puttenham

from *The Art of English Poesy* 1589

I will not reach above the time of King Edward the Third and Richard the Second for any that wrote in English metre, because before their times, by reason of the late Norman Conquest, which had brought into this realm much alteration both of our language and laws, and therewithal a certain martial barbarousness, whereby the study of all good learning was so much decayed as long time after no man or very few intended to write in any laudable science: so as beyond that time there is little or nothing worth commendation to be found written in this art. And those of the first age were Chaucer and Gower, both of them, as I suppose, knights. After whom followed John Lydgate, the monk of Bury, and that nameless who wrote the satire called *Piers Plowman*; next him followed Hardyng, the chronicler; then in King Henry the Eighth's time, Skelton, I wot not for what great worthiness surnamed the Poet Laureate. In the latter end of the same king's reign sprang up a new company of courtly makers, of whom Sir Thomas Wyatt the elder and Henry Earl of Surrey were the two chieftains, who having travelled into Italy, and there tasted the sweet and stately measures and style of the

1 scholarly   2 men learned in the liberal arts   3 accurate

Italian poesy, as novices newly crept out of the schools of Dante, Ariosto and Petrarch, they greatly polished our rude and homely manner of vulgar poesy from that it had been before, and for that cause may justly be said the first reformers of our English metre and style. . . . And in her Majesty's time that now is[1] are sprung up another crew of courtly makers, noblemen and gentlemen of her Majesty's own servants, who have written excellently well, as it would appear if their doings could be found out and made public with the rest; of which number is first that noble gentleman Edward Earl of Oxford, Thomas Lord of Buckhurst when he was young, Henry Lord Paget, Sir Philip Sidney, Sir Walter Raleigh, Master Edward Dyer, Master Fulke Greville, Gascoigne, Breton, Turbervile, and a great many other learned gentlemen, whose names I do not omit for envy, but to avoid tediousness, and who have deserved no little commendation.

But of them all particularly, this is mine opinion, that Chaucer, with Gower, Lydgate and Hardyng, for their antiquity ought to have the first place, and Chaucer, as the most renowned of them all, for the much learning appeareth to be in him, above any of the rest. And though many of his books be but bare translations out of the Latin and French, yet are they well handled, as his books of *Troilus and Criseyde*[2] and the *Romance of the Rose*, whereof he translated but one half (the device was Jean de Meun's, a French poet). The *Canterbury Tales* were Chaucer's own invention, as I suppose, and where he showeth more the natural of his pleasant wit than in any other of his works. His similitudes, comparisons and all other descriptions are such as can not be amended. His metre heroical of *Troilus and Criseyde* is very grave and stately, keeping the staff of seven and the verse of ten;[3] his other verses of the *Canterbury Tales* be but riding rhyme,[4] nevertheless very well becoming the matter of that pleasant pilgrimage, in which every man's part is played with much decency.[5]

(Book 1, Chapter 31)

---

1 Queen Elizabeth I   2 Puttenham, following Chaucer's own reference to 'myn auctour Lollius', supposes that *Troilus* was translated from Latin. 3 i.e. stanza of seven lines and line of ten syllables   4 decasyllabic couplets, considered an unelevated verse form by sixteenth-century writers 5 appropriateness, decorum

Sir Philip Sidney

from *Apology for Poetry* 1595 (but written about 1581)

Chaucer, undoubtedly, did excellently in his *Troilus and Criseyde;* of whom, truly, I know not whether to marvel more, either that he in that misty time could see so clearly, or that we in this clear age walk so stumblingly after him. Yet had he great wants, fit to be forgiven in so reverend antiquity.

(196)

Edmund Spenser

from *The Faerie Queene* 1596

> Whylome, as antique stories tellen us,
> Those two[1] were foes the fellonest on ground,
> And battell made the dreddest daungerous
> That ever shrilling trumpet did resound;
> Though now their acts be nowhere to be found,
> As that renowmed poet them compyled
> With warlike numbers and heroicke sound,
> Dan Chaucer, well of English undefyled,
> On Fame's eternall beadroll[2] worthie to be fyled.

(IV ii 32)

Sir Francis Beaumont

from a letter to Thomas Speght June 1597 (as printed in the 1602 edition of Speght's Chaucer)

Touching the incivility Chaucer is charged withal: what Roman poet hath less offended this way than he? Virgil in his *Priapus* is worse by a thousand degrees, and Ovid in his book *De Arte Amandi*

1 Cambel and Triamond. Cambalo is one of the sons of Cambyuskan in Chaucer's unfinished *Squire's Tale*. 2 a list of persons to be prayed for

and Horace in many places as deep as the rest; but Catullus and Tibullus in unclean wantonness beyond measure pass them all. Neither is Plautus nor Terence free in this behalf; but these two last are excused above the rest for their due observation of decorum, in giving to their comical persons such manner of speeches as did best fit their dispositions. And may not the same be said for Chaucer? How much had he swerved from decorum if he had made his Merchant, his Miller, his Cook, his Carpenter tell such honest and civil tales as were told of his Knight, his Squire, his Lawyer and his Scholar? But showing the disposition of the baser sort of people, he declareth in their prologues and tales that their chief delight was in undecent speeches of their own and in their false defamations of others, as in these verses appeareth:

'Lat be thy lewed dronken harlotrye.
It is a synne and eek a greet folye
To apeyren any man, or hym defame,
And eek to bryngen wyves in swich fame.'
                    (I 3145-8)

And in excuse of himself for uttering those broad speeches of theirs, he useth these words:

But first I pray yow, of youre curteisye,
That ye n'arette it nat my vileynye,
Thogh that I pleynly speke in this mateere,
To telle yow hir wordes and hir cheere,
Ne thogh I speke hir wordes proprely.
For this ye knowen al so wel as I,
Whoso shal telle a tale after a man,
He moot reherce as ny as evere he kan
Everich a word, if it be in his charge,
Al speke he never so rudeliche and large,
Or ellis he moot telle his tale untrewe,
Or feyne thyng, or fynde wordes newe. . . .
                    (I 725-36)

For no man can imagine in his so large compass, purposing to describe all Englishmen's humours living in those days, how it had been possible for him to have left untouched their filthy delights; or in discovering their desires, how to have expressed them without some of their words.

And now to compare him with other poets. His *Canterbury Tales* contain in them almost the same argument that is handled in comedies;[1] his style therein for the most part is low and open and like unto theirs; but herein they differ: the comedy writers do all follow and borrow one from another, as Terence from Plautus and Menander, Plautus from Menander and Demophilus, Statius Caecilius from Diphilus, Apollodorus and Philemon, and almost all the last comedians from that which was called *antiqua comoedia*. The ring they beat is this, and out of the same track they go not: to show the looseness of many young men, the lewdness of some young women, the crafty school-points of old bawds, the little regard of honest-disposed serving-men, the miserable wretchedness of divers old fathers and their folly in countenancing, and committing their sons to the charge and government of, most impudent and flattering parasites – such as in Terence is prating Davus and Geta and bold, bawdy Phormio. Chaucer's device of his Canterbury pilgrimage is merely his own. His drift is to touch all sorts of men and to discover all vices of that age, which he doth so feelingly and with so true an aim, as he never fails to hit whatsoever mark he levels at.

In his five books of *Troilus and Criseyde*, in the *Romance of the Rose*, in his *Black Knight*, in the *Merciless Lady*, in some few also of his *Tales*, in his *Dream* and in that of Blanche (which is in your hands, and was never yet imprinted), and in other his discourses, he soareth much higher;[2] and is in his *Troilus* so sententious as there be few staves in those books which include not some principal sentence,[3] most excellently imitating Homer and Virgil, and borrowing often of them, and of Horace also, and other the rarest both orators and poets that have written. Of whom for the sweetness of his

1 Beaumont refers to the comedy of Greece (Menander, Diphilus, Apollodorus, Philemon and Demophilus) and Rome (Terence, Plautus and Statius Caecilius).
2 Lydgate's *Complaint of the Black Knight*, the *Belle Dame Sans Merci* of Roos and the anonymous *Isle of Ladies* ('Chaucer's Dream') were all included by Speght among the works of Chaucer.
3 Few stanzas in the five books of *Troilus* are without some important maxim or proverb.

poetry may be said that which is reported of Stesichorus;[1] and as Marcus Cethegus was termed by Ennius *Suadae medulla*,[2] so may Chaucer rightly be called the pith and sinews of Eloquence, and very life itself of all mirth and pleasant writing. Besides, one gift he hath above other authors, and that is by excellency of his descriptions to possess his readers with a more forcible imagination of seeing that (as it were) done before their eyes which they read, than any other that ever hath written in any tongue.

Thomas Speght

from his edition, *Works of our Ancient and Learned English Poet Geoffrey Chaucer* 1598

Argument to *General Prologue* to the *Canterbury Tales*

The author in these prologues to his *Canterbury Tales* doth describe the reporters thereof for two causes. First, that the reader, seeing the quality of the person, may judge of his speech accordingly, wherein Chaucer hath most excellently kept that decorum which Horace requireth in that behalf. Secondly, to show how even in our language that may be performed for descriptions which the Greek and Latin poets in their tongues have done at large. And surely this poet, in the judgement of the best learned, is not inferior to any of them in his descriptions, whether they be of persons, times, or places. Under the pilgrims, being a certain number and all of differing trades, he comprehendeth all the people of the land, and the nature and disposition of them in those days – namely, given to devotion rather of custom than of zeal. In the tales is showed the state of the Church, the Court and Country, with such art and cunning that, although none could deny himself to be touched, yet none durst complain that he was wronged.

1 Hermogenes, an ancient rhetorician, said of the early Greek poet Stesichorus: 'he appears extremely sweet because of his frequent use of epithets'.
2 literally 'the marrow of Eloquence'. Marcus Cethegus was an early Roman orator.

Argument to *Sir Thopas*

A Northern tale of an outlandish knight, purposely uttered by
Chaucer in a different rhyme and style from the other tales, as
though he himself were not the author but only the reporter of the
rest.

Two Versions of the Wife of Bath
(Wife of Bath's Prologue, III 469-502)

Richard Brathwait

from *A Comment upon . . . the 'Miller's Tale' and the Wife of Bath*
1665 (but begun before 1617)

But, Lord Crist! whan that it remembreth me
Upon my yowthe, and on my jolitee,
It tikleth me aboute myn herte roote.
Unto this day it dooth myn herte boote
That I have had my world as in my tyme.

It delights her to remember the pranks of her youth; and no doubt
it would highly content her to have a taste of Aeson's herb, and so
become young again. For her desires continue strong, though her
strength be weak; her thoughts green, though her hairs be grey.

But age, allas! that al wole envenyme,
Hath me biraft my beautee and my pith.
Lat go, farewel! the devel go therwith!

A charitable old trader! Age, like a venom, hath crept upon her;
the beauty and strength of her youth have left her; both which
seeing she cannot recover, she freely bequeaths the Devil that which
she cannot keep with her. Yet holds she on in her old trade of folly.

The flour is goon, ther is namoore to telle;
The bren, as I best kan, now moste I selle.

Few or none but they will leave Sin, when Sin hath left them; but
this merry gossip will scarcely leave it, when she is now left by it.

Though the flower of her youth be lost, the bran of her age is left, and that must now be bolted, or she will never rest contented.

But yet to be right myrie wol I fonde.
Now wol I tellen of my fourthe housbonde.

All this which hath been said last must serve for a preamble to her fourth husband; of whom her discourse must be but short, according (as may be supposed) to the length of his life and height of her love.

I seye, I hadde in herte greet despit
That he of any oother had delit.

He was of a wanton life himself, and therefore looks for his wife in the oven where himself had been. Ill-doers are ever ill-deemers. None are more suspicious than such as are most vicious. A licentious man's eye is in every corner; to whom the very least occasion will minister apparent ground of suspicion.

But he was quit, by God and by Seint Joce!
I made hym of the same wode a croce;
Nat of my body, in no foul manere . . .

Truth was, he could not for his heart be more jealous of me than I was of him. Neither, indeed, had he any just cause to suspect me of wantonness. Here she excuseth herself that she never consorted with any good fellows for her own bodily pleasure in all this husband's time. Only she invited them to good cheer, being now turned professed gossiper. And all this, perchance, (so perverse was her disposition) rather to nettle and sting her husband than any singular delight she took, either in respect of her comrades, or delicacy of tooth: as may be probably gathered by those verses immediately following:

But certeinly, I made folk swich cheere
That in his owene grece I made hym frye
For angre, and for verray jalousye.

Out of a jealousy, or rather a constant persuasion, that she was as liberal of her flesh as of her fare, he fried himself in his own grease. He wasted himself with anger, seeing both a weakening of his fortune and impeaching of his honour (as he verily suspected) cope so closely one with another.

By God! in erthe I was his purgatorie,
For which I hope his soule be in glorie.

It seems she was good for something, if it were but to become her
husband's purgatory – more properly, the touchstone of his patience.
By this means she thinks he had his purgatory on earth; and consequently, without any rub or stay in his way, he may go directly to
heaven. Afflictions being exercises, he needed not suffer his body to
rust for want of them, having both at bed and at board such plenty
of them.

For, God it woot, he sat ful ofte and song,
Whan that his shoo ful bitterly hym wrong.
Ther was no wight, save God and he, that wiste,
In many wise, how soore I hym twiste.

Like a downright honest man, he set the best face he could on't. Yet
when he feigned most mirth, he had greatest cause to mourn. Every
man knew not where his shoe wrenched him. He might laugh till
his heart ached again, yet never a whit nearer relief. She had
vowed to be his executioner, purposely to become his executor.

He deyde whan I cam fro Jerusalem,
And lith ygrave under the roode beem.

This good-wife, belike, had taken her pilgrimage to Jerusalem, either
voluntarily or by injunction. No doubt, had she played pilgrim all
her time her husband had a lighter heart. But now, coming home, she
finds her husband drawing near his last home; whom she sees no
sooner departed than she takes course to prevent his revival, to have
him no less suddenly than solemnly buried. Under the rood-loft
(a place of especial reverence in former times) she causeth his grave
to be made; albeit in no sumptuous manner, as ancient heroes have
been interred, as she after expressed:

Al is his tombe noght so curyus
As was the sepulcre of hym Daryus,
Which that Appelles wroghte subtilly;
It nys but wast to burye hym preciously.

To bestow on him so gorgeous or sumptuous a sepulchre as was that which was erected in honour of Darius, formed by the curious art of famous Apelles, or as that of Artimisia in the memory of her Mausolus, were but (as she thinks) lost labour. So much cost would make a poor executor, and too much impoverish the survivor.

Lat hym fare wel, God yeve his soul reste!
He is now in his grave and in his cheste.

He is now laid in earth, and his soul, I hope, at rest. He had my leave to be gone before he went. To grieve for that which cannot be remedied is bootless. I will spare then to shed any tears, seeing they are no less foolish than fruitless. And so goodnight to my fourth husband.

(54–6)

Alexander Pope

from *The Wife of Bath her Prologue* 1714[1]

But oh good Gods! whene'er a thought I cast
On all the joys of youth and beauty past,
To find in pleasures I have had my part
Still warms me to the bottom of my heart.
This wicked world was once my dear delight;
Now all my conquests, all my charms good night!
The flour consumed, the best that now I can
Is e'en to make my market of the bran.
   My fourth dear spouse was not exceeding true;
He kept, 'twas thought, a private miss or two;
But all that score I paid – As how? you'll say,
Not with my body, in a filthy way –
But I so dressed, and danced, and drank, and dined,
And viewed a friend with eyes so very kind,
As stung his heart, and made his marrow fry
With burning rage, and frantic jealousy.
His soul, I hope, enjoys eternal glory,

1 This extract appears out of chronological sequence to enable comparison with Brathwait's commentary. [Ed.]

For here on earth I was his purgatory.
Oft, when his shoe the most severely wrung,
He put on careless airs, and sat and sung.
How sore I galled him, only Heaven could know,
And he that felt, and I that caused the woe.
He died when last from pilgrimage I came,
With other gossips, from Jerusalem,
And now lies buried underneath a rood,
Fair to be seen, and reared of honest wood.
A tomb, indeed, with fewer sculptures graced
Than that Mausolus' pious widow placed,
Or where enshrined the great Darius lay;
But cost on graves is merely thrown away.
The pit filled up, with turf we covered o'er,
So bless the good man's soul, I say no more.

(221–52)

Edward Phillips

from *Theatrum Poetarum* 1675

True it is that the style of poetry till Henry the Eighth's time, and partly also within his reign, may very well appear uncouth, strange and unpleasant to those that are affected only with what is familiar and accustomed to them; not but there were even before those times some that had their poetical excellencies, if well examined; and chiefly among the rest Chaucer, who through all the neglect of former aged poets still keeps a name, being by some few admired for his real worth, to others not unpleasing for his facetious way, which, joined with his old English, entertains them with a kind of drollery.

(263)

Joseph Addison

from *Account of the Greatest English Poets*   1694

Long had our dull forefathers slept supine,
Nor felt the raptures of the tuneful nine;
Till Chaucer first, a merry bard, arose,
And many a story told in rhyme and prose.
But age has rusted what the poet writ,
Worn out his language, and obscur'd his wit.
In vain he jests in his unpolish'd strain
And tries to make his readers laugh in vain.

(9–16)

John Dryden

from the Preface to *Fables*   1700

I proceed to Ovid and Chaucer; considering the former only in relation to the latter. With Ovid ended the golden age of the Roman tongue; from Chaucer the purity of the English tongue began. The manners of the poets were not unlike. Both of them were well-bred, well-natured, amorous, and libertine, at least in their writings, it may be also in their lives. Their studies were the same, philosophy and philology. Both of them were knowing in astronomy; of which Ovid's books of the Roman Feasts, and Chaucer's *Treatise of the Astrolabe*, are sufficient witnesses. But Chaucer was likewise an astrologer, as were Virgil, Horace, Persius, and Manilius. Both writ with wonderful facility and clearness; neither were great inventors: for Ovid only copied the Grecian fables, and most of Chaucer's stories were taken from his Italian contemporaries, or their predecessors. Boccace his *Decameron* was first published, and from thence our Englishman has borrowed many of his *Canterbury Tales:* yet that of Palamon and Arcite was written, in all probability, by some Italian wit, in a former age, as I shall prove hereafter. The tale of Grizild was the invention of Petrarch; by him sent to Boccace, from whom it came to Chaucer. *Troilus and Criseyde* was also written by a Lombard author, but much amplified by our English translator, as well as beautified; the genius of our countrymen in general being rather to improve an invention than to invent themselves, as is evident not only in our poetry, but in many of our manufactures. I find I have anticipated already, and taken up from Boccace before I come to him: but there is so much less behind; and I am of the temper of most kings, who love to be in debt, are all for present money, no matter how they pay it afterwards: besides, the nature of a preface is rambling, never wholly out of the way, nor in it. This I have learned from the practice of honest Montaigne, and return at my pleasure to Ovid and Chaucer, of whom I have little more to say.

Both of them built on the inventions of other men; yet since Chaucer had something of his own, as the *Wife of Bath's Tale*, the *Cock and the Fox*, which I have translated, and some others, I may justly give our countryman the precedence in that part; since I can remember nothing of Ovid which was wholly his. Both of them understood the manners; under which name I comprehend the passions, and, in a larger sense, the descriptions of persons, and their very habits. For an example, I see Baucis and Philemon as perfectly before me, as if some ancient painter had drawn them; and all the Pilgrims in the *Canterbury Tales*, their humours, their features, and the very dress, as distinctly as if I had supped with them at the Tabard in Southwark. Yet even there too the figures of Chaucer are much more lively, and set in a better light; which though I have not time to prove, yet I appeal to the reader, and am sure he will clear me from partiality. The thoughts and words remain to be considered, in the comparison of the two poets, and I have saved myself one-half of the labour, by owning that Ovid lived when the Roman tongue was in its meridian; Chaucer, in the dawning of our language: therefore that part of the comparison stands not on an equal foot, any more than the diction of Ennius and Ovid, or of Chaucer and our present English. The words are given up as a post not to be defended in our poet, because he wanted the modern art of fortifying. The thoughts remain to be considered: and they are to be measured only by their propriety; that is, as they flow more or less naturally from the persons described, on such and such occasions. The vulgar judges, which are nine parts in ten of all nations, who call conceits and jingles wit, who see Ovid full of them, and Chaucer altogether without

them, will think me little less than mad for preferring the Englishman to the Roman. Yet, with their leave, I must presume to say,
that the things they admire are only glittering trifles, and so far from
being witty, that in a serious poem they are nauseous, because they
are unnatural. Would any man who is ready to die for love, describe
his passion like Narcissus? Would he think of *inopem me copia fecit*,[1]
and a dozen more of such expressions, poured on the neck of one
another, and signifying all the same thing? If this were wit, was this
a time to be witty, when the poor wretch was in the agony of death?
This is just John Littlewit in *Bartholomew Fair*, who had a conceit (as
he tells you) left him in his misery; a miserable conceit. On these
occasions the poet should endeavour to raise pity; but, instead of
this, Ovid is tickling you to laugh. Virgil never made use of such
machines when he was moving you to commiserate the death of
Dido: he would not destroy what he was building. Chaucer makes
Arcite violent in his love, and unjust in the pursuit of it; yet, when he
came to die, he made him think more reasonably: he repents not of
his love, for that had altered his character; but acknowledges the
injustice of his proceedings, and resigns Emilia to Palamon. What
would Ovid have done on this occasion? He would certainly have
made Arcite witty on his deathbed; he had complained he was
further off from possession, by being so near, and a thousand such
boyisms, which Chaucer rejected as below the dignity of the subject.
They who think otherwise, would, by the same reason, prefer Lucan
and Ovid to Homer and Virgil, and Martial to all four of them. As
for the turn of words, in which Ovid particularly excels all poets, they
are sometimes a fault, and sometimes a beauty, as they are used
properly or improperly; but in strong passions always to be shunned,
because passions are serious, and will admit no playing. The French
have a high value for them; and, I confess, they are often what they
call delicate, when they are introduced with judgement; but Chaucer
writ with more simplicity, and followed Nature more closely, than
to use them. I have thus far, to the best of my knowledge, been an
upright judge betwixt the parties in competition, not meddling with
the design nor the disposition of it; because the design was not their
own; and in the disposing of it they were equal. It remains that I say
somewhat of Chaucer in particular.

1 Wealth has made me poor (*Metamorphoses*, III). [Ed.]

In the first place, as he is the father of English poetry, so I hold him in the same degree of veneration as the Grecians held Homer, or the Romans Virgil. He is a perpetual fountain of good sense; learned in all sciences; and, therefore, speaks properly on all subjects. As he knew what to say, so he knows also when to leave off; a continence which is practised by few writers, and scarcely by any of the ancients, excepting Virgil and Horace. One of our late great poets is sunk in his reputation, because he could never forgive any conceit which came in his way; but swept like a drag-net, great and small. There was plenty enough, but the dishes were ill sorted; whole pyramids of sweetmeats, for boys and women; but little of solid meat, for men. All this proceeded not from any want of knowledge, but of judgement. Neither did he want that in discerning the beauties and faults of other poets, but only indulged himself in the luxury of writing; and perhaps knew it was a fault, but hoped the reader would not find it. For this reason, though he must always be thought a great poet, he is no longer esteemed a good writer; and for ten impressions, which his works have had in so many successive years, yet at present a hundred books are scarcely purchased once a twelve-month; for, as my last Lord Rochester said, though somewhat profanely, *Not being of God, he could not stand.*

Chaucer followed Nature everywhere, but was never so bold to go beyond her; and there is a great difference of being *poeta* and *nimis poeta*, if we may believe Catullus, as much as betwixt a modest behaviour and affectation. The verse of Chaucer, I confess, is not harmonious to us; but 'tis like the eloquence of one whom Tacitus commends, it was *auribus istius temporis accommodata*:[1] they who lived with him, and some time after him, thought it musical; and it continues so even in our judgement, if compared with the numbers of Lydgate and Gower, his contemporaries: there is the rude sweetness of a Scotch tune in it, which is natural and pleasing, though not perfect. 'Tis true, I cannot go so far as he who published the last edition of him;[2] for he would make us believe the fault is in our ears,

1 Suited to the ears of those days. [Ed.]
2 Thomas Speght, whose edition was used throughout the seventeenth century, wrote: 'And for [Chaucer's] verses, although in divers places they seem to us to stand of unequal measures, yet a skilful reader who can scan them in their nature shall find it otherwise.' [Ed.]

and that there were really ten syllables in a verse where we find but nine: but this opinion is not worth confuting; 'tis so gross and obvious an error, that common sense (which is a rule in everything but matters of Faith and Revelation) must convince the reader, that equality of numbers, in every verse which we call *heroic*, was either not known, or not always practised, in Chaucer's age. It were an easy matter to produce some thousands of his verses, which are lame for want of half a foot, and sometimes a whole one, and which no pronunciation can make otherwise. We can only say, that he lived in the infancy of our poetry, and that nothing is brought to perfection at the first. We must be children before we grow men. There was an Ennius and in process of time a Lucilius, and a Lucretius, before Virgil and Horace; even after Chaucer there was a Spenser, a Harrington, a Fairfax, before Waller and Denham were in being; and our numbers were in their nonage till these last appeared. I need say little of his parentage, life, and fortunes; they are to be found at large in all the editions of his works. He was employed abroad, and favoured, by Edward the Third, Richard the Second, and Henry the Fourth, and was poet, as I suppose, to all three of them. In Richard's time, I doubt, he was a little dipped in the rebellion of the Commons; and being brother-in-law to John of Gaunt, it was no wonder if he followed the fortunes of that family; and was well with Henry the Fourth when he had deposed his predecessor. Neither is it to be admired, that Henry, who was a wise as well as a valiant prince, who claimed by succession, and was sensible that his title was not sound, but was rightfully in Mortimer, who had married the heir of York; it was not to be admired, I say, if that great politician should be pleased to have the greatest Wit of those times in his interests, and to be the trumpet of his praises. Augustus had given him the example, by the advice of Maecenas, who recommended Virgil and Horace to him; whose praises helped to make him popular while he was alive, and after his death have made him precious to posterity. As for the religion of our poet, he seems to have some little bias towards the opinions of Wycliffe, after John of Gaunt his patron; somewhat of which appears in the tale of Piers Plowman: yet I cannot blame him for inveighing so sharply against the vices of the clergy in his age: their pride, their ambition, their pomp, their avarice, their worldly interest, deserved the lashes which he gave them, both in that, and in most of his *Canterbury Tales*. Neither has his contemporary Boccace spared them: yet both those poets lived in much esteem with good and holy men in orders; for the scandal which is given by particular priests reflects not on the sacred function. Chaucer's Monk, his Canon, and his Friar, took not from the character of his Good Parson. A satirical poet is the check of the laymen on bad priests. We are only to take care, that we involve not the innocent with the guilty in the same condemnation. The good cannot be too much honoured, nor the bad too coarsely used; for the corruption of the best becomes the worst. When a clergyman is whipped, his gown is first taken off, by which the dignity of his order is secured. If he be wrongfully accused, he has his action of slander; and 'tis at the poet's peril if he transgress the law. But they will tell us, that all kind of satire, though never so well deserved by particular priests, yet brings the whole order into contempt. Is then the peerage of England anything dishonoured when a peer suffers for his treason? If he be libelled, or any way defamed, he has his *scandalum magnatum*[1] to punish the offender. They who use this kind of argument, seems to be conscious to themselves of somewhat which has deserved the poet's lash, and are less concerned for their public capacity than for their private; at least there is pride at the bottom of their reasoning. If the faults of men in orders are only to be judged among themselves, they are all in some sort parties; for, since they say the honour of their order is concerned in every member of it, how can we be sure that they will be impartial judges? How far I may be allowed to speak my opinion in this case, I know not; but I am sure a dispute of this nature caused mischief in abundance betwixt a King of England and an Archbishop of Canterbury; one standing up for the laws of his land, and the other for the honour (as he called it) of God's Church; which ended in the murder of the prelate, and in the whipping of his Majesty from post to pillar for his penance. The learned and ingenious Dr Drake has saved me the labour of inquiring into the esteem and reverence which the priests have had of old; and I would rather extend than diminish any part of it: yet I must needs say, that when a priest provokes me without any occasion given him, I have no reason, unless it be the charity of a Christian, to forgive him: *prior laesit* is justification sufficient in the civil law. If I answer him

1 Slander of great ones – a cause for legal action. [Ed.]

in his own language, self-defence I am sure must be allowed me; and if I carry it further, even to a sharp recrimination, somewhat may be indulged to human frailty. Yet my resentment has not wrought so far, but that I have followed Chaucer, in his character of a holy man, and have enlarged on that subject with some pleasure; reserving to myself the right, if I shall think fit hereafter, to describe another sort of priests, such as are more easily to be found than the Good Parson; such as have given the last blow to Christianity in this age, by a practice so contrary to their doctrine. But this will keep cold till another time. In the meanwhile, I take up Chaucer where I left him.

He must have been a man of a most wonderful comprehensive nature, because, as it has been truly observed of him, he has taken into the compass of his *Canterbury Tales* the various manners and humours (as we now call them) of the whole English nation, in his age. Not a single character has escaped him. All his pilgrims are severally distinguished from each other; and not only in their inclinations, but in their very physiognomies and persons. Baptista Porta could not have described their natures better, than by the marks which the poet gives them. The matter and manner of their tales, and of their telling, are so suited to their different educations, humours, and callings, that each of them would be improper in any other mouth. Even the grave and serious characters are distinguished by their several sorts of gravity: their discourses are such as belong to their age, their calling, and their breeding; such as are becoming of them, and of them only. Some of his persons are vicious, and some virtuous; some are unlearned or (as Chaucer calls them) lewd, and some are learned. Even the ribaldry of the low characters is different: the Reeve, the Miller, and the Cook, are several men, and distinguished from each other as much as the mincing Lady-Prioress and the broad-speaking, gap-toothed Wife of Bath. But enough of this; there is such a variety of game springing up before me, that I am distracted in my choice, and know not which to follow. 'Tis sufficient to say according to the proverb, that here is God's plenty. We have our forefathers and great-grand-dames all before us, as they were in Chaucer's days; their general characters are still remaining in mankind, and even in England, though they are called by other names than those of Monks, and Friars, and Canons, and Lady Abbesses, and Nuns; for mankind is ever the same, and nothing lost out of

Nature, though everything is altered. May I have leave to do myself the justice (since my enemies will do me none, and are so far from granting me to be a good poet, that they will not allow me so much as to be a Christian, or a moral man), may I have leave, I say, to inform my reader, that I have confined my choice to such tales of Chaucer as savour nothing of immodesty. If I had desired more to please than to instruct, the Reeve, the Miller, the Shipman, the Merchant, the Sumner, and, above all, the Wife of Bath, in the *Prologue* to her Tale, would have procured me as many friends and readers, as there are *beaux* and ladies of pleasure in the town. But I will no more offend against good manners: I am sensible as I ought to be of the scandal I have given by my loose writings; and make what reparation I am able, by this public acknowledgement. If anything of this nature, or of profaneness, be crept into these poems, I am so far from defending it, that I disown it. *Totum hoc indictum volo.*[1] Chaucer makes another manner of apology for his broad speaking, and Boccace makes the like; but I will follow neither of them. Our countryman, in the end of his Characters, before the *Canterbury Tales*, thus excuses the ribaldry, which is very gross, in many of his novels:

But first I pray yow, of youre curteisye,
That ye n'arette it nat my vileynye,
Thogh that I pleynly speke in this mateere,
To telle yow hir wordes and hir cheere,
Ne thogh I speke hir wordes proprely.
For this ye knowen al so wel as I,
Whoso shal telle a tale after a man,
He moot reherce as ny as evere he kan
Everich a word, if it be in his charge,
Al speke he never so rudeliche and large,
Or ellis he moot telle his tale untrewe,
Or feyne thyng, or fynde wordes newe.
He may nat spare, althogh he were his brother;
He moot as wel seye o word as another.
Crist spak hymself ful brode in hooly writ,
And wel ye woot no vileynye is it.

1 I wish all this unsaid. [Ed.]

Eek Plato seith, whoso that kan hym rede,
The wordes moote be cosyn to the dede.

(I 725–42)

Yet if a man should have inquired of Boccace or of Chaucer, what need they had of introducing such characters, where obscene words were proper in their mouths, but very undecent to be heard; I know not what answer they could have made; for that reason, such tales shall be left untold by me. You have here a specimen of Chaucer's language, which is so obsolete, that his sense is scarce to be understood; and you have likewise more than one example of his unequal numbers, which were mentioned before. Yet many of his verses consist of ten syllables, and the words not much behind our present English: as for example, these two lines, in the description of the Carpenter's young wife:

Wynsynge she was, as is a joly colt,
Long as a mast, and upright as a bolt.

(I 3263–4)

I have almost done with Chaucer, when I have answered some objections relating to my present work. I find some people are offended that I have turned these tales into modern English; because they think them unworthy of my pains, and look on Chaucer as a dry, old-fashioned wit, not worth reviving. I have often heard the late Earl of Leicester say, that Mr Cowley himself was of that opinion; who, having read him over at my Lord's request, declared he had no taste of him. I dare not advance my opinion against the judgement of so great an author; but I think it fair, however, to leave the decision to the public. Mr Cowley was too modest to set up for a dictator; and being shocked perhaps with his old style, never examined into the depth of his good sense. Chaucer, I confess, is a rough diamond, and must first be polished ere he shines. I deny not likewise, that, living in our early days of poetry, he writes not always of a piece; but sometimes mingles trivial things with those of greater moment. Sometimes also, though not often, he runs riot, like Ovid, and knows not when he has said enough. But there are more great wits besides Chaucer, whose fault is their excess of conceits, and those ill sorted. An author is not to write all he can, but only all he ought.

Having observed this redundancy in Chaucer, (as it is an easy matter for a man of ordinary parts to find a fault in one of greater,) I have not tied myself to a literal translation; but have often omitted what I judged unnecessary, or not of dignity enough to appear in the company of better thoughts. I have presumed further in some places, and added somewhat of my own where I thought my author was deficient, and had not given his thoughts their true lustre, for want of words in the beginning of our language. And to this I was the more emboldened, because (if I may be permitted to say it of myself) I found I had a soul congenial to his, and that I had been conversant in the same studies. Another poet, in another age, may take the same liberty with my writings; if at least they live long enough to deserve correction. It was also necessary sometimes to restore the sense of Chaucer, which was lost or mangled in the errors of the press. Let this example suffice at present: in the story of *Palamon and Arcite*, where the temple of Diana is described, you find these verses, in all the editions of our author:

Ther saugh I Dane, yturned til a tree, –
I mene nat the goddesse Diane,
But Penneus doghter, which that highte Dane.

(I 2062–4)

Which after a little consideration I knew was to be reformed into this sense, that Daphne the daughter of Peneus was turned into a tree. I durst not make thus bold with Ovid, lest some future Milbourne should arise, and say, I varied from my author, because I understood him not.

But there are other judges, who think I ought not to have translated Chaucer into English, out of a quite contrary notion: they suppose there is a certain veneration due to his old language; and that it is little less than profanation and sacrilege to alter it. They are further of opinion, that somewhat of his good sense will suffer in this transfusion, and much of the beauty of his thoughts will infallibly be lost, which appear with more grace in their old habit. Of this opinion was that excellent person whom I mentioned, the late Earl of Leicester, who valued Chaucer as much as Mr Cowley despised him. My Lord dissuaded me from this attempt, (for I was thinking of it some years before his death,) and his authority prevailed so far with me, as to defer my undertaking while he lived, in deference to him: yet my reason was not convinced with what he urged against it. If the first end of a writer be to be understood, then, as his language grows obsolete, his thoughts must grow obscure –

Multa renascentur, quae nunc cecidere; cadentque
Quae nunc sunt in honore vocabula, si volet usus,
Quem penes arbitrium est et jus et norma loquendi.

When an ancient word for its sound and significancy deserves to be revived, I have that reasonable veneration for antiquity to restore it. All beyond this is superstition. Words are not like landmarks, so sacred as never to be removed; customs are changed, and even statutes are silently repealed, when the reason ceases for which they were enacted. As for the other part of the argument, that his thoughts will lose of their original beauty by the innovation of words; in the first place, not only their beauty, but their being is lost, where they are no longer understood, which is the present case. I grant that something must be lost in all transfusion, that is, in all translations; but the sense will remain, which would otherwise be lost, or at least be maimed, when it is scarce intelligible, and that but to a few. How few are there who can read Chaucer, so as to understand him perfectly? And if imperfectly, then with less profit, and no pleasure. 'Tis not for the use of some old Saxon friends, that I have taken these pains with him: let them neglect my version, because they have no need of it. I made it for their sakes who understand sense and poetry as well as they, when that poetry and sense is put into words which they understand. I will go further, and dare to add, that what beauties I lose in some places, I give to others which had them not originally: but in this I may be partial to myself; let the reader judge, and I submit to his decision. Yet I think I have just occasion to complain of them, who because they understand Chaucer, would deprive the greater part of their countrymen of the same advantage, and hoard him up, as misers do their grandam gold, only to look on it themselves, and hinder others from making use of it. In sum, I seriously protest, that no man ever had, or can have, a greater veneration for Chaucer than myself. I have translated some part of his works, only that I might perpetuate his memory, or at least refresh it, amongst my countrymen. If I have altered him anywhere for the better, I must at the same time acknowledge, that I could have done nothing without him. *Facile est inventis addere*[1] is no great commendation; and I am not so vain to think I have deserved a greater. I will conclude what I have to say of him singly, with this one remark: a lady of my acquaintance, who keeps a kind of correspondence with some authors of the fair sex in France, has been informed by them, that Mademoiselle de Scudéry, who is as old as Sibyl, and inspired like her by the same God of Poetry, is at this time translating Chaucer into modern French. From which I gather, that he has been formerly translated into the old Provençal; for how she should come to understand old English, I know not. But the matter of fact being true, it makes me think that there is something in it like fatality; that, after certain periods of time, the fame and memory of great Wits should be renewed, as Chaucer is both in France and England. If this be wholly chance, 'tis extraordinary; and I dare not call it more, for fear of being taxed with superstition.

Boccace comes last to be considered, who, living in the same age with Chaucer, had the same genius, and followed the same studies. Both writ novels, and each of them cultivated his mother tongue. But the greatest resemblance of our two modern authors being in their familiar style, and pleasing way of relating comical adventures, I may pass it over, because I have translated nothing from Boccace of that nature. In the serious part of poetry, the advantage is wholly on Chaucer's side; for though the Englishman has borrowed many tales from the Italian, yet it appears, that those of Boccace were not generally of his own making, but taken from authors of former ages, and by him only modelled; so that what there was of invention, in either of them, may be judged equal. But Chaucer has refined on Boccace, and has mended the stories, which he has borrowed, in his way of telling; though prose allows more liberty of thought, and the expression is more easy when unconfined by numbers. Our countryman carries weight, and yet wins the race at disadvantage. I desire not the reader should take my word; and, therefore, I will set two of their discourses, on the same subject, in the same light, for every man to judge betwixt them. I translated Chaucer first, and, amongst the rest, pitched on the *Wife of Bath's Tale;* not daring, as I have said,

1 It is easy to add to things already conceived. [Ed.]

to adventure on her *Prologue*, because 'tis too licentious. There Chaucer introduces an old woman, of mean parentage, whom a youthful knight, of noble blood, was forced to marry, and consequently loathed her. The crone being in bed with him on the wedding-night, and finding his aversion, endeavours to win his affection by reason, and speaks a good word for herself, (as who could blame her?) in hope to mollify the sullen bridegroom. She takes her topics from the benefits of poverty, the advantages of old age and ugliness, the vanity of youth, and the silly pride of ancestry and titles, without inherent virtue, which is the true nobility. When I had closed Chaucer, I returned to Ovid, and translated some more of his fables; and, by this time, had so far forgotten the *Wife of Bath's Tale*, that, when I took up Boccace, unawares I fell on the same argument, of preferring virtue to nobility of blood and titles, in the story of *Sigismonda*; which I had certainly avoided, for the resemblance of the two discourses, if my memory had not failed me. Let the reader weigh them both; and, if he thinks me partial to Chaucer, 'tis in him to right Boccace.

I prefer, in our countryman, far above all his other stories, the noble poem of *Palamon and Arcite*, which is of the epic kind, and perhaps not much inferior to the *Ilias*, or the *Æneis*. The story is more pleasing than either of them, the manners as perfect, the diction as poetical, the learning as deep and various, and the disposition full as artful: only it includes a greater length of time, as taking up seven years at least; but Aristotle has left undecided the duration of the action; which yet is easily reduced into the compass of a year, by a narration of what preceded the return of Palamon to Athens. I had thought, for the honour of our narration, and more particularly for his, whose laurel, though unworthy, I have worn after him, that this story was of English growth, and Chaucer's own: but I was undeceived by Boccace; for, casually looking on the end of his seventh *Giornata*, I found Dioneo, (under which name he shadows himself,) and Fiametta, (who represents his mistress, the natural daughter of Robert, King of Naples,) of whom these words are spoken: *Dioneo e Fiametta gran pezza cantarono insieme d'Arcita, e di Palemone*; by which it appears, that this story was written before the time of Boccace; but the name of its author being wholly lost, Chaucer is now become an original; and I question not but the poem has received many beauties, by passing through his noble hands. Besides this tale, there is another of his own invention, after the manner of the Provençals, called *The Flower and the Leaf*, with which I was so particularly pleased, both for the invention and the moral, that I cannot hinder myself from recommending it to the reader.

(254–70)

Alexander Pope

in conversation 1730 (from Joseph Spence, *Observations, Anecdotes and Characters*, first published 1820)

I read Chaucer still with as much pleasure as almost any of our poets. He is a master of manners and of description, and the first tale-teller in the true enlivened natural way.

(1 179)

Elizabeth Cooper

from *The Muses' Library* 1737

Chaucer . . . encountered the follies of mankind as well as their vices, and blended the acutest raillery with the most insinuating humour. By his writings it plainly appears that poetry and politeness grew up together, and had like to have been buried in his grave.

(1 xi)

Samuel Johnson

from 'The History of the English Language', *Dictionary of the English Language* 1755

The history of our language is now brought to the point at which the history of our poetry is generally supposed to commence, the time of the illustrious Geoffrey Chaucer, who may perhaps, with great justice, be styled the first of our versifiers who wrote poetically. He does not, however, appear to have deserved all the praise which he has received, or all the censure that he has suffered. Dryden, who mistakes genius for learning and, in confidence of his abilities, ventured to write of what he had not examined, ascribes to Chaucer the first refinement of our numbers, the first production of easy and natural rhymes, and the improvement of our language by words borrowed from the more polished languages of the Continent. Skinner, contrarily, blames him in harsh terms for having vitiated his native speech by *whole cartloads of foreign words*. But he that reads the works of Gower will find smooth numbers and easy rhymes, of which Chaucer is supposed to have been the inventor, and the French words, whether good or bad, of which Chaucer is charged as the importer. Some innovations he might probably make, like others, in the infancy of our poetry, which the paucity of books does not allow us to discover with particular exactness; but the works of Gower and Lydgate sufficiently evince that his diction was in general like that of his contemporaries. And some improvements he undoubtedly made, by the various dispositions of his rhymes, and by the mixture of different numbers, in which he seems to have been happy and judicious.

Richard Hurd

from *Letters on Chivalry and Romance* 1762

Dan Chaucer . . . in a reign that almost realized the wonders of romantic chivalry not only discerned the absurdity of the old romances, but has even ridiculed them with incomparable spirit.

His *Rhyme of Sir Thopas*, in the *Canterbury Tales*, is a manifest banter on these books, and may be considered as a sort of prelude to the adventures of Don Quixote. I call it *a manifest banter*, for we are to observe that this was Chaucer's own tale, and that, when in the progress of it the good sense of the Host is made to break in upon him and interrupt him, Chaucer approves his disgust and, changing his note, tells the simple instructive *Tale of Melibeus*, 'a moral tale virtuous', as he chooses to characterize it, to show what sort of fictions were most expressive of real life, and most proper to be put into the hands of the people.

One might further observe that the *Rhyme of Sir Thopas* itself is so managed as with infinite humour to expose the leading impertinences of books of chivalry, and their impertinences only; as may be

seen by the different conduct of this tale from that of Cambuscan,
which Spenser and Milton were so pleased with, and which with
great propriety is put into the mouth of the Squire.
                                                           (107-8)

Thomas Warton

from *History of English Poetry* 1774

Hitherto our poets had been persons of a private and circumscribed
education; and the art of versifying, like every other kind of composition, had been confined to recluse scholars. But Chaucer was a man
of the world; and from this circumstance we are to account, in great
measure, for the many new embellishments which he conferred on
our language and our poetry. The descriptions of splendid proces-
sions and gallant carousals with which his works abound are a
proof that he was conversant with the practices and diversions of
polite life. Familiarity with a variety of things and objects, opportunities of acquiring the fashionable and courtly modes of speech,
connexions with the great at home, and a personal acquaintance with
the vernacular poets of foreign countries, opened his mind and
furnished him with new lights.
                                                           (1 341-2)

Pathetic description is one of Chaucer's peculiar excellences.
                                                           (1 387)

Pope has imitated this piece [the *House of Fame*] with his usual
elegance of diction and harmony of versification. But in the meantime
he has not only misrepresented the story, but marred the character
of the poem. He has endeavoured to correct its extravagancies by new
refinements and additions of another cast; but he did not consider
that extravagancies are essential to a poem of such a structure, and
even constitute its beauties. An attempt to unite order and exactness
of imagery with a subject formed on principles so professedly
romantic and anomalous is like giving Corinthian pillars to a Gothic
palace. When I read Pope's elegant imitation of this piece, I think I
am walking among the modern monuments unsuitably placed in
Westminster Abbey.
                                                           (1 396)

But Chaucer's vein of humour, although conspicuous in the *Canterbury Tales*, is chiefly displayed in the characters with which they are
introduced. In these his knowledge of the world availed him in a
peculiar degree, and enabled him to give such an accurate picture of
ancient manners as no contemporary nation has transmitted to
posterity. It is here that we view the pursuits and employments, the
customs and diversions of our ancestors, copied from the life and
represented with equal truth and spirit by a judge of mankind whose
penetration qualified him to discern their foibles or discriminating
peculiarities, and by an artist who understood that proper selection
of circumstances and those predominant characteristics which form a
finished portrait. We are surprised to find, in so gross and ignorant
an age, such talents for satire and for observation on life, qualities
which usually exert themselves at more civilized periods, when the
improved state of society, by subtilizing our speculations and establishing uniform modes of behaviour, disposes mankind to study
themselves, and renders deviations of conduct and singularities of
character more immediately and necessarily the objects of censure
and ridicule. These curious and valuable remains are specimens of
Chaucer's native genius, unassisted and unalloyed. The figures are
all British, and bear no suspicious signatures of classical, Italian or
French imitation. The characters of Theophrastus are not so lively,
particular and appropriated.

(I 435)

Joseph Warton

from *Essay on the Genius and Writings of Pope* 1782

But whatever Chaucer might copy from the Italians, yet the artful
and entertaining plan of his *Canterbury Tales* was purely original and
his own. This admirable piece, even exclusive of its poetry, is highly
valuable, as it preserves to us the liveliest and exactest picture of the
manners, customs, characters and habits of our forefathers, whom he
has brought before our eyes acting as on a stage, suitably to their
different orders and employments. With these portraits the driest
antiquary must be delighted; by this plan he has more judiciously
connected these stories which the guests relate than Boccace has

done in his novels; whom he has imitated, if not excelled, in the variety of the subjects of his tales. It is a common mistake that Chaucer's excellence lay in his manner of treating light and ridiculous subjects; for whoever will attentively consider the noble poem of Palamon and Arcite will be convinced that he equally excels in the pathetic and the sublime.

(I 351-2)

William Blake

from *A Descriptive Catalogue of Pictures, Poetical and Historical Inventions, Painted by William Blake* . . . 1809

The characters of Chaucer's Pilgrims are the characters which compose all ages and nations: as one age falls, another rises, different to mortal sight, but to immortals only the same; for we see the same characters repeated again and again, in animals, vegetables, minerals, and in men; nothing new occurs in identical existence; Accident ever varies, Substance can never suffer change nor decay.

Of Chaucer's characters, as described in his *Canterbury Tales*, some of the names or titles are altered by time, but the characters themselves for ever remain unaltered, and consequently they are the physiognomies or lineaments of universal human life, beyond which Nature never steps. Names alter, things never alter. I have known multitudes of those who would have been monks in the age of monkery, who in this deistical age are deists. As Newton numbered the stars, and as Linneus numbered the plants, so Chaucer numbered the classes of men.

The Painter has consequently varied the heads and forms of his personages into all Nature's varieties; the Horses he has also varied to accord to their Riders; the costume is correct according to authentic monuments.

The Knight and Squire with the Squire's Yeoman lead the procession, as Chaucer has also placed them first in his prologue. The Knight is a true Hero, a good, great, and wise man; his whole length

portrait on horseback, as written by Chaucer, cannot be surpassed.
He has spent his life in the field; has ever been a conqueror, and is
that species of character which in every age stands as the guardian of
man against the oppressor. His son is like him with the germ of
perhaps greater perfection still, as he blends literature and the arts
with his warlike studies. Their dress and their horses are of the first
rate, without ostentation, and with all the true grandeur that unaffected simplicity when in high rank always displays. The Squire's
Yeoman is also a great character, a man perfectly knowing in his
profession:

And in his hand he baar a myghty bowe.

(I 108)

Chaucer describes here a mighty man; one who in war is the worthy
attendant on noble heroes.

The Prioress follows these with her female chaplain:

Another Nonne with hire hadde she,
That was hir chapeleyne, and preestes thre.

(I 163-4)

This Lady is described also as of the first rank, rich and honoured.
She has certain peculiarities and little delicate affectations, not un-
becoming in her, being accompanied with what is truly grand and
really polite; her person and face Chaucer has described with minuteness; it is very elegant, and was the beauty of our ancestors, till after
Elizabeth's time, when voluptuousness and folly began to be accounted beautiful.

Her companion and her three priests were no doubt all perfectly
delineated in those parts of Chaucer's work which are now lost; we
ought to suppose them suitable attendants on rank and fashion.

The Monk follows these with the Friar. The Painter has also
grouped with these the Pardoner and the Sompnour and the Manciple, and has here also introduced one of the rich citizens of London:
Characters likely to ride in company, all being above the common
rank in life or attendants on those who were so.

For the Monk is described by Chaucer, as a man of the first rank
in society, noble, rich, and expensively attended; he is a leader of
the age, with certain humorous accompaniments in his character,

that do not degrade, but render him an object of dignified mirth, but also with other accompaniments not so respectable.

The Friar is a character also of a mixed kind:

A Frere ther was, a wantowne and a merye.
(I 208)

but in his office he is said to be a 'full solemn man': eloquent, amorous, witty, and satyrical; young, handsome, and rich; he is a complete rogue, with constitutional gaiety enough to make him a master of all the pleasures of the world.

His nekke whit was as the flour-de-lys;
Therto he strong was as a champioun.
(I 238-9)

It is necessary here to speak of Chaucer's own character, that I may set certain mistaken critics right in their conception of the humour and fun that occurs on the journey. Chaucer is himself the great poetical observer of men, who in every age is born to record and eternize its acts. This he does as a master, as a father, and superior, who looks down on their little follies from the Emperor to the Miller; sometimes with severity, oftener with joke and sport.

Accordingly Chaucer has made his Monk a great tragedian, one who studied poetical art. So much so, that the generous Knight is, in the compassionate dictates of his soul, compelled to cry out:

'Hoo!' quod the Knyght, 'good sire, namoore of this!
That ye han seyd is right ynough, ywis,
And muchel moore; for litel hevynesse
Is right ynough to muche folk, I gesse.
I seye for me, it is a greet disese,
Whereas men han been in greet welthe and ese,
To heeren of hire sodeyn fal, allas!
And the contrarie is joye and greet solas . . .'
(VII 2767-74)

The Monk's definition of tragedy in the proem to his tale is worth repeating:

Tragedie is to seyn a certeyn storie,
As olde bookes maken us memorie,
Of hym that stood in greet prosperitee,
And is yfallen out of heigh degree
Into myserie, and endeth wrecchedly.

(VII 1973-7)

Though a man of luxury, pride and pleasure, he is a master of art
and learning, though affecting to despise it. Those who can think
that the proud Huntsman and Noble Housekeeper, Chaucer's Monk,
is intended for a buffoon or burlesque character, know little of
Chaucer.

For the Host who follows this group, and holds the center of the
cavalcade, is a first rate character, and his jokes are no trifles; they
are always, though uttered with audacity, and equally free with the
Lord and the Peasant, they are always substantially and weightily
expressive of knowledge and experience; Henry Baillie, the keeper
of the greatest Inn of the greatest City; for such was the Tabarde
Inn in Southwark, near London: our Host was also a leader of the
age.

By way of illustration, I instance Shakspeare's Witches in
Macbeth. Those who dress them for the stage, consider them as
wretched old women, and not as Shakspeare intended, the Goddesses
of Destiny; this shews how Chaucer has been misunderstood in his
sublime work. Shakspeare's Fairies also are the rulers of the vegetable
world, and so are Chaucer's; let them be so considered, and then the
poet will be understood, and not else.

But I have omitted to speak of a very prominent character, the
Pardoner, the Age's Knave, who always commands and domineers
over the high and low vulgar. This man is sent in every age for a
rod and scourge, and for a blight, for a trial of men, to divide the
classes of men; he is in the most holy sanctuary, and he is suffered by
Providence for wise ends, and has also his great use, and his grand
leading destiny.

His companion, the Sompnour, is also a Devil of the first magnitude, grand, terrific, rich and honoured in the rank of which he holds
the destiny. The uses to Society are perhaps equal of the Devil and
of the Angel, their sublimity, who can dispute.

In daunger hadde he at his owene gise
The yonge girles of the diocise,
And knew hir conseil, etc.

(1 663-5)

The principal figure in the next groupe is the Good Parson; an Apostle, a real Messenger of Heaven, sent in every age for its light and its warmth. This man is beloved and venerated by all, and neglected by all: He serves all, and is served by none; he is, according to Christ's definition, the greatest of his age. Yet he is a Poor Parson of a town. Read Chaucer's description of the Good Parson, and bow the head and the knee to him, who, in every age, sends us such a burning and a shining light. Search, O ye rich and powerful, for these men and obey their counsel, then shall the golden age return: But alas! you will not easily distinguish him from the Friar or the Pardoner; they, also, are 'full solemn men', and their counsel you will continue to follow.

I have placed by his side the Sergeant at Lawe, who appears delighted to ride in his company, and between him and his brother, the Plowman; as I wish men of Law would always ride with them, and take their counsel, especially in all difficult points. Chaucer's Lawyer is a character of great venerableness, a Judge, and a real master of the jurisprudence of his age.

The Doctor of Physic is in this groupe, and the Franklin, the voluptuous country gentleman, contrasted with the Physician, and on his other hand, with two Citizens of London. Chaucer's characters live age after age. Every age is a Canterbury Pilgrimage; we all pass on, each sustaining one or other of these characters; nor can a child be born, who is not one of these characters of Chaucer. The Doctor of Physic is described as the first of his profession; perfect, learned, completely Master and Doctor in his art. Thus the reader will observe, that Chaucer makes every one of his characters perfect in his kind; every one is an Antique Statue; the image of a class, and not of an imperfect individual.

This groupe also would furnish substantial matter, on which volumes might be written. The Franklin is one who keeps open table, who is the genius of eating and drinking, the Bacchus; as the Doctor of Physic is the Esculapius, the Host is the Silenus, the Squire is the

Apollo, the Miller is the Hercules, etc. Chaucer's characters are a description of the eternal Principles that exist in all ages. The Franklin is voluptuousness itself, most nobly pourtrayed:

It snewed in his hous of mete and drynke.

(I 345)

The Plowman is simplicity itself, with wisdom and strength for its stamina. Chaucer has divided the ancient character of Hercules between his Miller and his Plowman. Benevolence is the plowman's great characteristic; he is thin with excessive labour, and not with old age, as some have supposed:

He wolde thresshe, and therto dyke and delve,
For Cristes sake, for every povre wight,
Withouten hire, if it lay in his myght.

(I 536–8)

Visions of these eternal principles or characters of human life appear to poets, in all ages; the Grecian gods were the ancient Cherubim of Phoenicia; but the Greeks, and since them the Moderns, have neglected to subdue the gods of Priam. These gods are visions of the eternal attributes, or divine names, which, when erected into gods, become destructive to humanity. They ought to be the servants, and not the masters of man, or of society. They ought to be made to sacrifice to Man, and not man compelled to sacrifice to them; for when separated from man or humanity, who is Jesus the Saviour, the vine of eternity, they are thieves and rebels, they are destroyers.

The Plowman of Chaucer is Hercules in his supreme eternal state, divested of his spectrous shadow; which is the Miller, a terrible fellow, such as exists in all times and places for the trial of men, to astonish every neighbourhood with brutal strength and courage, to get rich and powerful to curb the pride of Man.

The Reeve and the Manciple are two characters of the most consummate worldly wisdom. The Shipman, or Sailor, is a similar genius of Ulyssean art; but with the highest courage superadded.

The Citizens and their Cook are each leaders of a class. Chaucer has been somehow made to number four citizens, which would make his whole company, himself included, thirty-one. But he says there was but nine and twenty in his company:

Wel nyne and twenty in a compaignye.
                    (I 24)

The Webbe, or Weaver, and the Tapiser, or Tapestry Weaver, appear to me to be the same person; but this is only an opinion, for full nine and twenty may signify one more or less. But I dare say that Chaucer wrote 'A Webbe Dyer', that is, a Cloth Dyer:

A Webbe Dyere and a Tapycer
                    (I 362)

The Merchant cannot be one of the Three Citizens, as his dress is different, and his character is more marked, whereas Chaucer says of his rich citizens:

They were clothed alle in o lyveree.
                    (I 363)

The characters of Women Chaucer has divided into two classes, the Lady Prioress and the Wife of Bath. Are not these leaders of the ages of men? The lady prioress, in some ages, predominates; and in some the wife of Bath, in whose character Chaucer has been equally minute and exact, because she is also a scourge and a blight. I shall say no more of her, nor expose what Chaucer has left hidden; let the young reader study what he has said of her: it is useful as a scarecrow. There are of such characters born too many for the peace of the world.

I come at length to the Clerk of Oxenford. This character varies from that of Chaucer, as the contemplative philosopher varies from the poetical genius. There are always these two classes of learned sages, the poetical and the philosophical. The painter has put them side by side, as if the youthful clerk had put himself under the tuition of the mature poet. Let the Philosopher always be the servant and scholar of inspiration and all will be happy.

Such are the characters that compose this Picture.

                    (567–72)

George Crabbe

from the Preface to *Tales* 1812

It may probably be remarked that tales, however dissimilar, might have been connected by some associating circumstance to which the whole number might bear equal affinity, and that examples of such union are to be found in Chaucer, in Boccace, and other collectors and inventors of tales which, considered in themselves, are altogether independent; and to this idea I gave so much consideration as convinced me that I could not avail myself of the benefit of such artificial mode of affinity. To imitate the English poet, characters must be found adapted to their several relations, and this is a point of great difficulty and hazard: much allowance seems to be required even for Chaucer himself; since it is difficult to conceive that on any occasion the devout and delicate Prioress, the courtly and valiant Knight, and 'the poure good man the Persone of a Towne' would be the voluntary companions of the drunken Miller, the licentious Sompnour and 'the wanton Wife of Bath', and enter into that colloquial and travelling intimacy which, if a common pilgrimage to the shrine of St Thomas may be said to excuse, I know nothing beside (and certainly nothing in these times) that would produce such effect. . . .

Be it then granted that (as Duke Theseus observes) 'such tricks hath strong imagination', and that such poets 'are of imagination all compact'; let it be further conceded that theirs is a higher and more dignified kind of composition, nay, the only kind that has pretentions to inspiration; still, that these poets should so entirely engross the title as to exclude those who address their productions to the plain sense and sober judgement of their readers rather than to their fancy and imagination, I must repeat that I am unwilling to admit – because I conceive that, by granting such right of exclusion, a vast deal of what has been hitherto received as genuine poetry would no longer be entitled to that appellation.

All that kind of satire wherein character is skilfully delineated must (this criterion being allowed) no longer be esteemed as genuine poetry; and for the same reason many affecting narratives which are founded on real events, and borrow no aid whatever from the imagination of the writer, must likewise be rejected. A considerable part of the poems, as they have hitherto been denominated, of Chaucer are of this naked and unveiled character; and there are in his Tales many pages of coarse, accurate and minute, but very striking description. Many small poems in a subsequent age, of most impressive kind, are adapted and addressed to the common sense of the reader, and prevail by the strong language of truth and nature. They amused our ancestors, and they continue to engage our interest and excite our feelings by the same powerful appeals to the heart and affections.

(xvi-xvii, xx-xxi)

William Hazlitt

from 'On Chaucer and Spenser', *Lectures on the English Poets*, Lecture 2 1818

While Chaucer's intercourse with the busy world, and collision with the actual passions and conflicting interests of others, seemed to brace the sinews of his understanding, and gave to his writings the air of a man who describes persons and things that he had known and been intimately concerned in; the same opportunities, operating on a differently constituted frame, only served to alienate Spenser's mind the more from the 'close-pent up' scenes of ordinary life, and to make him 'rive their concealing continents', to give himself up to the unrestrained indulgence of 'flowery tenderness'.

It is not possible for any two writers to be more opposite in this respect. Spenser delighted in luxurious enjoyment; Chaucer, in severe activity of mind. As Spenser was the most romantic and visionary, Chaucer was the most practical of all the great poets, the most a man of business and the world. His poetry reads like history. Everything has a downright reality; at least in the relator's mind. A simile, or a sentiment, is as if it were given in upon evidence. Thus he describes Criseyde's first avowal of her love.

And as the newe abaysed nyghtyngale,
That stynteth first whan she bygynneth to synge,
Whan that she hereth any herde tale,
Or in the hegges any wyght stirynge,
And after siker doth hire vois out rynge,

Right so Criseyde, whan hire drede stente,
Opned hire herte, and tolde hym hire entente.

> (*Troilus and Criseyde*, III 1233–9)

This is so true and natural, and beautifully simple, that the two
things seem identified with each other. Again, it is said in the *Knight's
Tale* –

This passeth yeer by yeer and day by day,
Till it fil ones, in a morwe of May,
That Emelye, that fairer was to sene
Than is the lylie upon his stalke grene,
And fressher than the May with floures newe –
For with the rose colour stroof hire hewe,
I noot which was the fyner of hem two …

> (*Canterbury Tales*, I 1033–9)

This scrupulousness about the literal preference, as if some question
of matter of fact was at issue, is remarkable. I might mention that
other, where he compares the meeting between Palamon and Arcite
to a hunter waiting for a lion in a gap,

That stondeth at the gappe with a spere,
Whan hunted is the leon or the bere,
And hereth hym come russhyng in the greves,
And breketh bothe bowes and the leves …

> (*Canterbury Tales*, I 1639–42)

or that still finer one of Constance, when she is condemned to death:

Have ye nat seyn somtyme a pale face,
Among a prees, of hym that hath be lad
Toward his deeth, wher as hym gat no grace,
And swich a colour in his face hath had,
Men myghte knowe his face that was bistad,
Amonges alle the faces in that route?
So stant Custance and looketh hire aboute.

> (*Canterbury Tales*, II 645–51)

The beauty, the pathos here does not seem to be of the poet's seeking,
but a part of the necessary texture of the fable. He speaks of what he
wishes to describe with the accuracy, the discrimination of one who

relates what has happened to himself, or has had the best information from those who have been eye-witnesses of it. The strokes of his pencil always tell. He dwells only on the essential, on that which would be interesting to the persons really concerned: yet as he never omits any material circumstance, he is prolix from the number of points on which he touches, without being diffuse on any one; and is sometimes tedious from the fidelity with which he adheres to his subject, as other writers are from the frequency of their digressions from it. The chain of his story is composed of a number of fine links, closely connected together, and riveted by a single blow. There is an instance of the minuteness which he introduces into his most serious descriptions in his account of Palamon when left alone in his cell:

Swich sorwe he maketh that the grete tour
Resouneth of his youlyng and clamour.
The pure fettres on his shynes grete
Weren of his bittre, salte teeres wete.

(*Canterbury Tales*, I 1277–80)

The mention of this last circumstance looks like a part of the instructions he had to follow, which he had no discretionary power to leave out or introduce at pleasure. He is contented to find grace and beauty in truth. He exhibits for the most part the naked object, with little drapery thrown over it. His metaphors, which are few, are not for ornament, but use, and as like as possible to the things themselves. He does not affect to show his power over the reader's mind, but the power which his subject has over his own. The readers of Chaucer's poetry feel more nearly what the persons he describes must have felt, than perhaps those of any other poet. His sentiments are not voluntary effusions of the poet's fancy, but founded on the natural impulses and habitual prejudices of the characters he has to represent. There is an inveteracy of purpose, a sincerity of feeling, which never relaxes or grows vapid, in whatever they do or say. There is no artificial, pompous display, but a strict parsimony of the poet's materials, like the rude simplicity of the age in which he lived. His poetry resembles the root just springing from the ground, rather than the full-blown flower. His muse is no 'babbling gossip of the air', fluent and redundant; but, like a stammerer, or a dumb person, that has just found the use of speech, crowds many things together with eager haste, with anxious pauses, and fond repetitions to prevent mistake. His words point as an index to the objects, like the eye or finger. There were none of the commonplaces of poetic diction in our author's time, no reflected lights of fancy, no borrowed roseate tints; he was obliged to inspect things for himself, to look narrowly, and almost to handle the object, as in the obscurity of morning we partly see and partly grope our way; so that his descriptions have a sort of tangible character belonging to them, and produce the effect of sculpture on the mind.

(20–22)

S. T. Coleridge

in conversation 15 March 1834

I take unceasing delight in Chaucer. His manly cheerfulness is especially delicious to me in my old age. How exquisitely tender he is, and yet how perfectly free from the least touch of sickly melancholy or morbid drooping! The sympathy of the poet with the subjects of his poetry is particularly remarkable in Shakespeare and Chaucer; but what the first effects by a strong act of imagination and mental metamorphosis, the last does without any effort, merely by the inborn kindly joyousness of his nature. How well we seem to know Chaucer! How absolutely nothing do we know of Shakespeare!

(433)

Francis Jeffrey, Lord Jeffrey

from a review of Sir James Mackintosh's *Memoirs, Edinburgh Review* October 1835

We stop here to remark that, though concurring in the substance of this masterly classification of our writers, we should yet be disposed to except to that part of it which represents the first introduction of soft, graceful and idiomatic English as not earlier than the period of the Restoration. In our opinion it is at least as old as Chaucer. The English Bible is full of it; and it is the most common, as well as the most beautiful, of the many languages spoken by Shakespeare.

(226)

Walter Savage Landor

from a letter to R. H. Horne   before 1841

Indeed I *do* admire him, or rather love him. In my opinion, he is fairly worth a score or two of Spensers. He had a knowledge of human nature and not of doll-making and *fantoccini* dressing.[1] . . . Pardon me if I say I would rather see Chaucer quite alone, in the dew of his sunny morning, than with twenty clever gentlefolks about him, arranging his shoe-strings and buttoning his doublet. I like even his *language*. I will have no hand in breaking his dun but rich-painted glass to put in (if clearer) much thinner panes.

Leigh Hunt

from *Imagination and Fancy* 1844

Chaucer's steed of brass, that was

so horsly, and so quyk of yc,

(*Canterbury Tales*, v 194)

is copied from the life. You might pat him and feel his brazen muscles.

(16)

1 dressing of puppets [Ed.]

Leigh Hunt

from *Wit and Humour* 1846

His humour is of a description the most thoroughly delightful; for it is at once entertaining, profound, and good-natured. If this last quality be thought a drawback by some, as wanting the relish of personality, they may supply even that (as some have supplied it) by supposing that he drew his characters from individuals, and that the individuals were very uncomfortable accordingly. I confess I see no ground for the supposition beyond what the nature of the case demands. Classes must of course be drawn, more or less, from the individuals composing them; but the unprofessional particulars added by Chaucer to his characters (such as the Merchant's uneasy marriage, and the Franklin's prodigal son) are only such as render the portraits more true, by including them in the general category of human kind. The gangrene which the Cook had on his shin, and which has been considered as a remarkable instance of the gratuitous, is, on the contrary (besides its masterly intimation of the perils of luxury in general), painfully in character with a man accustomed to breathe an unhealthy atmosphere, and to be encouraging bad humours with tasting sauces and syrups. Besides, the Cook turns out to be a drunkard.

(75)

Leigh Hunt

from the Preface to *Stories in Verse* 1855

There is a charming line in Chaucer:

Up roos the sonne and up roos Emelye.

> (*Canterbury Tales*, I 2273)

Now here are two simple matters of fact, which happen to occur simultaneously. The sun rises, and the lady rises at the same time. Well, what is there in that, some demanders of imaginative illustration will say? Nothing, answers one, but an hyperbole. Nothing, says another, but a conceit. It is a mere commonplace turn of gallantry, says a third. On the contrary, it is the reverse of all this. It is pure morning freshness, enthusiasm and music. Writers, no doubt, may repeat it till it becomes a commonplace, but that is another matter. Its first sayer, the great poet, sees the brightest of material creatures, and the beautifulest of human creatures, rising at dawn at the same time. He feels the impulse strong upon him to do justice to the appearance of both; and with gladness in his face and music on his tongue, repeating the accent on a repeated syllable, and dividing the *rhythm* into two equal parts, in order to leave nothing undone to show the merit on both sides, and the rapture of his impartiality, he utters, for all time, his enchanting record.[1]

Now it requires animal spirits, or a thoroughly loving nature, to enjoy that line completely; and yet, on looking well into it, it will be found to contain (by implication) simile, analogy, and indeed, every other form of imaginative expression, apart from that of direct illustrative words; which, in such cases, may be called needless commentary. The poet lets nature speak for herself. He points to the two beautiful objects before us, and is content with simply hailing them in their combination.

In all cases where Nature should thus be left to speak for herself (and they are neither mean nor few cases, but many and great) the imaginative faculty, which some think to be totally suspended at such times, is, on the contrary, in full activity, keeping aloof all irrelevancies and impertinence, and thus showing how well it understands its great mistress. When Lady Macbeth says she should have murdered Duncan herself,

> Had he not resembled
> Her father as he slept,

she said neither more nor less than what a poor criminal said long afterwards, and quite unaware of the passage, when brought before

---

1 The *Knight's Tale*, in which this line occurs, is an exquisite abridgment of a long and prolix poem, called *The Theseid* (*La Teseide*), by Boccaccio, who, great and grave, and Chaucer-like genius as he was in other respects, and subjected by the same causes to the same popular misconception, did not possess the art of writing verse. Though Boccaccio, however, supplied Chaucer with the original story, the line here quoted, with numberless other beauties, is our poet's own.

a magistrate from a midnight scuffle in a barge on the Thames – 'I should have killed him, if he had not looked so like my father while he was sleeping.' Shakespeare made poetry of the thought by putting it into verse – into modulation; but he would not touch it otherwise. He reverenced Nature's own simple, awful and sufficing suggestion too much to add a syllable to it for the purpose of showing off his subtle powers of imaginative illustration. And with no want of due reverence to Shakespeare be it said, that it is a pity he did not act invariably with the like judgement – that he suffered thought to crowd upon thought, where the first feeling was enough. So, what can possibly be imagined simpler, finer, completer, less wanting anything beyond itself, than the line in which poor old Lear, unable to relieve himself with his own trembling fingers, asks the bye-stander to open his waistcoat for him – not forgetting, in the midst of his anguish, to return him thanks for so doing, like a gentleman:

Pray you undo this button – Thank you, Sir.

The poet here presents us with two matters of fact, in their simplest and apparently most prosaical form; yet, when did ever passion or imagination speak more intensely? and this, purely because he has let them alone?

There is another line in Chaucer which seems to be still plainer matter of fact, with no imagination in it of any kind, apart from the simple necessity of imagining the fact itself. It is in the story of the Tartar king, which Milton wished to have had completed. The king has been feasting, and is moving from the feast to a ball-room:

Before him goeth the loud minstrelsy.

(*Canterbury Tales*, v 268)

Now, what is there in this line (it might be asked) which might not have been said in plain prose? which indeed is not prose? The king is preceded by his musicians, playing loudly. What is there in that?

Well, there is something even in that, if the prosers who demand so much help to their perceptions could but see it. But verse fetches it out and puts it in its proper state of movement. The line itself, being a line of verse, and therefore a musical movement, becomes processional, and represents the royal train in action. The word 'goeth', which a less imaginative writer would have rejected in favour of something which he took to be more spiritual and uncommon, is the soul of the continuity of the movement. It is put, accordingly, in its most emphatic place. And the word 'loud' is suggestive at once of royal power, and of the mute and dignified serenity, superior to that manifestation of it, with which the king follows.

Before him goeth the loud minstrelsy.

Any reader who does not recognize the stately 'go', and altogether noble sufficingness of that line, may rest assured that thousands of the beauties of poetry will remain forever undiscovered by him, let him be helped by as many thoughts and images as he may.

So in a preceding passage where the same musicians are mentioned.

And so bifel that after the thridde cours,
Whil that this kyng sit thus in his nobleye,
Herknynge his mynstralles hir thynges pleye
Biforn hym at the bord deliciously,
In at the halle dore al sodeynly
Ther cam a knyght upon a steede of bras,
And in his hand a brood mirour of glas.
Upon his thombe he hadde of gold a ryng,
And by his syde a naked swerd hangyng;
And up he rideth to the heighe bord.
In al the halle ne was ther spoken a word
For merveille of this knyght; hym to biholde
Ful bisily they wayten, yonge and olde.

(*Canterbury Tales*, v 76–88)

In some of these lines, what would otherwise be prose becomes, by the musical feeling, poetry. The king 'sitting in his nobleness', is an imaginative picture. The word 'deliciously' is a venture of animal spirits, which, in a modern writer, some critics would pronounce to be affected, or too familiar; but the enjoyment, and even incidental appropriateness and *relish* of it, will be obvious to finer senses. And in the pause in the middle of the last couplet but one, and that in the course of the first line of its successor, examples were given by this

supposed unmusical old poet, of some of the highest refinements of
versification.

(24-30)

John Ruskin

from *Lectures on Art* 1870

For there is one strange, but quite essential, character in us – ever
since the Conquest, if not earlier: a delight in the forms of burlesque
which are connected in some degree with the foulness of evil. I
think the most perfect type of a true English mind in its best possible
temper, is that of Chaucer; and you will find that, while it is for the
most part full of things of beauty, pure and wild like that of an April
morning, there are even in the midst of this sometimes momentarily
jesting passages which stoop to play with evil – while the power of
listening to and enjoying the jesting of entirely gross persons, whatever the feeling may be which permits it, afterwards degenerates into
forms of humour which render some of quite the greatest, wisest,
and most moral of English writers now almost useless for our youth.
And yet you find that whenever Englishmen are wholly without
this instinct, their genius is comparatively weak and restricted.

(15-16)

James Russell Lowell

from 'Chaucer' 1870, *My Study Windows* 1871

Chaucer never shows any signs of effort, and it is a main proof of his
excellence that he can be so inadequately sampled by detached
passages – by single lines taken away from the connexion in which
they contribute to the general effect. He has that continuity of
thought, that evenly prolonged power, and that delightful equanimity,
which characterize the higher orders of mind. There is something in
him of the disinterestedness that made the Greeks masters in art. His
phrase is never importunate. His simplicity is that of elegance, not of

poverty. The quiet unconcern with which he says his best things is peculiar to him among English poets, though Goldsmith, Addison, and Thackeray have approached it in prose.

(281–2)

The very form of the *Canterbury Tales* was imaginative. The garden of Boccaccio, the supper-party of Grazzini, and the voyage of Giraldi make a good enough thread for their stories, but exclude all save equals and friends, exclude consequently human nature in its wider meaning. But by choosing a pilgrimage, Chaucer puts us on a plane where all men are equal, with souls to be saved, and with another world in view that abolishes all distinctions. By this choice, and by making the Host of the Tabard always the central figure, he has happily united the two most familiar emblems of life – the short journey and the inn. We find more and more as we study him that he rises quietly from the conventional to the universal, and may fairly take his place with Homer in virtue of the breadth of his humanity.

(288)

Walter Bagehot

from 'Charles Dickens' 1858, *Literary Studies* 1879

If a symmetrical mind busy itself with the active side of human life, with the world of concrete men and real things, its principal quality will be a practical sagacity, which forms with ease a distinct view and just appreciation of all the mingled objects that the world presents, – which allots to each its own place, and its intrinsic and appropriate rank. Possibly no mind gives such an idea of this sort of symmetry as Chaucer's. Everything in it seems in its place. A healthy sagacious man of the world has gone through the world; he loves it, and knows it; he dwells on it with a fond appreciation; every object of the old life of 'merry England' seems to fall into its precise niche in his ordered and symmetrical comprehension. The *Prologue* to the *Canterbury Tales* is in itself a series of memorial tablets to medieval society; each class has its tomb, and each its apt inscription. A man without such an apprehensive and broad sagacity must fail in every extensive delineation of various life; he might attempt to describe what he did not penetrate, or if by a rare discretion he avoided that mistake, his works would want the *binding element;* he would be deficient in that distinct sense of relation and combination which is necessary for the depiction of the whole of life, which gives to it unity at first, and imparts to it a mass in the memory ever afterwards.

(77)

Matthew Arnold

from 'The Study of Poetry' 1880 (reprinted in *Essays in Criticism,* second series, 1888)

In the twelfth and thirteenth centuries, that seed-time of all modern language and literature, the poetry of France had a clear predominance in Europe. Of the two divisions of that poetry, its productions in the *langue d'oïl* and its productions in the *langue d'oc,* the poetry of the *langue d'oc,* of southern France, of the troubadours, is of importance because of its effect on Italian literature – the first literature of modern Europe to strike the true and grand note, and to bring forth, as in Dante and Petrarch it brought forth, classics. But the predominance of French poetry in Europe, during the twelfth and thirteenth centuries, is due to its poetry of the *langue d'oïl,* the poetry of northern France and of the tongue which is now the French language. In the twelfth century the bloom of this romance-poetry was earlier and stronger in England, at the court of our Anglo-Norman kings, than in France itself. But it was a bloom of French poetry; and as our native poetry formed itself, it formed itself out of this. The romance-poems which took possession of the heart and imagination of Europe in the twelfth and thirteenth centuries are French; 'they are', as Southey justly says, 'the pride of French literature, nor have we anything which can be placed in competition with them.' Themes were supplied from all quarters; but the romance-setting which was common to them all, and which gained the ear of Europe, was French. This constituted for the French poetry, literature, and language, at the height of the Middle Age, an unchallenged predominance. The Italian Brunetto Latini, the master of Dante, wrote his *Treasure* in French because, he says, 'la parleure en est plus délitable et plus commune à toutes gens.' In the same century, the thirteenth, the French romance-writer, Christian of Troyes, formulates the claims, in chivalry and letters, of France, his native country, as follows:

Or vous ert par ce livre apris,
Que Gresse ot de chevalerie
Le premier los et de clergie;
Puis vint chevalerie à Rome,
Et de la clergie la some,
Qui ore est en France venue.
Deix doinst qu'ele i soit retenue,
Et que li lius li abelisse
Tant que de France n'isse
L'onor qui s'i est arestée!

Now by this book you will learn that first Greece had the renown for chivalry and letters: then chivalry and the primacy in letters passed to Rome, and now it is come to France. God grant it may be kept there; and that the place may please it so well, that the honour which has come to make stay in France may never depart thence!

Yet it is now all gone, this French romance-poetry, of which the weight of substance and the power of style are not unfairly represented by this extract from Christian of Troyes. Only by means of the historic estimate can we persuade ourselves now to think that any of it is of poetical importance.

But in the fourteenth century there comes an Englishman nourished on this poetry, taught his trade by this poetry, getting words, rhyme, metre from this poetry; for even of that stanza which the Italians used, and which Chaucer derived immediately from the Italians, the basis and suggestion was probably given in France. Chaucer (I have already named him) fascinated his contemporaries, but so too did Christian of Troyes and Wolfram of Eschenbach. Chaucer's power of fascination, however, is enduring; his poetical importance does not need the assistance of the historic estimate; it is real. He is a genuine source of joy and strength, which is flowing still for us and will flow always. He will be read, as time goes on, far more generally than he is read now. His language is a cause of difficulty for us; but so also, and I think in quite as great a degree, is the language of Burns. In Chaucer's case, as in that of Burns, it is a difficulty to be unhesitatingly accepted and overcome.

If we ask ourselves wherein consists the immense superiority of Chaucer's poetry over the romance-poetry – why is it that in passing from this to Chaucer we suddenly feel ourselves to be in another world, we shall find that his superiority is both in the substance of his poetry and in the style of his poetry. His superiority in substance is given by his large, free, simple, clear yet kindly view of human life – so unlike the total want, in the romance-poets, of all intelligent command of it. Chaucer has not their helplessness; he has gained the power to survey the world from a central, a truly human point of view. We have only to call to mind the *Prologue* to the *Canterbury Tales*. The right comment upon it is Dryden's: 'It is sufficient to say, according to the proverb, that *here is God's plenty*.' And again: 'He is a perpetual fountain of good sense.' It is by a large, free, sound representation of things, that poetry, this high criticism of life, has truth of substance; and Chaucer's poetry has truth of substance.

Of his style and manner, if we think first of the romance-poetry and then of Chaucer's divine liquidness of diction, his divine fluidity of movement, it is difficult to speak temperately. They are irresistible, and justify all the rapture with which his successors speak of his 'gold dewdrops of speech'. Johnson misses the point entirely when he finds fault with Dryden for ascribing to Chaucer the first refinement of our numbers, and says that Gower also can show smooth numbers and easy rhymes. The refinement of our numbers means something far more than this. A nation may have versifiers with smooth numbers and easy rhymes, and yet may have no real poetry at all. Chaucer is the father of our splendid English poetry; he is our 'well of English undefiled', because by the lovely charm of his diction, the lovely charm of his movement, he makes an epoch and founds a tradition. In Spenser, Shakespeare, Milton, Keats, we can follow the tradition of the liquid diction, the fluid movement, of Chaucer; at one time it is his liquid diction of which in these poets we feel the virtue, and at another time it is his fluid movement. And the virtue is irresistible.

Bounded as is my space, I must yet find room for an example

of Chaucer's virtue, as I have given examples to show the virtue of the great classics. I feel disposed to say that a single line is enough to show the charm of Chaucer's verse; that merely one line like this –

O martir, sowded[1] in virginitee!

(*Canterbury Tales*, VII 579)

has a virtue of manner and movement such as we shall not find in all the verse of romance-poetry; – but this is saying nothing. The virtue is such as we shall not find, perhaps, in all English poetry, outside the poets whom I have named as the special inheritors of Chaucer's tradition. A single line, however, is too little if we have not the strain of Chaucer's verse well in our memory; let us take a stanza. It is from the *Prioress's Tale*, the story of the Christian child murdered in a Jewry –

'My throte is kut unto my nekke boon,'
Scyde this child, 'and, as by wey of kynde,
I sholde have dyed, ye, longe tyme agon.
But Jesu Crist, as ye in bookes fynde,
Wil that his glorie laste and be in mynde,
And for the worship of his Mooder deere
Yet may I synge O *Alma* loude and cleere.'

(*Canterbury Tales*, VII 649–55)

Wordsworth has modernized this Tale, and to feel how delicate and evanescent is the charm of verse, we have only to read Wordsworth's first three lines of this stanza after Chaucer's –

My throat is cut unto the bone, I trow,
Said this young child, and by the law of kind
I should have died, yea, many hours ago.

The charm is departed. It is often said that the power of liquidness and fluidity in Chaucer's verse was dependent upon a free, a licentious dealing with language, such as is now impossible; upon a liberty, such as Burns too enjoyed, of making words like *neck*, *bird*, into a dissyllable by adding to them, and words like *cause*, *rhyme*, into a dissyllable by sounding the *e* mute. It is true that Chaucer's fluidity is

1 The French *soudé*: soldered, fixed fast.

conjoined with this liberty, and is admirably served by it; but we ought not to say that it was dependent upon it. It was dependent upon his talent. Other poets with a like liberty do not attain to the fluidity of Chaucer; Burns himself does not attain to it. Poets, again, who have a talent akin to Chaucer's, such as Shakespeare or Keats, have known how to attain to his fluidity without the like liberty.

And yet Chaucer is not one of the great classics. His poetry transcends and effaces, easily and without effort, all the romance-poetry of Catholic Christendom; it transcends and effaces all the English poetry contemporary with it, it transcends and effaces all the English poetry subsequent to it down to the age of Elizabeth. Of such avail is poetic truth of substance, in its natural and necessary union with poetic truth of style. And yet, I say, Chaucer is not one of the great classics. He has not their accent. What is wanting to him is suggested by the mere mention of the name of the first great classic of Christendom, the immortal poet who died eighty years before Chaucer – Dante. The accent of such a verse as

In la sua volontade è nostra pace . . .[1]

is altogether beyond Chaucer's reach; we praise him, but we feel that this accent is out of the question for him. It may be said that it was necessarily out of the reach of any poet in the England of that stage of growth. Possibly; but we are to adopt a real, not a historic, estimate of poetry. However we may account for its absence, something is wanting, then, to the poetry of Chaucer, which poetry must have before it can be placed in the glorious class of the best. And there is no doubt what that something is. It is the σπουδαιότης, the high and excellent seriousness, which Aristotle assigns as one of the grand virtues of poetry. The substance of Chaucer's poetry, his view of things and his criticism of life, has largeness, freedom, shrewdness, benignity; but it has not this high seriousness. Homer's criticism of life has it, Dante's has it, Shakespeare's has it. It is this chiefly which gives to our spirits what they can rest upon; and with the increasing demands of our modern ages upon poetry, this virtue of giving us what we can rest upon will be more and more highly esteemed. A voice from the

1 In his will is our peace (*Paradiso*, III 85). [Ed.]

slums of Paris, fifty or sixty years after Chaucer, the voice of poor Villon out of his life of riot and crime, has at its happy moments (as, for instance, in the last stanza of *La Belle Heaulmière*[1]) more of this important poetic virtue of seriousness than all the productions of Chaucer. But its apparition in Villon, and in men like Villon, is fitful; the greatness of the great poets, the power of their criticism of life, is that their virtue is sustained.

To our praise, therefore, of Chaucer as a poet there must be this limitation; he lacks the high seriousness of the great classics, and therewith an important part of their virtue. Still, the main fact for us to bear in mind about Chaucer is his sterling value according to that real estimate which we firmly adopt for all poets. He has poetic truth of substance, though he has not high poetic seriousness, and corresponding to his truth of substance he has an exquisite virtue of style and manner. With him is born our real poetry.

(23–34)

A. C. Swinburne

from 'Short Notes on English Poets' 1880, *Miscellanies* 1886

Of all whose names may claim anything like equality of rank on the roll of national poets – not even excepting Virgil – we may say that Chaucer borrowed most from abroad, and did most to improve whatever he borrowed. I believe it would be but accurate to admit

1 The name *Heaulmière* is said to be derived from a headdress (helm) worn as a mark by courtesans. In Villon's ballad, a poor old creature of this class laments her days of youth and beauty. The last stanza of the ballad runs thus –

'Ainsi le bon temps regretons
Entre nous, pauvres vieilles sottes,
Assises bas, à croppetons,
Tout en ung tas comme pelottes;
A petit feu de chenevottes
Tost allumés, tost estainctes.
Et jadis fusmes si mignottes!
Ainsi en prend à maintz et maintes.'

'Thus amongst ourselves we regret the good time, poor silly old things, low-seated on our heels, all in a heap like so many balls; by a little fire of hemp-stalks, soon lighted, soon spent. And once we were such darlings! So fares it with many and many a one.'

that in all his poems of serious or tragic narrative we hear a French or Italian tongue speaking with a Teutonic accent through English lips. It has utterly unlearnt the native tone and cadence of its natural inflections; it has perfectly put on the native tone and cadence of a stranger's; yet is it always what it was at first – *lingua romana in bocca tedesca*.[1] It speaks not only with more vigour but actually with more sweetness than the tongues of its teachers; but it speaks after its own fashion no other than the lesson they have taught. Chaucer was in the main a French or Italian poet, lined thoroughly and warmly throughout with the substance of an English humorist. And with this great gift of specially English humour he combined, naturally as it were and inevitably, the inseparable twin-born gift of peculiarly English pathos. In the figures of Arcite and Grisilde, he has actually outdone Boccaccio's very self for pathos: as far almost as Keats was afterwards to fall short of the same great model in the same great quality. And but for the instinctive distaste and congenital repugnance of his composed and comfortable genius from its accompanying horror, he might haply have come nearer than he has cared or dared to come even to the unapproachable pathos of Dante. But it was only in the world of one who stands far higher above Dante than even Dante can on the whole be justly held to stand above Chaucer, that figures as heavenly as the figures of Beatrice and Matilda could move unspotted and undegraded among figures as earthly as those of the Reeve, the Miller, and the Wife of Bath: that a wider if not keener pathos than Ugolino's or Francesca's could alternate with a deeper if not richer humour than that of Absolon and Nicholas.

It is a notable dispensation of chance – one which a writer who might happen to be almost a theist might designate in the deliciously comical phrase of certain ambiguous pietists as 'almost providential' – that the three great typical poets of the three great representative nations of Europe during the dark and lurid lapse of the Middle Ages should each afford as complete and profound a type of a different and alien class as of a different and alien people. Vast as are the diversities of their national and personal characters, these are yet less radical than the divergences between class and class which mark off each from either of his fellows in nothing but in fame. Dante represents, at its

---

1 A romance tongue in a germanic mouth. [Ed.]

best and highest, the upper class of the dark ages not less than he represents their Italy; Chaucer represents their middle class at its best and wisest, not less than he represents their England; Villon represents their lower class at its worst and its best alike, even more than he represents their France. And of these three the English middle class, being incomparably the happiest and the wisest, is indisputably, considering the common circumstances of their successive times, the least likely to have left us the highest example of all poetry then possible to men. And of their three legacies, precious and wonderful as it is, the Englishman's is accordingly the least wonderful and the least precious. The poet of the sensible and prosperous middle class in England had less to suffer and to sing than the theosophic aristocrat of Italy, or the hunted and hungry vagabond who first found articulate voice for the dumb longing and the blind love as well as for the reckless appetites and riotous agonies of the miserable and terrible multitude.

(2-4)

T. R. Lounsbury

from *Studies in Chaucer: His Life and Writings*　1892

There is about his method of work nothing of that blind creative impulse which, acting without reflection, characterizes, or is supposed to characterize, the poet of the earliest period. On the contrary, he knows precisely what he is aiming to accomplish. He has his attention steadily directed towards the best method of doing it. When he fails, it is not because he has not considered the matter. It is because he has been misled, either by the taste of his age or by the bad models he has set before himself. He has all the self-consciousness of the creative genius of later times, who has mastered his art as well as been mastered by it. He has precise and definite views about it. He criticizes and condemns not only tendencies in others, but tendencies in himself that conflict with what he has come to regard as essential to the development of his own power of expression in its purest and most perfect form.

(III 324)

W. P. Ker

from 'Chaucer and the Renaissance' (first published in *Form and Style in Poetry*, 1929) Clark Lecture   1912

The Renaissance is in many cases an excellent substitute for thinking, but it is not so easy as it sometimes looks. It is often made easy by blackening and belying the Middle Ages, describing them as ages of faith and slavery, impervious to reason, negligent of learning, and so forth.

But, when you look into the Renaissance, instead of freedom you find very often conventionality and superstition more thorough than anything in the Middle Ages, formalism more deliberate and determined. You also find some of the most characteristic things of the Middle Ages surviving undiminished and ratified by modern judges – allegory, for example.

Until you may be inclined to use about the Renaissance the phrase of an ancient Greek sceptic, and say, 'Concerning the Renaissance, whether it was or was not, or is or is not, I neither know nor do not know, nor care nor do not care.'

But if you go to the three Italians of the fourteenth century, Dante, Petrarch and Boccaccio, you will find some clear evidence of something new going on, a change of fashion, in literature at any rate, which agrees with what people commonly believe about the Renaissance. In so far as Chaucer was affected by those authors and by that change of fashion, it is allowable to speak of 'Chaucer and the Renaissance', to use that as a title for a lecture.

The change is due to a sense of the art of Latin poetry, an appreciation of the form of ancient poetry, and a wish to copy that in modern language, as well as in Latin.

Dante was the first poet to imitate in a modern language the classical use of the simile. Chaucer is the first English poet to use the epic simile, and he seems to have taken the suggestion, not from Virgil and Ovid, but from Dante, and from Boccaccio, who copied Dante.

From Petrarch Chaucer learned comparatively little. He does not seem to have attended to Petrarch's Latin works, except his Latin version of Boccaccio's story of Griselda; he translates one of the Sonnets, not into an English sonnet, but into three stanzas of his

Troilus. Petrarch, who is much more modern than Boccaccio, not to speak of Dante, is in his Italian verse not so strikingly new in manner as Boccaccio, to a foreign reader at any rate. The foreign reader finds in Petrarch Sonnets and *Canzoni*, and takes them easily as being like other Sonnets and *Canzoni* for a hundred years past; there is nothing surprising in their form, no advertised intention of following the ancients.

But with the *Teseide* of Boccaccio, the poem which held Chaucer for so long, it is impossible to make a mistake. Anyone can see in two minutes that this is different from all the narrative poems hitherto published. Boccaccio, to adapt a phrase of Shakespeare's Beatrice, has set up his bills and challenged the world at epic poetry. The *Teseide* is meant to compete with Virgil and Statius. It is a modern epic poem, in twelve books, with everything that an epic poem ought to have: gods and goddesses (technically called the machinery in later times), catalogues of the forces, similes, combats, funeral games – everything, except the visit to the infernal regions, for which there appears to have been no room. It is not wonderful that Chaucer was attracted by this brilliant and imposing piece. It touched him in many different ways.

Italian poetry must have struck Chaucer as being much more interesting and varied than the French poetry which he knew. He was fond of stories; he was also a judge of diction; but before he knew the Italian poets he knew hardly any narrative poetry, except the Latin, where there were both good stories and good style.

What he thought of the English romances he has revealed in *Sir Thopas*; in French the good stories were often clumsily told, and the masters of poetic style were often thin and conventional in argument. But here in Dante and Boccaccio there must have appeared to Chaucer an immense wealth of substance, together with beauty of form beyond what any of the French had attained. The great translator takes all he can. He imitates the phrasing and the figures of speech. Apparently he went over his poem of Constance, and put in a simile where he could, following the example of Dante. In the *Parliament of Fowls* he strengthened and enriched his conventional scheme with diction and ornament taken from the Italian school. And he began an epic poem of his own with an introduction partly copied from Boccaccio – the epic which so quickly turned into something quite different while he worked at it – the *Complaint of Anelida*, about which you may think I have already said enough. But there is still something curious about that poem which may bear some further study, in connexion with the modern epic of Boccaccio on which it is founded.

Chaucer makes much more of Boccaccio than of Dante, and one reason for that is that Boccaccio is much more French than Dante, and in his reading and his poetical tastes much nearer to Chaucer. Chaucer would not have been attracted so much by Boccaccio's epic if that had been a great heroic poem. But the *Teseide* is really a short novel of the French type enormously magnified and diversified into the likeness of epic, with exceedingly clever and ingenious use of literary artifices like the Olympian machinery and the catalogues.

The story of it we all know, because it is Chaucer's *Knight's Tale* – Palamon and Arcite, the two noble kinsmen. No original has been found for it older than Boccaccio; but either there was a French original which has been lost, or Boccaccio has exactly followed the general receipt for a short problem story as that was understood by the French. The plot is a piece of casuistry, such as the French understood and still understand better than most other people. Given two gentlemen who have sworn eternal friendship, and who at the same moment fall in love with the same lady – the problem resembles mathematics; there is no irrelevance in saying so, for that is indeed the character of a good deal of French fiction; the story is an abstract case of opposite irresistible forces – like *Le Cid*, like *Hernani*.

Chaucer paid his regard to the *Teseide* because it offered him both the epic magnificence, which was a new thing in a modern language, and the casuistical story, with which as a type he was well acquainted. Now, it seems to me, we can understand what he aimed at when he set out to write *Anelida*, and what is implied in that undertaking. I take it all to mean this (which is of no small interest as showing the working of Chaucer's mind and his skill in criticism), namely, that he had found out the secret of Boccaccio's epic and the way in which it had been composed, and was going to match it in English by borrowing not the story but the method, together with as much of Boccaccio's literary scaffolding as he could transfer to his own use. He takes the epic setting of the *Teseide*, and into that frame he begins to put, not the story of the two noble kinsmen, but another sentimental

story of the same scale, another situation where the personages are
three in number. He reasoned in this way: my Italian author has
made a long narrative poem out of a comprehensible, not very intricate, situation – the opposition of two personages. I will go and make
a poem like it. I will borrow what I can of his framework, ornament,
descriptions of temples, and the like, but I will have a plot of my own.
It shall be no more complicated than his – but why should it not
succeed as well?

It did not succeed as well; partly because it is not as good to begin
with; abstract as it may be, the rivalry of Palamon and Arcite is
dramatic to the end; the tension is not relaxed as long as they are
both alive. But in *Anelida* there is no drama; the tension is all in the
spirit of Anelida alone, and so the proper expression of it is lyrical –
the finest and most elaborate of Chaucer's lyrics, which leaves the
epic scaffolding all in ruin, empty and meaningless. Does anyone want
to hear me describing a temple? says Chaucer. But he never really
had any hope, after the lyrical complaint was finished, and so he does
not go on. His critical reading of Boccaccio was perfect; he had found
the pulse of the machine. But in his own use of the secret he had
overlooked certain new elements, and the alchemist's furnace was
blown to shivers – though with no serious damage to the artist.

Chaucer belongs to the Renaissance, is caught by the Renaissance,
in so far as he began to think of poetical form with reference to
ancient models, especially Latin epic poetry. He would not have
thought in that way if he had not read Italian and come into contact
with the new Italian ambitions. The Renaissance element in his work
is not very large. He is almost entirely safe from the pure formalism
of the Renaissance, which is exemplified in Milton's list of subjects in
the Trinity MS. and in his deliberations over epic and tragedy. It was
common in Milton's time, and earlier – the idea of an epic poem or a
perfect tragedy without any filling in it, a mere frame or diagram.
Boccaccio had it when he wrote the *Teseide*; Chaucer had it only as
a reader of Boccaccio's epic, and in relation to the matter of Boccaccio's work. His ideal is never defecated to a pure transparency, if
we may use Coleridge's phrase to describe the pure formal pattern
of a poem which was an object of contemplation and reverence to
so many artists between Dante and Milton.

The interest of this sort of thing is that you see the artist, Chaucer, driven to use all his resources and applying his mind as hard as he can to what might be called a strategical and tactical problem. He is matched against Boccaccio; he has it in him to do something as good as the Italian. But it is not only the Italian poet who stands over against him; there is an impersonal opponent, what one might call the conditions of the ground, which are not clear to him, which there is no one to explain to him, and which he has to find out for himself, like a general who makes mistakes or gains partial and inconclusive victories until the situation clears itself, and the decisive moment arrives. Then, to use a memorable sentence of Napier's *Peninsular War*, he 'comes down with both feet on Ciudad Rodrigo', and everything is won. That is the use of studying an imperfect work like Chaucer's *Anelida*; you can make out where he failed and why he went back; you can see what was in his mind when it comes to his next move, and you can understand the nature of his success. Apart from all its other beauties, Chaucer's *Knight's Tale* brings out a quality in Chaucer's mind with which the Renaissance may have had something to do, but which is properly his own mind, working, after his partial failures and successes, freely, originally, with criticism and reflection at the service of imagination, and never a hindrance anywhere. The moral of the *Knight's Tale* for students of the literary art is that it is well to have a mind of one's own. It is founded on Boccaccio's epic poem, and partly a translation from it. But the form is of Chaucer's own invention, and it is got by criticism of Boccaccio and renunciation of the things which Boccaccio thought of main importance – the epic scheme. Chaucer sees the story in his own way; he throws overboard all the epic machinery that he does not want; he attends to the plot, and uses out of the Italian poem just as much as suits his purpose, which is enough to make a great difference in richness of detail between this poem and anything hitherto known in English. He is able, it may be remarked among other things, to describe a temple; even three temples; and so, that no one wishes to escape or object, and with greater success than his Italian model, as may be proved by comparison of the Italian and the English.

In all this there is something of the Renaissance. Boccaccio's poem is Renaissance work, and it is Boccaccio's poem that puts Chaucer on his mettle, and stimulates him to fence and scheme and plan for the best possible way of telling a story. In so far as Chaucer's *Knight's Tale* is a poem that will bear the most exacting tests with regard to its composition, ordonnance, whatever be the right name for that in which the classical poets are believed to excel, it is a classical poem. It comes up to the requirements; there is nothing weak or inharmonious or out of place. If such virtues as these are the ideal of the Renaissance, then Chaucer's poem belongs to the Renaissance. But, on the other hand, they are due to Chaucer's mind working critically on a Renaissance formula – the artificial epic poem – and rejecting many of the things on which the Renaissance poets and critics were disposed to set most value.

There is still something more to be considered in the example of Chaucer's imperfect work with which I set out: another reference justified by the poem of *Anelida* – a curious illustration of the tolerance of Chaucer, and his fondness for old fashions. I have compared the artistic problems with which he dealt to those of a general waiting for the situation to clear itself, and judging the place and time and manner of the decisive stroke. But Chaucer is not always straining for success, and does not always choose to watch for an opportunity. With all his critical skill, he is not really absorbed in questions of poetical art; he has clearly never formulated for himself any idea of a perfect poem separate from the particular matters in which he happens to be interested. And he continues to be interested in many things which are difficult to work into proper form, and in dealing with them he is sometimes careless. I would take the *Squire's Tale* as an example of this, and a contrast to the *Knight's Tale*, and, what is most curious, a repetition of the tactical mistake of the *Complaint of Anelida*. The *Squire's Tale*, like *Anelida*, is left unfinished –

> half told
> The story of Cambuscan bold,
> Of Camball and of Algarsife,
> And who had Canace to wife,
> That own'd the virtuous ring and glass,
> And of the wondrous horse of brass,
> On which the Tartar king did ride.

The reason why it is unfinished is of the same sort as the difficulty of *Anelida*, and there is a very close likeness between the poems in the arrangement of their stories. The *Squire's Tale* is not so obviously miscalculated as the other poem; it does not make the same false start with the heavy epic introduction. It is less pretentious at the beginning, and the incongruity is less marked. But the discordant motives are there, and they are of the same kind. Chaucer sets out to tell a story of adventures and enchantment; it promises well; everyone wishes to hear more of the horse of brass. But the romance changes to another theme, and the change is the same as in *Anelida*; from action and adventures to the distress of love, the sorrow of the true lover abandoned. It is a favourite subject with Chaucer, it is the theme of the *Legend of Good Women*. There he succeeded because there he kept to the ancient stories of the heroines. He failed in the *Squire's Tale*, as he had failed in *Anelida*, because he tried to bring matter and sentiment of this sort into a narrative frame which was not convenient, which had too much in it already to allow the proper development of the second subject. This I think is felt more or less by all readers of the *Squire's Tale*, though the story, the poem, is so good that everyone wishes it to go on. I think Chaucer's reason for stopping is a sound one. He was involved in the new pathetic sentiment; he had got too far away from the narrative, and could not attend to the romance of the flying horse, and he never found time to go back upon his work as he did with the story of Theseus and Hippolyta, of Palamon and Arcite.

There is little room left to speak of Chaucer's largest poem, *Troilus*, the strongest proof of his genius as a poet, in comparison with which the *Knight's Tale* and the *Squire's Tale* and all the rest are shadowy, visionary things.

But it is possible in a sentence or two to describe Chaucer's aim and procedure in this narrative work of his. Here again he had a sentimental story with two chief personages, and two or three more. It is much less of a plot than the *Knight's Tale*. It is hardly more complicated than the story of Anelida. It is the opposite of that story; here it is the man who is true, and the woman who appears to be true and is proved faithless. Out of this simple matter Chaucer has made a long story fully told, as solid as the strongest work in verse or prose in any age. He had Boccaccio here again to guide him: *Troilus* is taken from a narrative poem of Boccaccio. But that original is a slight thing, quite different in scale from the epic poem which is the original of the *Knight's Tale*. Chaucer has thought it all over for himself, and what he has added to it is what we roughly call reality. He sees the story acted, not in the limited selected world of romance, from which things are excluded that might interfere with the romantic impression, but in a scene as real as the Ithaca of Homer, the London of *Vanity Fair* and *Pendennis*. This reality is, of course, imagination, just as much as the limited world of romance of the *Faerie Queene*, for example, but real is the right name for it. Chaucer places his figures in a world where one has a sense of ordinary life going on all round about the sentimental story of the lovers, and, more than that, he has put the vulgar ordinary mind into the third chief personage, the next in importance after Troilus and Criseyde themselves, Pandarus. He is like the wise youth in *Richard Feverel* – a prosaic touchstone of romance.

Those who wish to find a modern counterpart to the story of *Troilus* will find it in the *Tragic Comedians*. The heroine of that story is a later incarnation of Criseyde. The art of Chaucer has nothing to fear by comparison with anything in modern fiction, and, over and above the strength of what one may call its prose imagination, it is also poetry.

Chaucer has come down with both feet on the real world.

What has this to do with the Renaissance?

(68–79)

Part Three **Modern Views**

Introduction

The three best pieces of Chaucer criticism before 1900 are all the
work of poets: Dryden's preface to his volume of translations,
Blake's catalogue to his exhibition of paintings, and Arnold's
introduction to Ward's anthology of English poetry. It would be
absurd to call any of these men 'amateurs'; yet as critics they were
not 'professionals', either. But Arnold was Professor of Poetry at
Oxford, and that, for Chaucer, represented the shape of things to
come. For the course of twentieth-century Chaucer criticism has
been determined by the growth, in England and America, of
Departments of English in the universities. In America, where so
much of the best work on Chaucer has been done in recent years,
the universities have a monopoly; and even in England non-
academic writers do not often dare – or care – to follow in the
footsteps of Dryden and Blake. G. K. Chesterton was the last
notable exception.

This university criticism lacks what W. P. Ker called the
'disengaged' note of Dryden's criticism; for its exponents are,
above all, engaged with their chosen author. So it is not easy for
them to pronounce – or even, sometimes, to reckon with – the
judgement of the common reader. Their criticism does not,
characteristically, place Chaucer in a broad literary context,
defining his weaknesses as well as his strengths, as Dryden's does.
It is sometimes rather parochial. Yet it has many compensating
virtues. It is, above all, scholarly and (in a good sense) eclectic.
We know far more about Chaucer than did earlier generations,
we read him in better texts and with better dictionaries, and we
can see his work from many more points of view. Most of the
old approaches have either survived or been revived; and these
are available alongside newer, distinctively twentieth-century
views. So it is not easy – or not from this distance – to perceive
the outlines of a single twentieth-century Chaucer. In the
selections which follow, the reader will find many Chaucers: the
realist, the scholar, the philosopher, the humorist, the courtly

maker, the stylist, the craftsman, the ironist, the moralist. These images are not all equally good for all purposes, by any means; but it is in the nature of modernism that they should all be available in the imaginary museum.

The academic phase of Chaucer criticism runs from the time of Professor G. L. Kittredge (an extract from whose influential lectures, published in 1915 as *Chaucer and his Poetry*, opens this section) to the present day. But there have been advances in knowledge and changes in fashion during this period of more than fifty years. It is necessary, therefore, to distinguish between an older and a newer academic criticism.

Kittredge himself is the chief representative of the former. He and his colleagues studied and taught a Chaucer who, as one would expect, has much in common with the Chaucer of the Victorians and Romantics. We recognize this when Kittredge speaks of Chaucer's 'profound sense of the joy and beauty, the sadness and irony, of human life'. Yet because Kittredge is giving a whole series of lectures on Chaucer – in contrast, say, to the single lecture which Hazlitt devoted to Chaucer and Spenser – he is able to illustrate such general observations with that more detailed and leisurely analysis which is characteristic of critics working under academic conditions. And what most of all shows up, under Kittredge's scrutiny, is the realistic or 'dramatic' detail in Chaucer's work, the felicity with which he shows 'life as it is' (see p. 123). Where Dryden simply says that he 'sees' Chaucer's pilgrims 'as distinctly as if I had supped with them at the Tabard', Kittredge says just what he sees – what the pilgrims thought of themselves and each other, what they meant by their tales, and so on. Kittredge was well able to appreciate earlier poems of Chaucer such as the *Book of the Duchess;* but the *Canterbury Tales* convinced him that the conventions of dream poetry and allegory – indeed, all literary conventions – were to be dispensed with in the final Chaucerian achievement, when the poet looked straight at 'life as it is'. Similar views were expressed by other scholars of the time. Thus J. M. Manly, in a lecture entitled 'Chaucer and the Rhetoricians', described how Chaucer, having formed his style according to the precepts of the medieval rhetoricians, achieved in his maturity 'methods of composition based upon close observation of life and the exercise of the creative imagination' (p. 129).

The newer critics of Chaucer take a quite different view of literary convention in his work. The conventions governing the *Book of the Duchess* – a rhetorical, courtly love vision – are by them regarded as dispensable only in the sense that other conventions may take their place. All art is conventional. What we call 'realism' can make no special claim to 'show life as it is': it is itself a literary mode, just as the plain or conversational style is a kind of rhetoric. C. S. Lewis, in his *Allegory of Love* (1936), made an important contribution to the development of such views, by his eloquent advocacy of the stylized conventions of allegory and courtly love, and equally by his somewhat chilly treatment of the realism of low-life comedy in Chaucer's poems (p. 151). Twenty years later Charles Muscatine, in his *Chaucer and the French Tradition* (1957), presented the case in its fullest and most systematic form. The 'courtly' and the 'bourgeois' traditions in medieval French poetry, according to Muscatine, furnished Chaucer with two basic 'styles': the courtly and the realistic or naturalistic. The latter is just as literary and conventionalized as the former, having its foundations in Jean de Meun's part of the *Romance of the Rose* and in the *fabliaux* (those very literary tales of sex and trickery which lie behind the tales of the Miller and the Reeve). Chaucer's originality lies in the way he brings these two traditions together and plays them off against each other: 'Chaucer's "new style" is a mixture of "old" ones'.

The New Criticism of Chaucer, so far as there has been such a thing, has remained up to now firmly within academic bounds. Indeed, it might well be argued that Muscatine's approach

to Chaucer is more, not less, academic than Kittredge's, since he
encapsulates *every* aspect of the poetry (or every significant one)
within 'styles', 'traditions', and 'conventions'; and the same
judgement might be passed on J. V. Cunningham's
excellent essay on the *General Prologue* (see p. 218). This is a field
where the impact of critics such as (in England) Leavis, Empson
and Richards, has been obscured and muffled – chiefly, no doubt,
by the language problem. Yet Muscatine and others, notably
E. T. Donaldson, do reflect the special sensibility of their time,
just as Chaucer critics have always done. The point is well made
by Muscatine: 'To use such terms as "irony", "ambiguity",
"tension" and "paradox" in describing Chaucer's poetry is to
bring to the subject our typical mid-century feeling for an
unresolved dialectic'.

Irony is indeed a favourite and distinctive theme of mid-
century writing on Chaucer. Discussions of the matter centre,
most often, on the figure of the narrator in Chaucer's poems –
the dreamer in the dream poems, the bookish man-who-tells-the-
story in *Troilus and Criseyde*, and the pilgrim Geoffrey in the
Canterbury Tales. Earlier critics paid little attention to this person,
or *persona;* but it is through him, according to many recent writers,
that Chaucer articulates his irony. Thus, the narrator sees what
there is to see and reports what there is to report in Chaucer's
narratives; and it is he who expresses those lively feelings of
sympathy and regret, enthusiasm and bewilderment, which are so
characteristic of the poems. But he is himself a fictional figure, one
of the *dramatis personae*, and his reactions represent, as it were, only
the ostensible voice in the irony. The other voice conveys – as is
usual in such cases – different and in some sense profounder and
more reliable judgements. So the tale of *Sir Thopas* is told by the
pilgrim Geoffrey (the 'ostensible voice') as 'the best rhyme I can';
but those who can hear the masked voice of Geoffrey's creator
recognize the thing immediately as incompetent hack-work.

This conception of the workings of Chaucer's irony has appealed
to readers of many different persuasions. Those who look to Chaucer
for fixed and final judgements of a moral kind can discount the
wayward sympathies of the ostensible voice as no more than
'pretty and pleasant coverts' (in an Elizabethan phrase), behind
which the work of the moralist and satirist goes on undisturbed.
So Professor D. W. Robertson, in his controversial *Preface to
Chaucer* (1963). On the other hand, those who share with Muscatine
'our typical mid-century feeling for an *unresolved* dialectic' can
find just such a dialectic in the two voices of Chaucer's poetry.
Neither voice, on this view, has a monopoly of wisdom: each
makes a contribution to a total poetic vision which is too complex
to be identified with any non-poetic world-picture, medieval or
otherwise. I have selected E. T. Donaldson's essay on *Troilus and
Criseyde* to represent this view here (see p. 190). His very subtle
analysis of the poem ends with the following characteristic summary
of the dialectic, or dialogue, between its voices: 'The simultaneous
awareness of the real validity of human values – and hence our
need to commit ourselves to them – and of their inevitable
transitoriness – and hence our need to remain uncommitted –
represents a complex, mature, truly tragic vision of mankind.'

It seems likely that the future course of Chaucer criticism will
be chiefly determined in the universities, for so long as those
institutions retain their present dominance in the field of higher
literary studies; but it is not easy to predict what this course will
be. Where do the new directions lie? Some would say, in D. W.
Robertson's so-called 'historical' criticism – illustrated here from
R. E. Kaske's defence of it – which sets out to interpret Chaucer
chiefly in terms of allegorical significances established by St
Augustine and other Church Fathers in their exegesis of Scripture.
This represents the most radical of all current reactions against
the humorous, realistic Chaucer of Victorian and early academic
times. Less radical, but more promising, is the attempt to see

Chaucer in his broad contemporary context, as a representative of international late Gothic culture. Since Chaucer's sources are now pretty well understood, scholars are beginning to look beyond them to other literary, and non-literary, art which may throw light on his work. It may be that Spanish literature or English miniature-painting will provide the insights of the future.

However this may be, we should expect future critics, like past and present ones, to reflect the preoccupations of their age. Good critics (unlike good scholars, perhaps) owe allegiance both to their author and to their own age. Their characteristic question is: how does he look *now*? The alternative to criticism which sheds light on both its subject and its own age, it would seem, is criticism which sheds light on neither.

G. L. Kittredge

from *Chaucer and his Poetry* 1915

Chaucer's adoption of a Canterbury pilgrimage was not a mere excuse for story-telling. Most readers, I am aware, treat this great masterpiece simply as a storehouse of fiction, and so do many critics. Yet everybody feels, I am sure, that Chaucer was quite as much interested in the Pilgrims themselves as in their several narratives. This, no doubt, is what Dryden had in mind when he wrote, comparing Chaucer with Ovid:

Both of them understood the manners; under which name I comprehend the passions, and, in a larger sense, the descriptions of persons, and their very habits. For an example, I see Baucis and Philemon as perfectly before me, as if some ancient painter had drawn them; and all the Pilgrims in the *Canterbury Tales*, their humours, their features, and the very dress, as distinctly as if I had supped with them at the Tabard in Southwark. Yet even there too the figures in Chaucer are much more lively, and set in a better light.

I am much deceived if Dryden is not here treading on the verge of the proposition that the *Canterbury Tales* is, to all intents and purposes, a Human Comedy. Certainly he is calling our attention to something that distinguishes Chaucer's work from every collection of stories that preceded it. It was much, as we have seen, that Chaucer had the judgement, among the infinite doings of the world, to select a pilgrimage, and to parcel out his tales to the miscellaneous company that met at the Tabard on the way to Canterbury. It was more, far more, that he had the genius to create the Pilgrims, endowing each of them with an individuality that goes much beyond the typical. If we had only the *Prologue*, we might, perhaps, regard the Pilgrims as types. The error is common, and venial. But we must not stop with the *Prologue*: we must go on to the play. The Pilgrims are not static: they move and live. The Canterbury Pilgrimage is, whether Dryden meant it or not, a Human Comedy, and the Knight and the Miller and the Pardoner and the Wife of Bath and the rest are the *dramatis personae*. The *Prologue* itself is not merely a prologue: it is the first act, which sets the personages in motion. Thereafter, they move by virtue of their inherent vitality, not as tale-telling puppets, but as men and women. From this point of view, which surely accords with Chaucer's intention, the Pilgrims do not exist for the sake of the stories, but *vice versa*. Structurally regarded, the stories are merely long speeches expressing, directly or indirectly, the characters of the several persons. They are more or less comparable, in this regard, to the soliloquies of Hamlet or Iago or Macbeth. But they are not mere monologues, for each is addressed to all the other personages, and evokes reply and comment, being thus, in a real sense, a part of the conversation.

Further – and this is a point of crucial significance – the action of the plot, however simple, involves a great variety of relations among the Pilgrims. They are brought together by a common impulse, into a casual and impermanent association, which is nevertheless, for the time being, peculiarly intimate. They move slowly along the road, from village to village and inn to inn, in groups that are ever shifting, but ever forming afresh. Things happen to them. They come to know each other better and better. Their personalities act and react. Friendships combine for the nonce. Jokes are cracked, like the Host's on the Pardoner, which are taken amiss. Smouldering enmities of class or profession, like that between the Summoner and the Friar, which was proverbial, blaze into flaming quarrels. Thus the story of any pilgrim may be affected or determined – in its contents, or in the manner of the telling, or in both – not only by his character in general, but also by the circumstances, by the situation, by his momentary relations to the others in the company, or even by something in a tale that has come before. We lose much, therefore, when we neglect the so-called prologues and epilogues, and the bits of conversation and narrative that link the tales together. Many more of these would have been supplied if Chaucer had not left his work in so fragmentary a condition; but such as we have are invaluable, both for their own excellence, and for the light they throw upon the scope and details of the great design.

Chaucer's contemporaries were quite aware of the dramatic nature of the Pilgrimage and the significance of the Pilgrims as characters in the comedy. Their appreciation is put beyond a peradventure by that highly interesting document, the *Tale of Beryn*, written not long after Chaucer's death by an anonymous versifier for insertion in the Canterbury scheme. The *Beryn* itself, which is assigned to the Merchant as the first story on the return journey, need not detain us. The prologue, however, is worth a moment's notice.

This describes the arrival of the party at the Checker inn at Canterbury, and their proceedings, grave and gay, until they set out for London. Much space is given to the adventures of the Pardoner with a tapster, which result in his losing some money and getting his head broken. The scene in the cathedral is more edifying, and equally vivid. Particularly diverting is the behaviour of the Miller and others of his sort. While the Knight and his compeers go straightway to the shrine of St Thomas to pray and make offering, these idle fellows stroll about the church, staring at the stained-glass windows, misinterpreting the scenes therein depicted, and pretending, like gentlemen, to blazon the coats of arms. The Host calls them to order and directs them to the martyr's tomb. By-and-by the company scatter, to see the sights of the town or to call upon their friends, while the Wife of Bath and the Prioress walk about the inn garden. They reassemble for supper, at which the Host acts as marshal.

All this is a poor substitute for what Chaucer would have given us, if he had lived to finish his work. But there is some merit in the performance, and it certainly evinces a lively sense of the actuality of Chaucer's Pilgrims. The author of *Beryn* did not mistake the *Canterbury Tales* for a volume of disconnected stories. He recognized the work for what it really is – a micro-cosmography, a little image of the great world.

Travel, as everybody knows, is for the time being a mighty leveller of social distinctions, particularly when its concomitants throw the voyagers together while at the same time isolating them from the rest of the world. Think of the smoking-room of a small steamship with only three or four dozen passengers. These men might live side by side in one row of brick houses for a hundred years and scarcely know each other's faces. Break the shaft, keep them at sea for an extra week, and, if they aren't careful and if the cigars hold out, they will empty their hearts to one another with an indiscretion that may shock them to death when they remember it ashore.

Now an organized company of Pilgrims – and Chaucer's Pilgrims had effected an organization at Harry Bailly's inn – were brought together in a similar intimacy, which was made especially close by the religious impulse that actuated them all in common. We must not be sceptical about the genuineness of this impulse, merely because some of the Pilgrims are loose fish, or because they do not always act and speak with propriety. If we let this consideration much affect us, it must be either because we are uninstructed in medieval manners, or because we apply our own religion to life in a deplorably wooden fashion. This score and a half of miscellaneous Englishmen and Englishwomen were fulfilling the vow they had made to St Thomas in sickness or danger or misfortune. However diverse their stations in life, their moral codes, or the sincerity of their religion in general – and in all these points there is variety so rich as almost to bewilder – here they were at one. The saint had helped them, and they were gratefully doing their duty in return.

But the occasion was not only religious, it was social. Listen to the Host, who has entertained hundreds of such companies at the Tabard Inn:

'Ye goon to Caunterbury – God yow speede,
The blisful martir quite yow youre meede!
And wel I woot, as ye goon by the weye,
Ye shapen yow to talen and to pleye;
For trewely, confort ne myrthe is noon
To ride by the weye doumb as a stoon.'

(I 769–74)

The occasion, then, was both religious and social; and the various Pilgrims, knowing that all men are equal in God's sight, were not indisposed to sink their differences of rank for the nonce, so far, at least, as to laugh and talk together without the stand-offish punctilio of rigid etiquette.

Chaucer's own birth and station, as I reminded you in my opening lecture, had brought him into easy contact with both high and low; and his experiences as burgher, soldier, courtier, officeholder, and diplomatic agent had given him unparalleled opportunities for observation, which his humorously sympathetic temperament had impelled him to use to the best advantage. Mankind was his specialty.

He was now a trained and practised writer, with a profound sense of the joy and beauty, the sadness and irony, of human life. He had already studied the whole world from the point of view of two of the ruling passions – the desire for reputation (in the *House of Fame*) and passionate love (in the *Troilus*). In both of these great works, however, his approach had been, so to speak, oblique or indirect: by symbolism or allegory in the one; in the other, by way of a return to the days of old. Now, at length, in this Canterbury Pilgrimage, with its nine-and-twenty contemporary human creatures, he has recognized his crowning opportunity. He will show life as it is; he will paint 'what he sees'! But I am wrong. It is not showing (or exhibition); it is not painting (or delineation): it is dramatic action. And so he makes himself one of the Pilgrims, in order that we may understand that they are as real as he is. Chaucer existed, thus we instinctively syllogize, and therefore the Prioress existed, and the Reeve, and the Manciple, and the Monk, and the Knight, and Harry Bailly, the incomparable innkeeper, to whom, and not to Geoffrey Chaucer, the conduct of the drama is entrusted. Chaucer reports, but Harry Bailly is the dynamic agent. The action of the piece is largely due to his initiative, and to him are referable the details again and again. Sometimes, to be sure, the play gets out of hand, but not for long; and usually, on such occasions, he is content to let go the reins, since the team is guiding itself.

The Host, as we know, is the appointed leader. He nominates himself for the office, as many a good politician has done before and since, but not until after supper, when his social qualities have been fully tested. He is well fitted for the office – a fine large man, handsome after his florid fashion, merry, afraid of nobody – 'of manhod hym lakkede right naught' – loud-voiced and free-spoken. It is not by accident that Chaucer calls him as fair a burgess as there is in Cheap; for London was an *imperium in imperio*,[1] and the citizens were persons of importance, not merely in their own eyes, but in the estimation of all orders and even of the king. Chaucer himself, who was always in politics – would that we had his political autobiography! – is a first-rate example of a 'king's man', a sort of courtier who was also a burgher by descent and in actuality. Once a Londoner, always a Londoner, no matter what else you might become.

1 An empire within an empire. [Ed.]

But Harry Bailly was not only a fair and seemly burgess, bold of his speech. He was 'wys, and wel ytaught': that is, in modern parlance, a discreet man, with plenty of tact, one who 'knew his way about'; he had some education and was thoroughly versed in the usages of society. His hearty and sometimes boisterous manner must not deceive us. It is partly professional technique, and he forces it a little now and then, for a very special purpose – to see if he cannot irritate some pilgrim or other into revolt; for whoever gainsays his judgement must pay an enormous forfeit, no less than the total travelling expenses of the company.

'And whoso wole my juggement withseye
Shal paye al that we spenden by the weye.'
(I 805–6)

Harry is the legitimate ancestor of many a jovial and autocratic innkeeper in our literature; but we must not confuse him with such roaring eccentrics as Blague the landlord of the George at Waltham in the *Merry Devil of Edmonton*, or even mine Host of the Garter in the *Merry Wives*. 'Ha!' cries Blague, 'I'll caper in my own fee simple. Away with punctilios and orthography! I serve the good Duke of Norfolk. Bilbo! *Tityre tu patulae recubans sub tegmine fagi.*' Blague, it appears, is 'wel ytaught', for he can quote Virgil, with a prophecy, one is tempted to conjecture, of the *Tityre-tu's* of the next generation; but after all he is only a kind of substantial and well-esteemed buffoon. He is not Harry Bailly – scarcely more so than Sir John Falstaff (rest his soul!) is Chaucer's Knight. For Harry has his own dignity: he knows the times and the manners. Here, as ever, Chaucer is quite specific. The landlord of the Tabard, so he tells us, was

a semely man . . . withalle
For to han been a marchal in an halle.
(I 751–2)

Such as he had been master of ceremonies many a time when our Knight had 'begun the board', or sat at the head of the table, at high chivalric festivals.
(153–63)

Virginia Woolf

from 'The Pastons and Chaucer', *The Common Reader* 1925

Chaucer fixed his eyes upon the road before him, not upon the world to come. He was little given to abstract contemplation. He deprecated, with peculiar archness, any competition with the scholars and divines:

The answere of this lete I to dyvynys,
But wel I woot that in this world greet pyne ys.

(*Canterbury Tales*, 1 1323-4)

What is this world? what asketh men to have?
Now with his love, now in his colde grave
Allone, withouten any compaignye.

(1 2777-9)

O crueel goddes that governe
This world with byndyng of youre word eterne,
And writen in the table of atthamaunt
Youre parlement and youre eterne graunt,
What is mankynde moore unto you holde
Than is the sheep that rouketh in the folde?

(1 1303-8)

Questions press upon him; he asks them, but he is too true a poet to answer them; he leaves them unsolved, uncramped by the solution of the moment, and thus fresh for the generations that come after him. In his life, too, it would be impossible to write him down a man of this party or of that, a democrat or an aristocrat. He was a staunch churchman, but he laughed at priests. He was an able public servant and a courtier, but his views upon sexual morality were extremely lax. He sympathized with poverty, but did nothing to improve the lot of the poor. It is safe to say that not a single law has been framed or one stone set upon another because of anything that Chaucer said or wrote; and yet, as we read him, we are absorbing morality at every pore. For among writers there are two kinds: there are the priests who take you by the hand and lead you straight up to the mystery; there are the laymen who imbed their doctrines in flesh and blood and make a complete model of the world without excluding the bad or laying stress upon the good. Wordsworth, Coleridge, and Shelley are among the priests; they give us text after text to be hung upon the wall, saying after saying to be laid upon the heart like an amulet against disaster –

Farewell, farewell, the heart that lives alone

He prayeth best that loveth best
All things both great and small

– such lines of exhortation and command spring to memory instantly. But Chaucer lets us go our ways doing the ordinary things with the ordinary people. His morality lies in the way men and women behave to each other. We see them eating, drinking, laughing, and making love, and come to feel without a word being said what their standards are and so are steeped through and through with their morality. There can be no more forcible preaching than this where all actions and passions are represented, and instead of being solemnly exhorted we are left to stray and stare and make out a meaning for ourselves. It is the morality of ordinary intercourse, the morality of the novel, which parents and librarians rightly judge to be far more persuasive than the morality of poetry.

(30–32)

J. M. Manly

from *Chaucer and the Rhetoricians*, Warton Lecture on English Poetry 1926

In that charming Canterbury Tale which reveals the family life of Chauntecleer the cock and his favourite wife, Dame Pertelote, there is a passage to which I invite your attention. The pride and confidence of Chauntecleer have just been betrayed by the subtle flattery of Dan Russell the fox, and Chauntecleer, having closed his eyes the better to imitate the crowing of his revered father, has been seized by the throat and is being hurried away to destruction on the fox's back. It is the most tragic moment of the delightful mock-heroic tale and calls for all the resources of the most accomplished rhetoric. In accordance

with the best theory and practice of the art, the narrator of the tale
bursts forth into a series of apostrophes, first to Destiny, then to
Venus, upon whose day, Friday, the tragic event occurred, and
finally, climactically, to a person whose name means nothing to the
uninstructed modern reader:

O Gaufred, deere maister soverayn,
That whan thy worthy kyng Richard was slayn
With shot, compleynedest his deeth so soore,
Why ne hadde I now thy sentence and thy loore,
The Friday for to chide, as diden ye?
For on a Friday, soothly, slayn was he.
Thanne wolde I shewe yow how that I koude pleyne
For Chauntecleres drede and for his peyne.
(Canterbury Tales, VII 3347–54)

The commentators tell us that the appeal and the allusion are to
Master Gaufred de Vinsauf – Galfridus Vinosalvensis – and a section
of his Nova Poetria, in which the death of Richard Cœur de Lion,
who received his fatal wound on a Friday, is lamented with all the
artifices of medieval rhetoric, and the fateful Friday is reproached in
terms which, though highly ingenious, are distinctly ludicrous.

But the prosperity of a jest lies as much in the readiness of the
hearer as in the facetiousness of the jester. Why did Chaucer expect
his hearers to recognize the literary gem alluded to, and to enjoy the
allusion? Nearly two hundred years had passed since King Richard
was slain, and only a few less since the Latin poet wrote his intention-
ally serious but actually comic lamentation. And yet Chaucer
assumed that his audience would understand at once, without even
mention of the surname of this Master Gaufred. He could not have
alluded more trippingly to the best known among his own contemporaries. And his confidence was justifiable. Every educated
man remembered Master Gaufred and some perhaps knew by heart
his famous lamentation, for the Nova Poetria was one of the principal
textbooks on rhetoric and was studied in the schools with a zeal
devoted perhaps to few modern school books.

That Chaucer's intention here was satirical admits of no doubt.
He felt and he made his readers feel the enormous absurdity of
Gaufred's rhetorical outburst. Are we to infer that he regarded

rhetorical theories in general only as objects of ridicule and, like the author of *Hudibras* in a later age, held that

All a rhetorician's rules
Teach nothing but to name his tools?

There are a score of other passages in which he or the characters through whom he speaks profess to care little and know nothing about rhetoric. Says the Franklin:

I lerned nevere rethorik, certeyn;
Thyng that I speke, it moot be bare and pleyn.
I sleep nevere on the Mount of Pernaso,
Ne lerned Marcus Tullius Scithero.
Colours ne knowe I none, withouten drede,
But swiche colours as growen in the mede,
Or elles swiche as men dye or peynte.
Colours of rethoryk been to me queynte.

(*Canterbury Tales*, v 719–26)

In like manner the Host says contemptuously to the Clerk of Oxenford:

Youre termes, youre colours, and youre figures,
Keepe hem in stoor til so be that ye endite
Heigh style, as whan that men to kynges write.

(*Canterbury Tales*, iv 16–18)

With most writers, medieval or modern, such passages would be conclusive as to the writer's scorn of rhetoricians and rhetorical theory, but the interpretation of Geoffrey Chaucer is not so simple a matter. One is not always safe in taking his words as having only their plain and obvious meanings. When, for example, he denies the Summoner's view that the archdeacon's curse need not be dreaded by anyone who was willing to pay, and says:

Of cursyng oghte ech gilty man him drede,
For curs wol slee right as assoillyng savith,

(*Canterbury Tales*, i 660–61)

many scholars think he was speaking ironically and meant that neither curse nor absolution had any validity. And certainly the humorous citation by Chauntecleer and Pertelote of 'Daun Catoun', and 'the hooly doctour Augustyn, | Or Boece, or the Bisshop Bradwardyn' does not imply any lack of respect for those eminent authorities. Moreover, in the passages adduced above from the Host and the Franklin, it is clear that we have the views of those two characters, not the views of Chaucer himself, for the Clerk responds to the admonition of the Host not only by telling a tale he had learned from that excellent rhetorician Francis Petrarch, but by delivering a panegyric on Petrarch's 'heigh stile' and 'rethorike sweete'; and the very terms of the Franklin's disclaimer of rhetorical skill are derived from that most rhetorical of Latin poets, Persius, no doubt through the medium of some medieval treatise on rhetoric.

To any student of his technique, Chaucer's development reveals itself unmistakably, not as progress from crude, untrained native power to a style and method polished by fuller acquaintance with rhetorical precepts and more sophisticated models, but rather as a process of gradual release from the astonishingly artificial and sophisticated art with which he began and the gradual replacement of formal rhetorical devices by methods of composition based upon close observation of life and the exercise of the creative imagination. His growth in artistic methods and in artistic power – a growth unequalled so far as I am aware among medieval authors – seems inexplicable unless we admit that he had thought long and deeply upon the principles of composition, the technique of diction and phrasing, methods of narration, description, and characterization, and numberless other details of the writer's art. The astonishing advance from the thin prettinesses of the *Book of the Duchess* to the psychologic depth of *Troilus and Criseyde*, the swift tragic power of the *Pardoner's Tale*, the rollicking exuberance of the tales of the Miller and the Reeve, the matchless humour of the first half of the *Summoner's Tale*, and the incomparable portraiture of the *Prologue* is inconceivable as mere vegetative growth. The great debt of Chaucer to the Italians – and I suspect that his debt to Dante was as great as that to either Petrarch or Boccaccio – was perhaps not so much because they furnished new materials and new models for imitation, as because they stimulated his powers of reflection by forms and ideals of art different from those with which he was familiar.

Without arguing this point, I shall merely suggest certain evidences of his fondness for experimentation. Unfortunately – or perhaps fortunately – most of his early writings have perished. The ballades, roundels, virelayes, and other hymns to the god of Love testified to in the *Legend of Good Women* are gone, but two of the extant minor poems are obviously experimental. The fragment entitled *A Complaint to his Lady*, possibly written when he was in search of a suitable form for narrative verse, preserves an experiment in *terza rima*, the measure of Dante's great poem. The much discussed and little understood *Anelida and Arcite* seems also purely an experiment in versification and is of interest, chiefly if not solely, because the formal Complaint is an even more remarkable *tour de force* in rhyming than the famous translations from Sir Otes de Granson.

In investigating the sources of Chaucer's notions of literature and his conceptions of style, scholars have hitherto discussed only the writings of other authors which may have served as models for imitation. The possibility of his acquaintance with formal rhetorical theory and the precepts of rhetoricians has not been considered, notwithstanding the hint that might have been derived from the allusion to Gaufred de Vinsauf and the other passages on rhetoric scattered through his works. Even *a priori* there would seem to be a high probability that Chaucer was familiar with the rhetorical theories of his time, that he had studied the textbooks and carefully weighed the doctrines. Whatever modern scholars may have said of the errors in his references and the shallowness of his classical learning – and there are few of his critics whose errors are less numerous than his – he was a man of scholarly tastes and of considerable erudition. His works bear witness to no small reading in astronomy and astrology, in alchemy, in medicine, and in philosophy and theology, as well as in the classical authors current in his day. The ancient tradition that he was educated, in part at any rate, in the law school of the Inner Temple has recently been shown to be possible, if not highly probable. The education given by the inns of court seems to have been remarkably liberal. What more likely than that the formal study of rhetoric not only was included in his academic curriculum, as one of the Seven Arts, but also occupied much of his thought and reflection in maturer years?

(95–8)

Walter Raleigh

from 'On Chaucer', *On Writing and Writers* 1926

It is impossible to overpraise Chaucer's mastery of language. Here at the beginning, as it is commonly reckoned, of Modern English literature, is a treasury of perfect speech. We can trace his themes, and tell something of the events of his life. But where did he get his style – from which it may be said that English literature has been (in some respects) a long falling away?

What is the ordinary account? I do not wish to cite individual scholars, and there is no need. Take what can be gathered from the ordinary textbooks – what are the current ideas? Is not this a fair statement of them?

English was a despised language little used by the upper classes. A certain number of dreary works written chiefly for homiletic purposes, or in order to appeal to the humble people, are to be found in the half century before Chaucer. They are poor and flat and feeble, giving no promise of the new dawn. Then arose the morning star! Chaucer adopted the despised English tongue and set himself to modify it, to shape it, to polish it, to render it fit for his purpose. He imported words from the French; he purified the English of his time from its dross; he shaped it into a fit instrument for his use.

Now I have no doubt that a competent philologist examining the facts could easily show that this account *must be* nonsense, from beginning to end. But even a literary critic can say something certain on the point – perhaps can even give aid by divination to the philologists, and tell them where it will best repay them to ply their pickaxes and spades.

No poet makes his own language. No poet introduces serious or numerous modifications into the language that he uses. Some, no doubt, coin words and revive them, like Spenser or Keats in verse, Carlyle or Sir Thomas Browne in prose. But least of all great English poets did Chaucer mould and modify the speech he found. The poets who take liberties with speech are either prophets or eccentrics. From either of these characters Chaucer was far removed. He held fast by communal and social standards for literary speech. He desired to be understood of the people. His English is plain, terse, homely, colloquial English, taken alive out of daily speech. He expresses his ideal again and again, as when the Host asks what is the use of telling a tale that sends the hearers to sleep:

For certeinly, as that thise clerkes seyn,
Whereas a man may have noon audience,
Noght helpeth it to tellen his sentence.

(Canterbury Tales, VII 2800–802)

The same admirable literary critic repeats Chaucer's creed when he instructs the Clerk:

Youre termes, youre colours, and youre figures,
Keepe hem in stoor til so be that ye endite
Heigh style, as whan that men to kynges write.
Speketh so pleyn at this tyme, we yow preye,
That we may understonde what ye seye.

(Canterbury Tales, IV 16–20)

Chaucer has expressed his views on the model literary style so clearly and so often, and has illustrated them so well in his practice, that no mistake is possible. His style is the perfect courtly style; it has all the qualities of ease, directness, simplicity, of the best colloquial English, in short, which Chaucer recognized, three centuries before the French Academy, as the English spoken by cultivated women in society. His 'facound', like Virginia's, is 'ful wommanly and pleyn'. He avoids all 'countrefeted termes', all subtleties of rhetoric, and addresses himself to the 'commune intente'.

Examples of his plain, terse brevity are easy to find. Take one, from the *Monk's Tale* – of Hugelin of Pisa. (The imprisoned father bites his hands for grief; his young sons think it is for hunger):

His children wende that it for hunger was
That he his armes gnow, and nat for wo,
And seyde, 'Fader, do nat so, allas!
But rather ete the flessh upon us two.
Oure flessh thou yaf us, take oure flessh us fro,
And ete ynogh,' – right thus they to hym seyde,

And after that, withinne a day or two,
They leyde hem in his lappe adoun and deyde.

> (*Canterbury Tales*, VII 2447–54)

Now a style like this, and in this perfection, implies a society at the back of it. If we are told that educated people at the Court of Edward III spoke French and that English was a despised tongue, we could deny it on the evidence of Chaucer alone. His language was shaped for him, and it cannot have been shaped by rustics. No English style draws so much as Chaucer's from the communal and colloquial elements of the language. And his poems make it certain that from his youth up he had heard much admirable, witty talk in the English tongue.

The conclusion is that Chaucer's language is the language of his own day, like Gower's, but used by a quicker intelligence, and freer from repetition, artificial tags, flatnesses, etc. It was his good fortune to live at a time when bookish learning had not yet severed classes. He broke loose from the literary fashions which at all time affect the 'educated classes', and wrote the good English of peers and peasants. In this respect he comes near to the poets of Dryden's age.

This language was his own, not painfully acquired. Ease and skill of this kind is not attainable save in the birth tongue. Too much has been made of French; and of the dates of the 'adoption' of English for public documents, law courts, schools. The English language had throughout a healthy, full-blooded existence. Chaucer had no adequate *literary* predecessors in English. But how partial and poor a thing the manuscript literature of the time compared with the riches of spoken lore, proverb, tale and romance! As Chaucer helps us, by his portrait of the age, to correct the formal annalists, so he helps us, by his writing, to a truer appreciation of literary history.

If there is to be any profitable investigation of Chaucer's language it must be remembered that he is at the *end* of an age, not at the beginning. His pupils could make nothing of him, and the Renaissance brought in ideals which made him unintelligible. Like Burns, Chaucer is a culmination and a close. We can understand Burns only by remembering his debts to Fergusson, Ramsay, and scores of nameless poets. If we are to understand Chaucer, it must be by reference to a tribe of story-tellers, songsters, traffickers in popular lore and moral maxims who, because they did not relate themselves to paper, have almost passed, except by inference, from our ken.

(114–19)

G. K. Chesterton

from *Chaucer* 1932

Now even if we consider Chaucer only as a humorist, he was in this very exact sense a great humorist. And by this I do not only mean a very good humorist. I mean a humorist in the grand style; a humorist whose broad outlook embraced the world as a whole, and saw even great humanity against a background of greater things. This quality of grandeur in a joke is one which I can only explain by an example. The example also illustrates that clinging curse of all the criticism of Chaucer; the fact that while the poet is always large and humorous, the critics are often small and serious. They not only get hold of the wrong end of the stick, but of the diminishing end of the telescope; and take in a detail when they should be taking in a design. The Chaucerian irony is sometimes so large that it is too large to be seen. I know no more striking example than the business of his own contribution to the tales of the Canterbury Pilgrims. A thousand times have I heard men tell (as Chaucer himself would put it) that the poet wrote the *Rime of Sir Topas* as a parody of certain bad romantic verse of his own time. And the learned would be willing to fill their notes with examples of this bad poetry, with the addition of not a little bad prose. It is all very scholarly, and it is all perfectly true; but it entirely misses the point. The joke is not that Chaucer is joking at bad ballad-mongers; the joke is much larger than that. To see the scope of this gigantic jest we must take in the whole position of the poet and the whole conception of the poem.

The Poet is the Maker; he is the creator of a cosmos; and Chaucer is the creator of the whole world of his creatures. He made the pilgrimage; he made the pilgrims. He made all the tales that are told by the pilgrims. Out of him is all the golden pageantry and chivalry of the Knight's Tale; all the rank and rowdy farce of the Miller's; he told through the mouth of the Prioress the pathetic legend of the

Child Martyr and through the mouth of the Squire the wild, almost Arabian romance of Cambuscan. And he told them all in sustained melodious verse, seldom so continuously prolonged in literature; in a style that sings from start to finish. Then in due course, as the poet is also a pilgrim among the other pilgrims, he is asked for his contribution. He is at first struck dumb with embarrassment; and then suddenly starts a gabble of the worst doggerel in the book. It is so bad that, after a page or two of it, the tolerant innkeeper breaks in with the desperate protest of one who can bear no more, in words that could be best translated as 'Gorlumme!' or 'This is a bit too thick!' The poet is shouted down by a righteous revolt of his hearers, and can only defend himself by saying sadly that this is the only poem he knows. Then, by way of a final climax or anticlimax of the same satire, he solemnly proceeds to tell a rather dull story *in prose*.

Now a joke of that scale goes a great deal beyond the particular point, or pointlessness, of the *Rime of Sir Topas*. Chaucer is mocking not merely bad poets but good poets; the best poet he knows; 'the best in this kind are but shadows'. Chaucer, having to represent himself as reciting bad verse, did very probably take the opportunity of parodying somebody else's bad verse. But the parody is not the point. The point is in the admirable irony of the whole conception of the dumb or doggerel rhymer who is nevertheless the author of all the other rhymes; nay, even the author of their authors. Among all the types and trades, the coarse miller, the hard-fisted reeve, the clerk, the cook, the shipman, the poet is the only man who knows no poetry. But the irony is wider and even deeper than that. There is in it some hint of those huge and abysmal ideas of which the poets are half-conscious when they write; the primal and elemental ideas connected with the very nature of creation and reality. It has in it something of the philosophy of a phenomenal world, and all that was meant by those sages, by no means pessimists, who have said that we are in a world of shadows. Chaucer has made a world of his own shadows, and, when he is on a certain plane, finds himself equally shadowy. It has in it all the mystery of the relation of the maker with things made. There falls on it from afar even some dark ray of the irony of God, who was mocked when He entered His own world, and killed when He came among His creatures.

That is laughter in the grand style, *pace* Matthew Arnold; and

Arnold, with all his merits, did not laugh but only smiled – not to say smirked. It is the presence of such things, behind the seeming simplicity of the fourteenth-century poet, which constitutes what I mean here by the greatness of Chaucer.

(20–22)

A. E. Housman

from *The Name and Nature of Poetry* 1933

The *Knight's Tale* of Palamon and Arcite is not one of Chaucer's most characteristic and successful poems: he is not perfectly at home, as in the *Prologue* and the tale of Chauntecleer and Pertelote, and his movement is a trifle languid. Dryden's translation shows Dryden in the maturity of his power and accomplishment, and much of it can be honestly and soberly admired. Nor was he insensible to all the peculiar excellence of Chaucer: he had the wit to keep unchanged such lines as 'Up rose the sun and up rose Emily' or 'The slayer of himself yet saw I there'; he understood that neither he nor anyone else could better them. But much too often in a like case he would try to improve, because he thought that he could. He believed, as he says himself, that he was 'turning some of the *Canterbury Tales* into our language, as it is now refined'; 'the words' he says again 'are given up as a post not to be defended in our poet, because he wanted the modern art of fortifying'; 'in some places' he tells us 'I have added somewhat of my own where I thought my author was deficient, and had not given his thoughts their true lustre, for want of words in the beginning of our language.'

Let us look at the consequences. Chaucer's vivid and memorable line

The smylere with the knyf under the cloke

(I 1999)

becomes these three:

Next stood Hypocrisy, with holy leer,
Soft smiling and demurely looking down,
But hid the dagger underneath the gown.

Again:

'Allas,' quod he, 'that day that I was bore!'

(1 1542)

So Chaucer, for want of words in the beginning of our language. Dryden comes to his assistance and gives his thoughts their true lustre thus:

Cursed be the day when first I did appear;
Let it be blotted from the calendar,
Lest it pollute the month and poison all the year.

Or yet again:

The queene anon, for verray wommanhede,
Gan for to wepe, and so dide Emelye,
And alle the ladyes in the compaignye.

(1 1748–50)

If Homer or Dante had the same thing to say, would he wish to say it otherwise? But to Dryden Chaucer wanted the modern art of fortifying, which he thus applies:

He said; dumb sorrow seized the standers-by.
The queen, above the rest, by nature good
(The pattern formed of perfect womanhood)
For tender pity wept: when she began
Through the bright quire the infectious virtue ran
All dropped their tears, even the contended maid.

Had there not fallen upon England the curse out of Isaiah, 'make the heart of this people fat, and make their ears heavy, and shut their eyes'?

(20–23)

John Livingston Lowes

from *Geoffrey Chaucer* 1934

Between the *Book of the Duchess* and the *House of Fame* as a whole some years had intervened, and much had happened. For the Second Book of the *House of Fame*, with its reference to Chaucer's 'rekeninges', was certainly written after 1374, when he became Controller of the Customs. From 1369, the date of the *Duchess*, until then he had been in attendance at court, had been more than once in France on diplomatic missions, and above all, in 1372, had visited Italy. And that meant for Chaucer not only six or seven more years of observation and action but also the entrance into his life of the most powerfully transforming influence which he experienced – the works of Dante and Boccaccio, and, in another fashion, of Petrarch. He had liked and admired the French poets, had played with them delightfully, and he never quite forgot them. But Dante, to borrow a comparison from Guillaume de Lorris, was to them like the moon, beside which the other stars seem but little candles. And Dante did for Chaucer what Greek a century later did for Europe. When the *House of Fame* was written its maker could draw at will on the *Divine Comedy* – *Inferno*, *Purgatorio*, and *Paradiso*, all three – and the *Convivio* as well. And what Chaucer read had to be said – impression and expression went hand in hand. 'Borrowing' is an inept and misleading word.

I suppose there could scarcely be a sharper contrast than that between Chaucer and Dante – between the austerity of the one and the other's buoyant and exhaustless zest in life; between an intensity like white flame, set over against an unrivalled lightness of touch; between a remorseless compression which packs stanzas into lines, lines into words, as contrasted with a lavishness for which Dryden's 'Here is God's plenty' is the only phrase; between a passion for the minutest, most circumstantial record of contemporary incidents, and a supreme indifference to such particulars. Dante's sense of artistic unity was as uncompromising as steel; Chaucer had been a practitioner of the loosely-linked court poetry of France. Dante, like Flaubert, was one of the inexorable seekers for the unique word; invincible patience was not one of Chaucer's gifts. Yet the two had characteristics in common. Both had the same unerring 'memory of the eye', and that sense for saliency of detail which, in Dante's case, bites like etcher's acid a picture into the memory. Both had (in Chaucer's case still latent) the gift of reading and rendering essential character through seeming accidents of garb, of gesture, of facial expression. And it was inevitable that Dante's influence should be profound. But it was effected above all, I think, through the impact upon a highly original genius of the *vivida vis animi*[1] of a supreme creative personality. Chaucer's recollections of Dante's words are the least of his debts to him. Those are, for us, little more than hints which keep us aware of something which never found expression in words – the silent workings of the *Divine Comedy*, not unlike those of life, within or beneath Chaucer's consciousness. And in the *House of Fame* we meet that influence explicitly for the first time.

(102–4)

Book II begins with a striking Invocation:

O Thought, that wrot al that I mette [dreamt].
(*House of Fame*, 523)

And that is Dante's Invocation at the opening of the second Canto of the *Inferno*:

O mente, che scrivesti ciò ch'io vidi –
O Mind, that didst write what I saw.

What was it that Dante saw? He had told it, and Chaucer had read it, some threescore lines earlier in the first Canto:

A poet I was, and sang of that just son of Anchises,
who came from Troy after proud Ilion was burnt.

And that is precisely what Chaucer too had sung in his own First Book. In a word, in that Invocation, present by no accident, he has now bound together, however baffling their relations otherwise, Books I and II, as if with hoops of steel.

But in Book II Chaucer must be carried, to fulfil his purpose, to the House of Fame, and that, as he knew from the twelfth *Metamorphosis*, which he quotes, is set between heaven, earth and sea, and is consequently inaccessible, save through the air, to mortals. How,

1 Liveliness and strength of soul. [Ed.]

then, is he to reach it? It was once more in Dante, whom he was reading with a falcon's eye, that he found the suggestion of the way.

For in the ninth Canto of the *Purgatorio* Dante saw in a dream an eagle poised in the sky, with plumes of gold and wings outspread, intent to swoop. And Dante seemed, in his dream, to be where Ganymede had been snatched up in an eagle's talons, and carried to Jove's house. Then it seemed to him that the eagle, having wheeled a while, descended, terrible as lightning, and snatched him up as far as the sphere of fire. Precisely so Chaucer's eagle, that shone like gold, first soared, then came down like a thunderbolt, and

Me, fleynge, in a swap he hente,
And with hys sours ayen up wente,
Me caryinge in his clawes starke
As lyghtly as I were a larke.

(House of Fame, 543–6)

And Dante's lightning recalls to Chaucer a thunderbolt in a poem of Machaut, which he had read when he wrote the *Duchess*, and Machaut and Dante blend in Chaucer's thunderbolt – as if unconsciously to symbolize the passing and the coming sway.

But that is not quite all. There are few passages which Chaucer read that made so indelible an impression on his mind, and came so often back to memory, as the opening Canto of the *Paradiso* – the canto which ushered in the supreme ascent in all literature through the seven spheres and the starry heavens and the empyrean. And when Chaucer first saw the eagle, its golden plumage

. . . shon so bryghte
That never sawe men such a syghte,
But yf the heven had ywonne
Al newe of gold another sonne.

(House of Fame, 503–6)

And that is a line of the First Canto of the *Paradiso:*

Avesse il ciel d'un altro sole adorno.

Chaucer and Coleridge, in so many respects antipodal, were endowed with the same insatiable appetite for books, and the same prehensile, amalgamating memory.

(107–9)

Ezra Pound

from *A B C of Reading* 1934

Chaucer really does comprehend the thought as well as the life of his time.

The Wife of Bath's theology is not a mere smear. Her attention to the meaning of terms is greater than we find in Lorenzo Medici's imaginary dialogue with Ficino about platonism. This is, in Chaucer, the remains of the Middle Ages, when men took some care of their terminology.

When she says:

conseillyng is no comandement,
> (*Canterbury Tales*, III 67)

she has a meaning in each of her terms.

Chaucer wrote while England was still a part of Europe. There was one culture from Ferrara to Paris and it extended to England. Chaucer was the greatest poet of his day. He was more compendious then Dante.

He participated in the same culture with Froissart and Boccaccio, the great humane culture that went into Rimini, that spoke Franco-Veneto, that is in the roundels of Froissart and in the doggerel of the Malatesta.

In Shakespeare's time England is already narrowing. Shakespeare as supreme lyric technician is indebted to the Italian song-books, but they are already an EXOTIC.

Chaucer uses French art, the art of Provence, the verse art come from the troubadours. In his world there had lived both Guillaume de Poictiers and Scotus Erigena. But Chaucer was not a foreigner. It was HIS civilization.

He made fun of the hrimm hramm ruff, the decadence of Anglo-Saxon alliteration, the verse written by those who had forgotten the WHY of the Anglo-Saxon bardic narration, and been too insular to learn French. True, Chaucer's name *is* French and not English, his mind is the mind of Europe, not the mind of an annex or an outlying province.

He is *Le Grand Translateur*. He had found a new language, he had it largely to himself, with the grand opportunity. Nothing spoiled, nothing worn out.

(88–9)

C. S. Lewis

from 'Chaucer', *The Allegory of Love* 1936

For many historians of literature, and for all general readers, the great mass of Chaucer's work is simply a background to the *Canterbury Tales*, and the whole output of the fourteenth century is simply a background to Chaucer. Whether such a view is just, or whether it has causes other than the excellence of the *Tales*, need not here be inquired; for us, at any rate, Chaucer is a poet of courtly love, and he ceases to be relevant to our study when he reaches the last and most celebrated of his works. Nor does he stand, for us, in isolation from his century; he stands side by side with Gower and the translators of the *Romance of the Rose* – of whom, he himself was one – and co-operates with them in the work of assimilating the achievements of French poetry, and thus determining the direction of English poetry for nearly two hundred years.

By considering Chaucer in this light we shall lose much; but we shall have the advantage of seeing him as he appeared to his contemporaries, and to his immediate successors. When the men of the fourteenth or fifteenth centuries thought of Chaucer, they did not think first of the *Canterbury Tales*. Their Chaucer was the Chaucer of dream and allegory, of love-romance and erotic debate, of high style and profitable doctrine. To Deschamps, as every one remembers, he was the 'great translator' – the gardener by whom a French poet might hope to be transplanted – and also the English god of Love.[1] To Gower, he is the poet of Venus: to Thomas Usk, Love's 'owne trewe servaunt' and 'the noble philosophical poete'.[2] In the age that followed the names of Gower and Chaucer are constantly coupled. Chaucer's comic and realistic style is imitated by Lydgate in the

1 See Deschamps' *Ballade to Chaucer*, lines 11 and 31.
2 Gower, *Conf. Amantis*, Book VIII, 1st version, 2941; Usk, *Testament of Love*, Book III, Chapter 4.

Prologue to the *Book of Thebes*, and by an unknown poet in the Prologue to the *Tale of Beryn;* but this is a small harvest beside the innumerable imitations of his amatory and allegorical poetry. And while his successors thus show their admiration for his love poetry, they explicitly praise him as the great model of style. He is to them much what Waller and Denham were to the Augustans, the 'firste finder' of the true way in our language, which before his time was 'rude and boystous'.[1] Where we see a great comedian and a profound student of human character, they saw a master of noble sentiment and a source of poetic diction.

It is tempting to say that if Chaucer's friends and followers were dunces who treasured the chaff and neglected the grain, yet this is no reason why we should do likewise. But the temptation should be resisted. To grow impatient with the critical tradition of the earliest lovers of Chaucer is to exclude ourselves from any understanding of the later Middle Ages in England; for the literature of the fifteenth and sixteenth centuries is based (naturally enough) not on our reading of Chaucer, but on theirs. And there is something to be said for them.

In the first place, we must beware of condemning them for not working the vein which Chaucer had opened up in the *Canterbury Tales*, lest in so doing we condemn the whole course of English poetry. What they have left undone, their successors have left undone likewise. The *Canterbury Tales* are glorious reading, but they have always been sterile. If the later Middle Ages can offer us only the Prologue to *Thebes* and the Prologue to *Beryn*, we ourselves are not in much better plight. William Morris's discipleship to Chaucer was an illusion. Crabbe and Mr Masefield are good writers; but they are hardly among the greatest English poets. If Chaucer's *Tales* have had any influence, it is to be sought in our prose rather than in our verse. Our great and characteristic poets – our Spenser, Milton, Wordsworth, and the like – have much more in common with Virgil, or even with *Beowulf*, then with the *Prologue* and the *Pardoner's Tale*. Perhaps none of our early poets has so little claim to be called the father of English poetry as the Chaucer of the *Canterbury Tales*.

1 Hoccleve, *Regement of Princes*, 4978 (cf. ibid. 1973, *Bookes of his ornat endyting That is to al this land enlumynyng*); Lydgate, *Troy Book*, III, 4237. 'For he (sc. Chaucer) oure English gilt with his sawes, Rude and boistous firste be olde dawes That was ful fer from al perfeccioun Til that he cam.'

But even if the first Chaucerians were dunces, it would not be safe to neglect their testimony. The stupidest contemporary, we may depend upon it, knew certain things about Chaucer's poetry which modern scholarship will never know; and doubtless the best of us misunderstand Chaucer in many places where the veriest fool among his audience could not have misunderstood. If they all took Chaucer's love poetry *au grand sérieux*, it is overwhelmingly probable that Chaucer himself did the same; and one of the advantages of keeping the *Canterbury Tales* out of sight, as I have proposed to do, will be that we may thus hope to rid ourselves of a false emphasis which is creeping into the criticism of Chaucer. We have heard a little too much of the 'mocking' Chaucer. Not many will agree with the critic who supposed that the laughter of Troilus in heaven was 'ironical'; but I am afraid that many of us now read into Chaucer all manner of ironies, slynesses, and archnesses, which are not there, and praise him for his humour where he is really writing with 'ful devout corage'. The lungs of our generation are so very 'tickle o' the sere'.

There is one respect in which the severest critic will admit that the old Chaucerians were right; that is, in their recognition of Chaucer as a great model of poetical style. It is true that the Chaucerian style, imitated ill, and with gross exaggeration of its foreign and polysyllabic elements, may have been one of the sources of the later 'aureate' style, which, along with some beauties, has many vices. But Chaucer is not to blame for this. The history of his influence on the fifteenth century is closely parallel to that of Milton's on the eighteenth; in each we see the work of a great poet partially vulgarized, and hardened into a mannerism, by indiscreet imitation. The original style is to be judged on its own merits; and it is one of the pleasures of studying Chaucer to trace its development. That development is from a style essentially prosaic and yet pretentious, to a style which has since become almost the norm of English poetry. Examples will make all plain:

To speke of godnesse, trewly she
Had as moche debonairte
As ever had Hester in the Bible,
And more, yif more were possyble.

And, soth to seyne, therwythal
She had a wyt so general,
So hool enclyned to alle goode,
That al hir wyt was set, by the rode,
Withoute malyce, upon gladnesse.

(Book of the Duchess, 985–93)

This is the old, bad manner. A man could forgive, as mere honest
debility, the lumber of expletives – 'as *ever* had Hester' – 'and more,
yif more were possyble' – 'by the rode'; what is radically bad is the
fussy prolixity, the air of saying so much while so little is said, the
pseudo-legal or pseudo-logical pretentiousness. 'To speke of godnesse,' he begins; like a lecturer turning to a new head. 'She had a
wyt so general', he continues; and who would not expect that some
real consequence was coming? Such a style makes the worst of both
worlds: it is as heavy as the prose of instruction, and as empty as an
Elizabethan song, while yet it neither sings nor instructs. It is a style
which Lydgate in his worst places may be said to have brought to its
own terrible perfection. To turn from such a passage to the preludings
of the new style is like passing from the engine-room of a ship to the
deck.

Gladeth, ye foules, of the morowe gray!
Lo! Venus, rysen among yon rowes rede!
And floures fressh, honoureth ye this day . . .

(Complaint of Mars, 1–3)

Throgh Phebus, that was comen hastely
Within the paleys yates sturdely,
With torche in honde, of which the stremes bryghte
On Venus chambre knokkeden ful lyghte.

(Complaint of Mars, 81–4)

And then at erst hath he
Al his desir, and therwith al myschaunce.

(Complaint of Mars, 240–41)

But Chaucer's conversion is gradual, and in the same poem he can
suddenly plunge us back into the old manner at its very worst –

The ordre of compleynt requireth skylfully
That yf a wight shal pleyne pitously,
Ther mot be cause wherfore that men pleyne, . . .

(155–7)

which is sheer nonentity yawning in thirty syllables. Even in the
Parliament of Fowls, side by side with the calculated and comic
prosiness of the goose, we find the unintentionally and unjustifiably
prosaic verbiage of

      . . . foules of ravyne
Han chosen fyrst, *by pleyn eleccioun*,
The tercelet of the faucoun *to diffyne*
Al here sentence, and as him lest, termyne.

(527–30)

It seems ungracious to hunt out the faults of a great poet. But
Chaucer's achievement in style cannot be understood, cannot be
praised so sincerely as contemporaries praised it, until we realize
the depth from which he raised himself, and, at times, raised his
disciples also.

The form and sentiment of Chaucer's love poems well illustrate
what I said at the beginning of this chapter about the living and therefore ever-changing influence of the *Romance of the Rose*. They are all
recognizable descendants of it, but none of them is a poem of the
same type. Nowhere in Chaucer do we find what can be called a
radically allegorical poem. The point is of some importance; for it is
in Chaucer that many readers make their first acquaintance with
allegory, and Chaucer thus becomes the innocent cause of a deep-
seated misunderstanding. By a radical allegory I mean a story which
can be translated into literal narration, as I translated the first part of
the *Romance of the Rose* in the preceding chapter, without confusion,
but not without loss. Thus, if there is no story – if the literal version,
when extracted, proves to be a mere maxim or description, and not
the 'imitation of an action', then the work in question does not pass
my test. If, again, there are passages which cannot be so 'translated' –
episodes for which no *significacio* can be found – then, again, it fails.
Still more if there are passages which need no translation, being
already literal in the original text, then the original is to that extent

unallegorical. Above all, if we lose nothing by our 'translation', the original work must be bad. If the story, literally told, pleases as much as the original, and in the same way, to what purpose was allegory employed? For the function of allegory is not to hide but to reveal, and it is properly used only for that which cannot be said, or so well said, in literal speech. The inner life, and specially the life of love, religion, and spiritual adventure, has therefore always been the field of true allegory; for here there are intangibles which only allegory can fix and reticences which only allegory can overcome. The poem of Guillaume de Lorris is a true allegory of love; but no poem of Chaucer's is. In Chaucer we find the same subject-matter, that of chivalrous love; but the treatment is never truly allegorical. Traces of the allegorical poem survive. Thus we have poems set in the framework of a dream after the manner of Guillaume; but what happens in the dream is not allegorical. Or we have allegory itself used as a framework for something else. We have allegorical persons, each with a brief description, used as a kind of pageantry to decorate a background, in the Renaissance manner; or again we have personifications which have become a mere characteristic of style, a form of poetic diction, after the manner of the eighteenth century. Finally, in his greatest work, we have the courtly conceptions of love, which Chaucer learned from the French allegory, put into action in poetry which is not allegorical at all. Chaucer achieves the literal presenta tion; but it is Guillaume's allegory which has rendered the achievement possible.

The *Complaint unto Pity* and the *Complaint to his Lady* illustrate the use of personification at its lowest level – the most faint and frigid result of the popularity of allegory. Not only do the allegorical figures fail to interact, as in a true allegory; they even fail to be pictorial: they become a mere catalogue:

And fresshe Beaute, Lust, and Jolyte,
Assured Maner, Youthe, and Honeste,
Wisdom, Estaat, Drede, and Governaunce.

(*Complaint unto Pity*, 39–41)

– where it is not only the cadence of the last line that reminds us of Lydgate.

In the *Book of the Duchess* we have the poem framed in a dream, and we have courtly love; but allegory has disappeared. We dream in order to hear a bereaved lover give just such a literal account of his past happiness and present sorrow as he might have given in waking life. The dream is not, however, useless to Chaucer. It casts over his conversation with the lover a certain remoteness, it transfers the responsibility for what was said from his waking self to the vagaries of dream, and thus renders possible a more intimate picture of his patron's loss than would have been seemly on any other terms. But it would be rash to assume that Chaucer consciously chose it with this in view. The use of the dream for all sorts of purposes which hardly seem to justify it, and even for elegy, appears to have been a device of the French poets,[1] and I think that Chaucer followed it chiefly because he enjoyed it. Machaut had already shown how a poetic dream could be made much more like a dream than Guillaume de Lorris had attempted to make it;[2] and Chaucer, delighted, as any good workman must be delighted, with the task of capturing the most elusive, yet familiar, of experiences, has probably bettered his model. His 'dream psychology' has been described as 'flawless'.[3] Our own concern is naturally more with his psychology of love, for it is in this that Chaucer shows at once his own genius and his faithful discipleship to the *Rose* tradition. In this poem the bereaved lover has passed through all the same phases as the dreamer in the *Roman*: that he has passed also through one more is his tragedy. At first, like the dreamer, he had wandered unattached though in the garden of love,

And this was longe, and many a yer,
Or that myn herte was set owher,
That I dide thus, and nyste why;
I trowe hit cam me kyndely.

(*Book of the Duchess*, 775–8)

He knows well enough, however, who really sits as portress at the garden gate,

1 See C. L. Rosenthal, 'A possible source of Chaucer's *Book of the Duchess*', *Mod. Language Notes*, vol. 48 (1933).
2 Compare Machaut, *Dit dou Vergier*, 1199 ff., where the waking of the dreamer is convincingly managed: also *Dit dou Lyon*, 279 ff.
3 See J. Livingston Lowes, *Geoffrey Chaucer*, 1934, pp. 94–9.

For that tyme Yowthe, my maistresse,
Governed me *in ydelnesse*.

                    (797-8)

When, at length, he falls in love, it is because he has looked into the
well of Narcissus,

            . . . I ne tok
No maner counseyl but at hir lok
And at myn herte; for-why hir eyen
So gladly, I trow, myn herte seyen.

                    (839-41)

When he first attempts to approach the rose, however, he is repulsed
and driven to lament on the wrong side of the thorny hedge (1236-57).
In all this Chaucer agrees with the tradition, but he is not therefore
'conventional' in the bad sense of the word. How fine and fresh his
treatment is may be judged from the very remarkable fact that
though the poem is a true elegy, yet the abiding impression it leaves
upon us is one of health and happiness. There is no concealment of
the loss: the pain rings true in –

            'Farewel, swete, ywys,
And farewel al that ever ther ys'

                    (657-8)

and in the mourner's return upon himself (anticipating *Lycidas*)
when he calls back his fruitless wish – 'And thogh wherto?' (670).
But Chaucer's praise of the dead and his picture of the happiness that
has been lost are so potent that we remember them when everything
else in the poem is forgotten. Successful panegyric is the rarest of all
literary achievements, and Chaucer has compassed it. I believe in the
'goode faire White' (948), as I have never believed in Edward King,
or Arthur Hallam, or Clough. I seem to have seen her 'Laughe and
pleye so womanly' (850) and to have heard 'which a goodly, softe
speche' (919) she uttered; and now that she is dead I seem to realize
with more poignancy how 'hir lyste so wel to lyve, | That dulnesse
was of hir adrad' (879). Not because the poem is a bad elegy, but
because it is a good one, the black background of death is always
disappearing behind these iridescent shapes of satisfied love; and
because of these, all its attendant imagery – the harmony of birds,

the sun just rising in the 'blew, bright, clere' air, the glades starry
with flowers that have forgotten winter's poverty and alive with
happy animals – all these have a symbolic fitness that is beyond the
contract of conscious allegory. If the poem has any faults, apart from
its occasional lapses in style and metre, they arise from Chaucer's
anxiety to do better than he is yet able. Thus he has the happy idea
of trying to show dramatically in his dialogue the impatient self-
absorption of grief on the part of the lover, and his demands on the
dreamer's close attention. But he does this so clumsily that he sometimes makes the one seem a bore, and the other a fool, thus producing
comic effects which are disastrous, and which were certainly not
intended (749 ff., 1042 ff. and 1127 ff.).

From the *Complaint of Mars* I have already quoted lines that
illustrate the growth of Chaucer's poetic style; and when we have
noticed these, we have, perhaps, given this poem all the attention it
deserves. The astronomical allusions are, I confess, too hard for me:
the topical allegory is now difficult to recover and hardly worth
recovering.[1] The relation of mistress and lover in what was then conceived to be its normal or healthy condition is well described in the
lines

And thus she brydeleth him in hir manere,
With nothing but with scourging of her chere.

(41–2)

The poem is otherwise remarkable because it contains, agreeably
with the example of Jean de Meun, a hint of the opposite point of
view. One stanza which is put into the mouth of Mars draws the
contrast between Divine and earthly love, apparently to the advantage
of the former (218 ff.). But we are now prepared for such losses of
confidence at the end, or even in the midst, of an amorous poem.

The *Balade to Rosemounde* is interesting for two reasons. The first
stanza shows Chaucer's style at the point where it approaches most
nearly to the aureate style of his successors. The third stanza presents
a problem. Is this 'pyk walwed in galauntyne' intended to be comic
or not? The modern reader is tempted to reply at once in the affirma-
tive, but I feel no confidence. The conception of the 'mocking'

1 See Skeat's *Chaucer*, I, pp. 64 ff., and G. H. Cowling, 'Chaucer's Complaintes
of Mars and of Venus', *Review of English Studies*, vol. 2, no. 8, Oct. 1926.

Chaucer must not be so used as to render it impossible for us to say Chaucer ever wrote ill – which is what follows if everything that cannot please as poetry is immediately set down as humour. And what will be very funny if it is meant to be serious, may often be very feeble as a deliberate joke. The pike is a case in point. As serious poetry it is bathos: as jest it is flat. What effect Chaucer intended is just one of those things which, as I conceive, we shall never know, but which Gower or Scogan or John of Gaunt would have known at once and without question.

Passing over the ambitious and soon abandoned *Anelida*, and the exquisite *Merciles Beaute* (where the comic intention of the palinode is not doubtful), I come to the masterpiece among Chaucer's early poems, the *Parliament of Fowls*. The occasion and purport of this work have been the subject of a good deal of discussion.[1] The occasion, if discovered, would be but an 'unconcerning thing', a 'matter of fact'. There is, indeed, no necessity to assume any such external stimulus as a royal or noble marriage for the *Parliament*. The species to which the poem belongs – the debate on a hard question of love – is a familiar one. Two of Machaut's poems are *jugements;* and in earlier French poetry – not to mention our own *Owl and Nightingale* – birds had already debated.[2] What concerns us much more is the dispute about the purport or tendency – the emotional and imaginative upshot – of the poem as a whole. It is here that the exaggerated conception of the 'mocking' Chaucer has produced its most disastrous results. Critics have been found to support the view that Chaucer – now herkeneth which a reason I will bring – wrote the *Parliament* in order to ridicule the courtly sentiment of the nobler birds through the criticism of 'the lewednesse behynde'. It would almost be better to miss every joke in Chaucer than to believe that the Goose and the Duck are his spokesmen, and the Turtle and the Eagles his butt. I will not insist on my conviction that to believe thus is to attribute to Chaucer a square-headed vulgarity of thought and feeling which would be regrettable in any age and all but impossible to a

1 See Skeat, *Chaucer*, vol. 1, p. 75; E. Rickert, 'A new interpretation of the *Parliament of Fowls*', *Mod. Philology*, vol. 18, no. 1, May, 1920; D. Patrick 'The satire in Chaucer's Parliament', etc., *Philological Quarterly*, vol. 9, Jan., 1930; J. Livingston Lowes, *Geoffrey Chaucer*, 1934, pp. 124 ff.
2 See Langlois, *Origines et Sources*, chap. 2.

court poet of the age of Froissart: all may not share that conviction. But surely this view is based on a misunderstanding of the whole procedure of medieval love poetry? The courtly sentiment is, from the outset, an escape, a truancy, alike from vulgar common sense and from the ten commandments. Chrétien, and Guillaume de Lorris, and every one else had always known that Reason was on the other side. Yet the truancy is felt to be, in some flawed and fragile way, a noble thing: the source of every virtue except chastity, the 'flemer' of every vice save one. Hence those strange comings and goings in every medieval love-book. The delicate dream protects itself against moral or common-sensible attack by every kind of concession and tergiversation – by ambiguities in the sense of the word Love, as in Gower's *Prologue*, by a blending of love earthly and love heavenly as in Dante, or (less successfully) in Thomas Usk, by direct palinode, as in Andreas. Above all it protects itself against the laughter of the vulgar – that is, of all of us in certain moods – by allowing laughter and cynicism their place *inside* the poem; as some politicians hold that the only way to make a revolutionary safe is to give him a seat in Parliament. The Duck and Goose have their seats in Chaucer's *Parliament* for the same reason; and for the same reason we have satire on women in Andreas, we have the shameless Vekke in the *Rose*, we have Pandarus in the *Book of Troilus*, and Dinadan in Malory, and Godfrey Gobelive in Hawes, and the Squire of Dames in the *Faerie Queene*. Even so, long after the original reasons for the tradition have been forgotten, the *homme sensuel moyen* with his fair, large ears appears in the *Midsummer Night's Dream*, and Papageno, the child of nature, parallels and, in a sense, parodies, the loves and trials of Tamino. The appearance of such figures in a poem does not mean that the main tendency of the work is satiric: it almost means the opposite. When the soldiers followed Caesar in his triumph singing *calvum moechum adducimus*,[1] this did not mean that the purpose of a triumph was to ridicule the general. It meant precisely the opposite: the Fescennine licence was included as a concession to Nemesis, and Nemesis needed to be placated just because the ceremony as a whole aimed at the glorification of the general. In the same way, the comic figures in a medieval love poem are a cautionary concession – a libation made to

1 '[Look to your wives,] we bring the bald adulterer.' A song sung by Caesar's men at his Gallic triumph. [Ed.]

the god of lewd laughter precisely because he is not the god whom we
are chiefly serving – a sop to Silenus and Priapus lest they should
trouble our lofty hymns to Cupid. When this has been understood
(and not till then) we may, indeed, safely admit that Chaucer has
sympathy with the Goose and the Duck. So had every knight and
dame among his listeners. There would be no need to make a concession to the 'lewd' point of view if it were not present in the minds
of all. Chaucer and his audience knew, better than some know now,
that human life is not simple. They were able to think of two things
at once. They see the common world outside the charmed circle of
courtly love; they also have been in that common world and will be
there again; and they let it have its say, its 'large golee', for a moment,
even amidst their ardours and idealisms.

All this may seem over-subtle. But Chaucer, whatever we may
think of him, was not a 'regular fellow', *un vrai businessman*, or a
rotarian. He was a scholar, a courtier, and a poet, living in a highly
subtle and sophisticated civilization. It is only natural that we, who
live in an industrial age, should find difficulties in reading poetry that
was written for a scholastic and aristocratic age. We must proceed
with caution, lest our thick, rough fingers tear the delicate threads
that we are trying to disentangle.

When these confusions have been removed, every reader who loves
poetry may safely be left alone with the *Parliament of Fowls*. No
such reader will misunderstand the mingling of beauty and comedy
in this supremely happy and radiant work – a hearty and realistic
comedy, and a beauty without effort or afterthought, like Mozartian
music. It is not a radical allegory, by my standard, for it allegorizes
no inner action. Its *significacio*, if extracted, would prove to be a
state and not a story. Here, as in the *Book of the Duchess*, the old garden
of the *Rose* is used to paint a picture of love itself, of love at rest. If a
man will compare the beauties of this garden – the almost imperceptible wind, the darting fish, the rabbits playing in the grass, and
the 'ravishing sweetness' of stringed instruments – with any literal
portrayal of the same thing, he will find out what allegory was made
for. This is the kind of symbolism that never grows old. But suddenly,
in the middle of the poem, we come on something else. In this
matter I may claim to have made (quite accidentally) an imaginative
experiment. When I was last reading the *Parliament*, and came to the

description of its various inhabitants, which begins at line 211, I said to myself, 'Now this is very strange. These are not like Chaucer, nor like the Middle Ages at all. They are mere pageant figures put in for decoration.' A moment later, I remembered that I was in that part of the poem which is borrowed from Boccaccio.

This little story, on my bare word, is naturally not offered as a proof of anything; but it may serve to direct the reader's attention to something of importance. Boccaccio's Cupid, Pleasaunce, Beautee, Peace, Priapus, and the rest are Renaissance allegory, not medieval allegory. They are neither, on the one hand, a mere catalogue (like the abstractions in Chaucer's *Complaints*); nor are they true incarnations of inner experience, like the characters of the *Romance of the Rose*. They have nothing to do, but each has his little bit of description and his recognizable emblems. They are pure decoration – things to be carved on a mantelpiece, or pulled along the streets in a pageant, 'posed' each in his cart with anchors, scales, and other apparatus. They are pretty enough, but they have given the word 'allegory' a meaning from which it will, perhaps, never recover – with what injustice to certain great poets, it is one purpose of this book to show. And the odd thing is that Chaucer does not seem to be aware of the difference. He is too true a child of the Middle Ages even to resent the alien Renaissance quality in his model. That it is alien to him is proved by his treatment of it, for his omissions and alterations are all in the medieval direction; but he does not reach the point of throwing the Boccaccio over, as he might have done if he had read it with our eyes. In the *Teseide* Boccaccio takes a personified Prayer – readers of Homer will remember that prayers are among the oldest personifications – to the home of Venus (VII 51, 52). Chaucer goes thither himself. On arriving in the garden, Chaucer follows the Italian closely for two stanzas, because the Italian is here describing what every medieval poet wished to describe – the joyous life of the place (183–96). In the next stanza, after two lines on the music heard among the trees, he deserts his model; and where Boccaccio tells us how the Prayer went to and fro admiring the *bell' ornamento*, Chaucer compares the music with the harmonies of heaven, and mentions 'a wynd, unnethe it myghte be lesse' (197–203). He then proceeds to insert a stanza which has no counterpart in the original at all, and in which he explains how

'Th' air of that place so attempre was', that 'No man may there
waxe sek ne old.

(204–10)

Chaucer is, of course, remembering the garden in Guillaume de
Lorris, which 'semede a place espirituel' (*Roman de la Rose*, 642,
English version, 650) and the garden in Jean de Meun where there is
no time (*Roman de la Rose*, 20010 ff.). But while he thus makes his
garden more spiritual, with heavenly music and a dateless present,
he makes it more earthly too by the mention of his inaudible breeze;
he deepens the poetry every way. There is in Chaucer a far fuller
surrender of feeling and imagination to his theme than Boccaccio
was prepared to make. Chaucer was working with 'ful devout
corage': Boccaccio, for all his epic circumstance, feels in his heart of
hearts that all this stuff about gardens and gods of love is 'only poetry'.
And so Boccaccio will include a touch of satire and make his Beautee
go by *sè riguardando* (*Teseide*, VII 56), and Chaucer will naturally
omit this (*Parliament*, 225). Only false criticism will suppose that this
superior gravity in Chaucer is incompatible with the fact that he is a
great comic poet. Dryden went to the root of the matter when he
called him a perpetual fountain of good sense. A profound and
cheerful sobriety is the foundation alike of Chaucer's humour and of
his pathos. There is nothing of the renaissance frivolity in him.

(161–76)

Ezra Pound

from *A Guide to Kulchur* 1938

Chaucer's real civilization was three hundred years old. It inheres in
his sense of verbal melody, in the tonal leading of words meant to
be sung, or in sense of song modes worn smooth in the mind, so that
the words take the quality for singing.

The culture of Chrestien de Troyes and of Beroul, plus his own
humour.

(280–81)

Nevill Coghill

from *The Poet Chaucer* 1949

One of the most striking things about the *Canterbury Tales* is the enormous accession of new interests and energies, producing new styles to contain them, such as we have seen in the tales of the Miller and the Reeve and in the autobiography of the Wife of Bath. While these retain or advance the characteristic powers of his earlier work, the sharp intelligence, the conversational dexterity, the learnedness, and so forth, they would have been departures in poetry unpredictable in 1386.

Three other of his new interests are manifested in all that concerns the Pardoner, the Friar and the Summoner, that religious basilisk and those rival caterpillars. They are his interest in rogues, ecclesiastics and preachership. His studies in roguery are by no means confined to the Church, but are spread generally among the lower orders, instance the Miller, the Shipman and the Canon's Yeoman, and the professional classes have a taste of it too. But he has taken special care over these three ecclesiastical rogues and their sermons, which fit them so well that no interchange would be possible. For the Friar and the Summoner he has created a comedy of contempt, bordering in the case of the Summoner on hatred. His full comedy of hatred is reserved for the Pardoner, who is the centre of an ironic rather than a satiric vision. Fielding has some observations in the Preface to *Joseph Andrews* that help to clarify the principles underlying these kinds of comedy:

The only source of the true Ridiculous (as it appears to me) is affectation. . . . Now, affectation proceeds from one of these two causes, vanity or hypocrisy; for as vanity puts us on affecting false characters, in order to purchase applause; so hypocrisy sets us on an endeavour to avoid censure, by concealing our vices under an appearance of their opposite virtues. . . . From the discovery of this affectation arises the Ridiculous, which always strikes the reader with surprise and pleasure, and that in a higher and stronger degree when the affectation arises from hypocrisy, than from vanity; for to discover anyone to be the exact reverse of what he affects, is more surprising, and consequently more ridiculous, than to find him a little deficient in the quality he desires the reputation of.

The Friar and the Summoner have their vanities and hypocrisies and are made ridiculous enough, each in an appropriate degree. The Summoner is made to seem hateful even, but not importantly so; satirical exposure of the kind described by Fielding was a sufficient annihilation. But the basilisk Pardoner was more to be feared and therefore more to be hated. A monster of vanity and hypocrisy, he had a wider field of operation within the Church and a still deadlier technique. Pondering him, Chaucer moved beyond simple satire into irony, the most baleful form of militant poetry. In all that he says of the Pardoner he shows himself the first and subtlest ironist in English, for there are ironies within the irony.

The root principle of this figure of rhetoric is that the intended meaning is the opposite to that expressed in the words used, as in Swift's *A Modest Proposal*. Chaucer has used this in the *Prologue*:

But trewely to tellen atte laste
He was in chirche a noble ecclesiaste.

(*Canterbury Tales*, I 707–8)

In such a mood the Lord commended the Unjust Steward. By an extension this principle can also be applied to situation, and this Chaucer does in the Pardoner's sermon. The Three Rioters, seeking Death in order to slay him, find him without knowing that it is he, and are themselves slain by their own motive principle, cupidity. The personal situation of the Pardoner himself is equally ironical. It has often been said he is a lost soul, but he is more; he is a lost soul peddling a fake salvation for other souls, as if all salvation were a fake. Like Iago he knows all the right things to say, and says them for his private ends. The irony is that they are true while he supposes them a mockery:

For myn entente is nat but for to wynne,
And nothyng for correccioun of synne.
I rekke nevere, whan that they been beryed,
Though that hir soules goon a-blakeberyed!

(*Canterbury Tales*, VI 403–6)

He has taken the root of all evil to be his good; as the Maiorcan proverb has it, he is seeing black white.

But Chaucerian irony has a quality that I miss in Swift's and beyond the power of this root principle of opposition between what is said and meant or what is done and intended. It is the quality of doom, the sense that there are Higher Powers that see our wishes and doings and know them to be contrary to our own interests but congruent with Their quite other purposes for us. We are blind, but they see. And Chaucer lets us see them seeing. The power to do this arises from his long interest in the notion of Destiny, of 'simple' and 'conditional' necessity,[1] that he had so often argued. What is more ironical than a will supposed free, freely struggling to attain a pre-ordained doom, the opposite of its intention?

We witen nat what thing we preyen heere.

(*Canterbury Tales*, I 1260)

As early as in *Troilus and Criseyde* this theme is sounded. In that poem, over which there broods a fatal destiny, the Trojan Parliament clamoured for the return of Antenor, in exchange for Criseyde; Antenor, who was later to betray their city. They freely chose the doom the Gods had preordained for them. So in the ironies of the Pardoner and his tale there is a weaving sense of the supernal powers at work, and his sermon, given in the classic form of Text, Argument, *Exemplum*, and Exordium is as much a figure of his own doom as of the Three Rioters'. God is not mocked.

Nor indeed was Harry Bailey. Though Chaucer does not show us the doom on the Pardoner's hypocrisy, he lets us see a nemesis on his vanity. Confident of his spell-binding as he was (and a little drunk), he had bared the secrets of his profession in his preamble, sure that a sermon that had never failed would work the trick again. He preached it with unction and gusto. It ought to have worked, and with a true strategist's instinct he turned at the end of his peroration upon the most difficult of his hearers. If Harry Bailey collapsed, then all the rest were his. Harry Bailey did not collapse, but voiced the feelings

[1] e.g. *Simple necessity*: All men must die, they have no choice. *Conditional*: If a man freely chooses to take poison he must die; and God foresees his free choice.

of all England towards Pardoners in his annihilating retort. For once
the Pardoner had met defeat.

>   This Pardoner answerde nat a word;
> So wrooth he was, no word ne wolde he seye.
>
> (Canterbury Tales, VI 956–7)
> (158–62)

William Empson

from *The Structure of Complex Words* 1951

In Chaucer's time [the word 'honest'] meant 'deserving and receiving social honour', and any humour or irony put on top does not
affect this basic feeling. The poignant and in time cloying simplicity
of most of the characters in the *Canterbury Tales* comes out in a
steady vague use of it – 'I am speaking seriously and keeping moral
judgement in play'. Owing to this frequency it can come down to
mean hardly more than 'conventional', as when the Pardoner is
asked for a tale without 'ribaldry' and says he can't think of that
unless he had a drink:

> . . . I moot thynke
> Upon som honest thyng while that I drynke.
>
> (VI 327–8)

(The sense 'chaste' is already strong.) The nearest I could find to the
later rich uses comes about a man hiding himself abroad:

> And eek men broghte hym out of his contree,
> From yeer to yeer, ful pryvely his rente;
> But honestly and slyly he it spente,
> That no man wondred how that he it hadde . . .
>
> (I 1442–5)

'Sly' only meant clever, it seems, but that makes little difference.
The sense of 'honestly' seems to be 'not in the riotous pleasures that
attract attention', so 'in a respectable way', also 'steadily and carefully, like a good tradesman'. But it carries a kind of *interest* in this
process, which the story tells us no more about. He must have been a

very worthy capable man. And then there is the Monk who always brings 'some manere honest thyng' as a present to help the process of seduction (VII 49); something worthy of this generous giver. The sustained and always double irony of Chaucer can be felt in the word here but does not darken its simplicity.

(185–6)

Kemp Malone

from 'The *Legend of Good Women*', *Chapters on Chaucer* 1951

Wel ought us thanne honouren and beleve
These bokes, there we han noon other preve.
And as for me, though that I konne but lyte,
On bokes for to rede I me delyte,
And to hem yive I feyth and ful credence,
And in myn herte have hem in reverence
So hertely, that ther is game noon
That fro my bokes maketh me to goon,
But yt be seldom on the holyday,
Save, certeynly, whan that the month of May
Is comen, and that I here the foules synge,
And that the floures gynnen for to sprynge,
Farwel my bok, and my devocioun!

(*Legend of Good Women*, F 27–39)

Chaucer changed this passage a good deal, when he made his revision of the prologue:

Wel ought us thanne on olde bokes leve,
There as there is non other assay by preve.
And as for me, though that my wit be lyte,
On bokes for to rede I me delyte,
And in myn herte have hem in reverence,
And to hem yeve swich lust and swich credence
That there is wel unethe game noon
That fro my bokes make me to goon,
But it be other upon the halyday

Or ellis in the joly tyme of May:
Whan that I here the smale foules synge
And that the floures gynne for to sprynge
Farwel my stodye, as lastynge that sesoun!
                    (G 27-39)

The change in line 39 was surely made in a moment of poetical
aberration (though Robinson's pointing makes it worse and is unjust
to the poor poet). Most of the other changes were made to get rid
of the run-on lines. In the earlier version there were three of these:
27, 32, and 36. In the later version, all the lines are end-stopped. In
other passages of the revised version Chaucer did the same thing, and
he seems to have looked upon a run-on line as metrically inferior,
though not to be ruled out altogether.

It will be worth our while to look at the changes in this passage
more narrowly. By comparing the two versions we can look over
the poet's shoulder, so to speak, while he is at work and learn something about one aspect, at least, of his poetic art: his technique of
revision. It would be possible to write a whole book about this
technique of his in the *Legend of Good Women*. Here we have only a
few pages for the study of a single passage, and it would be perilous
to base any generalizations on our gatherings, but I think our time
will be well spent none the less.

We might as well begin at the beginning, with line 27. As it
stands, this line does not make a complete unit of thought; the
thought is completed by the first two words of line 28. Chaucer's
problem was to make the thought complete within the limits of the
line. He got the space needful for this by cancelling the verb *honouren*,
which was something of a metrical filler anyhow, and contenting
himself with one infinitive. The *and* after *honouren* had the function
of linking the two infinitives. Now that one of the infinitives was
cancelled, the link served no further purpose and had to be cancelled
too. These cancellations left Chaucer with two feet to fill in line 27.
He might have shifted 'these bokes' of the next line into the blank
space, but the line he would have made by so doing could have been
given a satisfactory scansion with difficulty if at all. He therefore gave
himself a little more leeway by cancelling the prefix *be-* of his second
infinitive, thus changing the verb-form into a simple *leve*. Into the

space of five syllables thereby made available in line 27, Chaucer put the phrase 'on olde bokes', filling the line neatly enough from a metrical point of view and completing the thought beautifully within the limits of the line. The phrase actually used, 'on olde bokes', was obviously inspired by the 'these bokes' of the earlier version, taking shape as it did to fit the metrical and syntactical conditions of Chaucer's problem.

In the foregoing I have made no effort to reconstruct the course of events in a sequence true to psychological reality. I do not know what this sequence was, and I see no way of finding out. Chaucer may perfectly well have started by deciding to shift 'these bokes' to line 27, and only then may he have looked at that line to see what he could dispense with there. But I am inclined to think that he began by brooding over his problem, and that he ended with a solution which came to him in a flash, all at once. Certainly he need not have gone through any such conscious procedure as that which I have outlined. But whether he analysed and then synthesized consciously or unconsciously, his mind worked on the problem before it solved it, and the elements which his mind had to consider before the problem could be solved are the elements which I have pointed out. Whether these elements were considered one at a time or together we shall never know, but we do know that they were all considered.

Chaucer's problem in line 28 differed greatly from the problem he solved in line 27. When he shifted 'these bokes' or their equivalent to line 27, he thereby made a blank space in line 28, a space which had to be filled to satisfy the metrical requirements of the line. His problem, then, was one of expansion or augmentation. What was left of line 28 had to be given a new wording which would fill up the line. The poet had to say the same thing in more words. A little prolixity was needed. He expanded *noon other preve* 'no other experience' to *non other assay by preve* 'no other test by experience'. This statement is more precise as well as longer than the earlier one, but the great reason for changing the wording was to make the statement longer, not to make it more precise. In other words, the problem here was metrical, not semantic. The same applies to the expansion of the first part of the line: from *there we han* 'where we have' to *there as there is* 'there where there is'. In this case the metrical requirements made it needful to cancel the pronoun and change the verb, but there is no real difference in the thought.

The change in line 29 amounts to little. There is no change at all in thought, but the wording of the revised version is such that the personal pronoun *I* does not come in. Chaucer also gets rid of the *I* in line 31. The earlier version has three *I*s in as many lines (29, 30, and 31), of which only one is kept in the later version, the one in line 30. This change is to be reckoned a stylistic improvement, an avoidance of repetition.

Line 30 is left unchanged. Lines 31 and 32 are made to change places, and the first two words of line 33 are cancelled. These words, 'so hertely', belong grammatically to line 32 and keep that line from being end-stopped. Their cancellation, then, turns line 32 (or line 31, as it becomes in the revised version) into an end-stopped line. But the idea behind the cancelled words needs expression, and Chaucer found means to get this idea in without giving up the systematic end-stopping which he liked to have. To express this idea he used the word *swich* 'such' (that is, 'so much'). He found he could not insert *swich* into line 32, because that would destroy the metrical pattern of the line. He therefore put line 32 right after line 30, and brought the old line 31 down to the position of line 32. The pattern of this line (the new 32) included a word-pair connected by the conjunction *and*, and Chaucer kept the pairing, though he changed one member of the pair. The second member of the pair was modified by the adjective *ful*, and it was easy to substitute *swich* for this *ful*; there is even a connexion in meaning, though of course not a complete equivalence. The first member of the pair had no modifier, but before it came an *I* which could be dispensed with, and Chaucer put another *swich* where the *I* had stood. He had to have two for the sake of symmetry, one modifier for each member of the word-pair. But 'swich feyth and swich credence' did not fully satisfy him, in spite of its symmetrical structure. The two words of the word-pair mean very much the same thing, and Chaucer saw no point in the semantic repetition. The second member of the pair, *credence*, was the rime word and could not be changed, but *feyth* was easier to handle. Chaucer replaced it with *lust* 'interest', a very satisfactory solution indeed.

With 'so hertely' cancelled, the rest of line 33 needed expansion, the problem here being like that in line 28. Chaucer turned the trick readily enough, by inserting the adverbs *wel* and *unethe* 'hardly' before *game*. This changed the meaning a little, but so little that the change hardly mattered. Line 34 was left as it was, except for one subtle change: the indicative *maketh* was replaced by the subjunctive *make*. This change goes with the expansion of line 33; in both cases the statement, unqualified in the earlier version, has become slightly less positive.

In both versions the rest of the passage specifies the exceptions to the rule set down in lines 33-4. These exceptions are two in number: the holiday and the month of May. In the earlier version the two exceptions are not on the same footing: Chaucer said he left his books seldom on holidays but he made no such qualification about his behaviour in May. In the later version, however, Chaucer treated the two exceptions in the same way: he marked their equality by using the correlative pair *other . . . or ellis* 'either . . . or else'. The first member of the correlation, *other*, replaces the 'seldom' of line 35; the second member, *or ellis*, replaces the 'save, certeynly' of line 36. The correlation carried with it a parallelism in the structure of the two lines, a parallelism not to be found in the earlier version, where line 35 ends with a prepositional phrase whereas line 36 ends with a clause which runs on into the next line. Chaucer took the consequences of the correlation which he had set up and made the two lines parallel in structure throughout: 'upon the halyday' (line 35) corresponds in formal pattern to 'in the joly tyme of May', though the correspondence is not absolutely rigid, since the second prepositional phrase has a somewhat more complicated structure than the first. Both lines, too, are end-stopped, whereas in the earlier version only line 35 is end-stopped. The change from *month* to *tyme* in line 36 has the effect of removing the alliteration, and this may have been Chaucer's reason for making the change; in line 1 of the poem the change he makes has the same effect. The insertion of *joly* makes a happy solution of the metrical problem here.

The last three lines of the passage are integrated with line 36 in the earlier version, but this integration could not be kept if lines 35 and 36 were to be correlated and made parallel. Chaucer therefore took the other tack and made the last three lines an independent grammatical unit, serving to make more specific what happened to him in the jolly time of May but without any syntactical linkage to line 36. The signi-

The Pilgrimage to Canterbury. A painting by Thomas Stothard.

The Canterbury Pilgrims. A painting by William Blake.

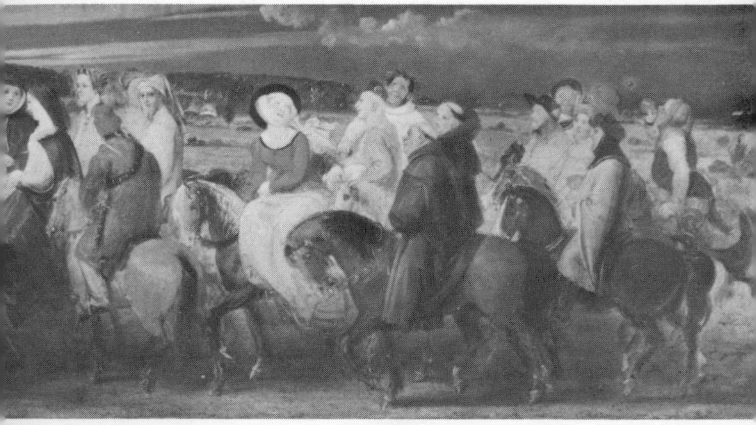

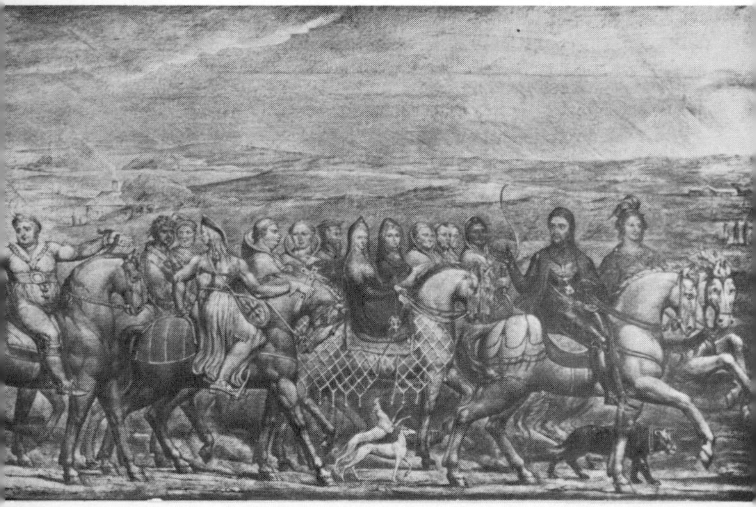

ficant changes here are the cancellation of *is comen* and the replacement
of *and* by *whan*. These two changes, both in line 37, remove the two
links which in the earlier version bind lines 36 and 37 together. Line
37, shortened by the cancellation, was made metrically complete
by inserting the adjective *smale* before *foules*. Line 38 was left
unchanged. The changes made in line 39 were not needed, so far
as I can see. I have already expressed my opinion of them. I wish
Chaucer had let the line stand as it was. But there is no accounting for
tastes.

(87–93)

John Speirs

from *Chaucer the Maker* 1951

The colloquial and highly dramatic character of the poetry of Chaucer
and Shakespeare implies that, for both of them, poetry was a developed
social art. Chaucer's poetry, though not like Shakespeare's intended
for the theatre, reads as if it had been intended – as no doubt it was –
to be read aloud to a company, the frequent dialogues being given
full value. The Court itself must have been a more sophisticated kind
of small-town community and the talk there a cultivated version of
small-town gossip; we seem, in listening to Chaucer's poetry, to
hear that talk organized into a poetic art that is the nearest thing to
dramatic art. The combination of easy familiarity and good breeding,
of colloquialism and courtesy, evidences a harmonious social relationship between cultivated poet and cultivated audience. But that poet
and that audience are, evidently, no more cut off than Shakespeare and
the more cultivated part of *his* audience are from the vigorous life
of the English people as a whole. Chaucer's poetry implies that
his English community was comparatively a homogeneous community in which folk of diverse 'degrees' (the Knight and the
Plowman) were interdependent and intimate, as by comparison
persons in the modern classless mass are isolated; it implies perhaps
the most nearly inclusive social order that has ever been implied in
English and (despite the Peasants' Revolt) the most harmoniously

integrated.[1] The scholarly and courtly Chaucer is a member of his whole contemporary English community; for the purposes of imaginative creation in language he had the same advantage as Shakespeare; his cultivated English is rooted in the speech – concrete, figurative, proverbial – of the agricultural English folk.

(20–21)

Raymond Preston

from 'The *Nun's Priest's Tale*', *Chaucer* 1952

Sir John's story of the Cock and the Fox is in medieval tradition of bestiary and follows a portion of the 'epic' of Reynard; yet it is not simply a fable, and *daun Russel* is not Reynard.[2] It is the literary equivalent of a jig fugue, or of a *quodlibet*. And here Chaucer comes nearest to expressing in a single tale the variety and comedy of the whole Canterbury sequence.

The most important thing that Dryden missed in his lively, inaccurate adaptation was the *sweete preest*. At one point in his transcript the nun's confessor even turns Restoration gallant:

Silence in times of Suff'ring is the best,
'Tis dang'rous to disturb a Hornet's Nest.
In other Authors you may find enough,
But all they say of Dames is idle Stuff.
Legends of lying Wits together bound,
The Wife of *Bath* would throw 'em to the Ground:
These are the words of Chanticleer, not mine,
I honour Dames, and think their Sex divine.

(*The Cock and the Fox*, 565–72)

1 R. J. Tiddy in his book *The Mummer's Play* stresses that, outside the villages, class distinctions were growing in importance in Chaucer's England, but 'the very clearness with which distinctions were recognized seems to have made easier the interplay of class with class. However great may have been the political inequality of Chaucer's times the classes have never afterwards been so completely fused in social intercourse. . . . This alone must have tended to preserve an identity of taste in literature. . . . I doubt very much whether there was any great difference in the tastes of the different classes till the time of the Renaissance, when classical themes and elaborate psychology were introduced.'
2 In spite of Dryden: *The Cock and the Fox: or, the Tale of the Nun's Priest* 480 ff.

Chaucer, on the other hand, holds us with the voice, the versatility of tone, of the admirable father who can attempt anything from mimicry to morality and lyricism to mock-heroic, and prefer nothing to the *heighe blisse* of God. If Sir John is a preacher on holiday, telling *exempla* and letting the sermon look after itself, his gaiety is a gift of the divine wisdom.

And the verse, for Chaucer, is simply the clearest means of expressing his range of tone, a convenient stave for melodic speech. Dryden makes the couplet a smart vehicle for wit. Thus Chaucer is improved:

> If, spurning up the Ground, he sprung a Corn,
> The Tribute in his Bill to her was born.
> But oh! what Joy it was to hear him sing
> In Summer, when the Day began to spring,
> Stretching his Neck, and warbling in his Throat,
> *Solus cum Sola*, then was all his Note.
> For in the Days of Yore, the Birds of Parts
> Were bred to Speak, and Sing, and learn the Lib'ral Arts.
>
> (85–92)

Chaunticleer, in Restoration costume, is a pantomime actor with a throaty delivery, and a satirical eye for Man like Dryden's for Achitophel:

> Thus numb'ring Times, and Seasons in his Breast,
> His second crowing the third Hour confess'd.
> Then turning, said to Partlet, See, my Dear,
> How lavish Nature has adorn'd the Year;
> How the pale Primrose, and blue Violet spring,
> And Birds essay their Throats disus'd to sing:
> All these are ours; and I with pleasure see
> Man strutting on two Legs, and aping me!
> An unfledg'd Creature, of a lumpish frame,
> Indew'd with fewer Particles of Flame:
> Our Dame sits couring o'er the Kitchen-fire,
> I draw fresh Air, and Nature's Works admire:
> And ev'n this Day, in more delight abound,
> Than, since I was an Egg, I ever found.
>
> (453–66)

This is good Dryden, generously expanded from four lines of the original. For an example, in a sentence, of what Chaucer can do, we must go back a little; but not very far.

Whan that the month in which the world bigan,
That highte March, whan God first maked man,
Was compleet, and passed were also,
Syn March bigan, thritty dayes and two,
Bifel that Chauntecleer in al his pryde,
His sevene wyves walkynge by his syde,
Caste up his eyen to the brighte sonne,
That in the signe of Taurus hadde yronne
Twenty degrees and oon, and somwhat moore,
And knew by kynde, and by noon oother loore,
That it was pryme; and crew with blisful stevene.[1]
(*Canterbury Tales*, VII 3187–97)

Into a single period, and without any suggestion of forcing, he has combined the Creation, Chaunticleer the born Astronomer Royal, the Royal Lover and Organ Voice, proud Chaunticleer seven times sinful, and the sound of Chaunticleer the golden spangled Hamburg. And in the whole tale there is the same easy mastery of the most diverse ideas: the sobriety of the respectable poor – the burlesque of time and pomp – the elegant fowls as strutting humans, complacently informed – the scholarly husband – O *Venus!* – the announcement of a moral, or at least a *soveregn notabilitee* (some dignified platitude from Geoffrey de Vinsauf). From a certain position, a cock may look as funny as a man with a little learning; a revolt of murderous peasants is not entirely dissimilar from an uproar in an English farmyard; which in turn may suggest that the end of the world has come. If for a moment you can look at these things from above, they all (even Talbot and Gerland and Malkin with a distaff in her hand) matter; and none of them matters, in isolation, at all; none is self-sufficient. And in Chaucer you *can* look, and for more than a moment. There is plenty of time, without violence or distraction of language, during which the mind is gently raised, and surrounded by a grace of comedy. 'This is easy', we say, '– easy mastery; the verse, for Chaucer, is simply –' But simplification is the hardest thing in the world: the

1 voice

last reward of any discipline, including poetics. How many major poets achieve it?

The Nun's Priest has amused us by re-arranging many modes of being, action, and expression, and without confounding them; without sentimentality or cynicism. This may be observed by comparison with the late George Orwell's *Animal Farm*. The Nun's Priest's fable is a masterpiece of mock-heroic verse, written out of medieval learning, the sermon-books, and oral tradition. It is even a very intelligent demonstration, six centuries in advance, of how far surrealism can go without incoherence. And yet Mr Orwell, having to rely upon Swift, children's fairytales, and the newspapers, wrote a very neat little piece.

(220–23)

W. K. Wimsatt

from 'One Relation of Rhyme to Reason', *The Verbal Icon* 1954

We come then to rhyme, the subject of our argument. And first it must be admitted that in certain contexts a high degree of parallel in sense may be found even in rhyme. Even identical words may rhyme. In the sestina, for example, the same set of rhyme words is repeated in six different stanzas. But here the order changes, and so does the relation of each rhyme word to the context. That is the point of the sestina. Somewhat the same may be said for a refrain when it does not rhyme with any other line of the context. In the broadest sense, difference of meaning in rhyme words includes difference of syntax. In fact, words have no character as rhymes until they become points in a syntactic succession. Hence rhyme words (even identical ones) can scarcely appear in a context without showing some difference of meaning. The point of this essay is therefore not to prove that rhyme words must exhibit difference of meaning, but to discuss the value of the difference and to show how a greater degree of difference harmonizes with a certain type of verse structure.

Under certain conditions (much more common than the sestina or refrain mentioned above) the opportunity and the demand for difference of meaning in rhyme may be slight.

Scogan, that knelest at the stremes hed
Of grace, of alle honour and worthynesse,
In th'ende of which strem I am dul as ded,
Forgete in solitarie wildernesse, –
Yet, Scogan, thenke on Tullius kyndenesse.

(*Lenvoy de Chaucer a Scogan*, 43–7)

The three identical 'nesse' rhymes could be mere prosy homoeoteleuton if the three words occurred in positions of nearly parallel logic or
syntax. But Chaucer's sense, meandering like the stream through the
stanza, makes no great demand upon these rhymes, and weak though
they are, they are strong enough. Even in Chaucer's couplets the same
continuity of sense through the verse may be discovered, and the
same tendency in rhyming, as we shall illustrate in the comparison
which follows.

Pope is the English poet whose rhyming shows perhaps the clearest
contrast to Chaucer's. Chaucer found, even in Middle English, a
'skarsete' of rhyme. There would come a day when an even greater
scarcity of easy rhymes would create a challenge to the English poet
and at the same time indicate one of his most subtle opportunities.
In the course of three hundred years English lost many of its easy
rhymes, stressed Germanic and Romance endings, *y*, *ing*, *ere*, *esse*, and
able, *age*, *al*, *aunce*, *aile*, *ain*, *esse*, *oun*, *ous*, *ure*, so that Pope perforce
rhymed words differing more widely in meaning. The characteristics
of Pope's couplet, as opposed to Chaucer's, are, of course, its closure
or completeness, its stronger tendency to parallel, and its epigrammatic, witty, intellectual point. One can hardly imagine such a
couplet rhyming 'wildernesse' and 'kyndenesse', or 'worthynesse'
and 'hethenesse', as Chaucer does in one couplet of the knight's
portrait.

Most likely it is neither feasible nor even desirable to construct a
scale of meaning differences to measure the cleverness of rhyme. The
analysis which I intend is not in the main statistical. But an obvious,
if rude, basis for classification is provided by the parts of speech. It
may be said, broadly, that difference in meaning of rhyme words can
be recognized in difference of parts of speech and in difference of
functions of the same part of speech, and that both of these differences
will be qualified by the degree of parallel or of obliquity appearing

between the two whole lines of a rhyming pair. The tenor of the comparison which follows will be to suggest that Pope's rhymes are characterized by difference in parts of speech or in function of the same parts of speech, the difference in each case being accentuated by the tendency of his couplets to parallel structure.

A large number of rhymes in both Pope and Chaucer, or indeed in any English poet, are rather neutral to our inquiry.

> Whan that Aprill with his shoures soote
> The droghte of March hath perced to the roote.
>
> (Canterbury Tales, 1 1–2)

Here the rhyme makes its contribution to difference of sense against equality of verse, but because the oblique phrases themselves make a fundamental contrast to the metrically equal lines, and the rhyming parts of speech are a function of the phrases, the rhyme is not likely to be felt as a special element of variation. There is a higher proportion of such rhymes in Chaucer than in Pope. In general Chaucer relies for variation more on continuous sense and syntax than on rhyme, and when his rhyme words are the same part of speech, he is apt to give us a dullish rhyme:

> Me thynketh it acordaunt to resoun
> To telle you al the condicioun . . .
>
> (Canterbury Tales, 1 37–8)

In similar constructions Pope is apt to find some quaint minor contrast in length and quality of words:

> What guards the purity of melting maids,
> In courtly balls, and midnight masquerades?

It is in couplets of parallel structure, however, that the rhyming of Pope is seen to best advantage. More of these couplets in Pope have rhymes of different parts of speech than in Chaucer, and their effect is more pronounced in Pope because the parallel within the closed couplet of Pope is likely to be smarter. Chaucer will write:

> And everemoore he hadde a sovereyn prys;
> And though that he were worthy, he was wys.
>
> (Canterbury Tales, 1 67–8)

Pope will write:

Oft, when the world imagine women stray,
The Sylphs thro' mystic mazes guide their way.
When Florio speaks, what virgin could withstand,
If gentle Damon did not squeeze her hand.

In these two examples, though the syntax is oblique, the sense is parallel and antithetic. Pope's couplets, no matter what their syntax, tend to hover on the verge of antithesis and hence to throw a stress upon whatever difference of meaning appears in the rhyme words.

One might expect to find that a parallel both of general sense and of rhyming parts of speech would produce a quality of flatness, a sort of minimum rhyme, such as we found in St Augustine – 'Lingua clamat, cor amat' – only the first step beyond homoeoteleuton. One thing that may prevent this and may lend the rhyme a value of variation is that through some irregularity or incompleteness of parallel the rhyming words have oblique functions. Thus Chaucer:

No deyntee morsel passed thurgh hir throte;
Hir diete was accordant to hir cote.

(Canterbury Tales, VII 2835–6)

And Pope:

From each she nicely culls with curious toil,
And decks the Goddess with the glitt'ring spoil.

There are more of these couplets in Pope than in Chaucer, and with Pope the rhyme difference is more likely to seem the result of some deft twist or trick.

Some are bewilder'd in the maze of schools,
And some made coxcombs Nature meant but fools.

There is a kind of inversion (from pupils to schools and back to the pupils in a new light) which in some couplets appears more completely as chiasmus, an effect concerning which I shall have more to say.

The two types of rhyme difference which characterize Pope's poetry (that of different parts of speech and that of the same part of speech in different functions) are a complement, as I have suggested, of his tendency to a parallel of lines. To recognize this may affect our opinion about how deliberately or consciously Pope strove for

difference of rhyme, but it should not diminish the impression which
the actual difference of rhyme makes upon us. Such rhyme difference
may be felt more clearly as a characteristic of Pope if we examine the
rhymes in a passage where the parallel is somewhat like that which
Chaucer at times employs. It is difficult to find passages of sustained
parallel in Chaucer. The usual narrative movement of his couplets
is the oblique forward movement of actions in a sequence. But in the
character sketches of the *Canterbury Prologue* a kind of loose parallel
often prevails for ten or twenty lines, as one feature of a pilgrim after
another is enumerated. The sense is continuous, in that the couplets
tend to be incomplete, but the lines are all members of a parallel
bundle. A clear example may be seen in the yeoman's portrait.

And he was clad in cote and hood of grene.
A sheef of pecok arwes, bright and kene,
Under his belt he bar ful thriftily,
(Wel koude he dresse his takel yemanly:

Upon his arm he baar a gay bracer,
And by his syde a swerd and a bokeler,
And on that oother syde a gay daggere
Harneised wel and sharp as point of spere;
A Christopher on his brest of silver sheene.
An horn he bar, the bawdryk was of grene

(I 103–6, 110–16)

'Thriftily' and 'yemanly', 'bracer' and 'bokeler', 'sheene' and
'grene', rhymes like these (aside even from the use of final syllables,
'ly' and 'er') I should call tame rhymes because the same parts of
speech are used in closely parallel functions. To see the difference in
this respect between Chaucer and Pope we may turn to the classic
lines of another portrait:

Bless'd with each talent and each art to please,
And born to write, converse, and live with ease;
Should such a man, too fond to rule alone,
Bear, like the Turk, no brother near the throne;
View him with scornful, yet with jealous eyes,
And hate for arts that caus'd himself to rise;
Damn with faint praise, assent with civil leer,

And without sneering teach the rest to sneer;
Willing to wound, and yet afraid to strike,
Just hint a fault, and hesitate dislike;
Alike reserv'd to blame or to commend,
A tim'rous foe, and a suspicious friend.

The parallel of lines is continuous, but the rhymes are always different parts of speech. The portrait continues:

Dreading ev'n fools; by flatterers besieged,
And so obliging that he ne'er obliged;
Like *Cato*, give his little Senate laws,
And sit attentive to his own applause.

Here the same parts of speech are rhymed, but one verb is passive, one active; one noun is plural, one singular. The functions are different, in each case what he does being set against what he receives.

It is to be noted that in the yeoman's portrait such rhymes as 'grene' and 'kene', 'thriftily' and 'yemanly' are of the sort which we described above as minimum rhyme, only one step away from homoeoteleuton. Rhymes of this type often escape the extreme, as we saw, by some irregularity of parallel. But it is significant to add now that even when Pope does not escape the extreme he has resources of piquancy. Here and there he will be guilty of a certain flatness:

Each motion guides, and every nerve sustains,
Itself unseen, but in th' effects remains.

Often, however, he conveys some nice contrast in the parallel.

True wit is Nature to advantage dress'd,
What oft was thought, but ne'er so well express'd.

Here the two rhyme verbs are not merely parallel examples. One is literal, one is figurative, and in being matched with each other they express in brief the metaphor on which this classic critical doctrine is based, that to express is to dress.

(156–61)

J. A. W. Bennett

from *The 'Parlement of Foules': An Interpretation*   1957

As to the acute and questioning intelligence, it is indicated by Chaucer's very decision to assess [in the *Parliament of Fowls*] the apparently conflicting claims of personal love, love of heavenly things, and love of the public weal, and to consider what Nature, as vicegerent of God, has to do with Venus. If Deschamps's praise of Chaucer as '*Socrates, pleins de philosophie*', smacks of rhetorical flamboyance, it was not out of flattery that Chaucer's first follower, Thomas Usk, called him a 'noble philosophical poet'. Usk, himself a sensitive analyst of love, uses the phrase in respect of *Troilus and Criseyde;* and in that poem, as in most of Chaucer's, all the philosophical passages are occasioned by climaxes or crises in a love-relation.[1] It is as a poet who is forever pondering the nature and effects of love that he introduces himself at the very beginning of the *Parliament:* 'Love ... my felynge | Astonyeth with his wonderful werkynge.' If there be a humorous flicker in the lines immediately following, there is certainly no hint that love can be smiled away. And if, adapting a common formula, he confesses 'I knowe nat Love in dede', this does not mean that the poem is in any sense second-hand, or superficial. By 'philosophical poet' Usk meant more than a skilful versifier of current doctrine. In his day (and long after) the epithet, which Chaucer was the first to use in English, implied learning in natural even more than in metaphysical science; and his *Astrolabe* – to say nothing of the new-found *Equatorie of the Planetes* – testifies to the poet's scientific interests, kindled perhaps by Oxford friends at the college of Walter de Merton, the centre of English science in the mid-century. Of natural philosophy there is, to be sure, little direct trace in our poem – though the power and dignity accorded to the Empress Nature is itself indicative of the admiring mind with which Chaucer surveyed the visible world. But there is much more than a trace of that speculative curiosity about the relation of men and women to each other and to this visible world, which in the two preceding centuries had issued in works as diverse as Bernardus Silvestris's *De Mundi Universitate*, Jean de Meun's continuation of the

---

1 See, for example, *Troilus and Criseyde*, IV 960 ff., *Canterbury Tales*, I 1251 ff.

Roman de la Rose, and Dante's *Commedia*. Behind them all lay the christianized Platonism of Chartres or the christianized Aristotelianism of St Thomas. The two movements had produced not only a sharpened sense of wonder (a sense far more characteristic of this earlier Renaissance than of the Romantic Revival to which Watts-Dunton attached the phrase), but a passion for understanding the world, for finding causes and natural laws: hence Dante's concern with the spots on the moon, de Meun's with the rainbow, Chaucer's (in the *House of Fame*) with the nature of sound – and of dreams. By this all-embracing curiosity their poetry is linked with the interpretations of Vincent of Beauvais and the speculations of Roger Bacon and William Ockham – and distinguished from the poetry of the sixteenth-century Renaissance, where we might expect, according to received ideas, to find a like interest; nothing in this later poetry has the encyclopedic range of Dante, de Meun, or even of the Seventh Book of the *Confessio Amantis;* we may find in the *Faerie Queene* a vision of Nature that resembles Chaucer's in its universality; but that is because, as we shall see, Spenser, almost alone among the Elizabethans, drank deeply from Chaucer's poetry and shared his vision.

(7–9)

Charles Muscatine

from 'The Mixed Style', *Chaucer and the French Tradition* 1957

The *Canterbury Tales* as a whole is an example of the mixed style. Each of the tales, by analogy and by contrast, takes meaning from others. The effect of the larger form, a structure of juxtapositions and tensions, is to place and control the attitudes evoked separately by its parts, to reveal their virtues and limitations in context. Some of this manipulation of attitudes is announced dramatically by rivalries among the pilgrims. The Miller and Reeve, the Summoner and Friar are at overt personal debate. The Clerk recognizes in his envoy a relationship to the Wife of Bath. The Cook promises a comment on an innkeeper. These dramatic relationships are in turn supported, and nondramatic ones are established mutely but no less powerfully,

by the choice and disposition of the literary materials themselves,
Thus the Miller's dramatic announcement of

> 'a noble tale for the nones
> With which I wol now quite the Knyghtes tale,'
>   (I 3126-7)

is underscored in his tale by a resemblance to the Knight's in plot and
in character grouping. The Reeve's rivalry with the Miller has similar
literary support. The Host's implied comparison of the Nun's Priest
with the Monk is followed by the Priest's recitation of a 'tragedy'
which comments on the Monk's collection of tragedies. Criticism has
detected (or suspected) a whole web of such relationships among the
tales, in genre, subject, plot, characterization, and so on.

It is hard to know where to draw the line between art and algebra
in these correspondences. The work is so great as to begin to generate
its own relationships. Does the description of the clerk Nicholas in
the *Miller's Tale*, with its verbal reminiscences of the Clerk's portrait
in the *General Prologue*, announce a comparative study of clerkships?
Is Chaucer's Clerk to be compared to the Wife of Bath's fifth husband? Is there a 'Marriage Group'? Had Chaucer extended his poem,
would the Merchant or the Monk have replied to the *Shipman's
Tale*? There are provocative resemblances between the *Miller's Tale*
and the *Merchant's*: do they support a philosophical comparison?
One could not begin to describe the relational possibilities suggested
by Chaucer's language, by phrases repeated – 'pitee renneth soone in
gentil herte', 'allone, withouten any compaignye',[1] – and by such
repeated figures as the rhetorical *comparatio* on the death of Priam,
which is used to describe both Constance's departure from Rome and
Chauntecleer's abduction from a chicken yard (II 288-94, VII 3355-
61). We need not pause to evaluate all these possibilities. Even what is
announced in the gross stylistics of the *Canterbury Tales* shows
Chaucer's tireless capacity for definition and comparison. He has a
passion for relationships, and the over-all structure of the work, the
linear sequence of discrete stories in various styles, meets this passion
perfectly.

1 See respectively I 1761, IV 1986, V 679 (compare *Legend of Good Women*
F 503); and I 2779, I 3204.

We are not surprised to find something of the same structure within the individual tales. Many of them can richly stand alone as containing significant measurement within themselves. The dominant attitudes they convey are habitually conjoined with other attitudes, idiosyncrasies with norms, norms with idiosyncrasies or other norms. The perspective is created variously; it is inserted, appended, implied, disguised, or worked plainly into the main pattern of the story. Sometimes it is a matter of plot and circumstance, the irony of a wrong turning that exposes an ignorance and prepares for a defeat. Often it comes with an internal shift of style.

Virtually all the *Canterbury Tales* have some mixture of styles. The poems of dominantly religious inspiration have a realism which, if the poem is successful, as I think the *Prioress' Tale* is, melts symbolically into the conventional frame without conflict or irony. This peaceful stylistic mixture has some of the quality of the religious paradox itself; naturalism and the supernatural make peace in miracle. But in other poems the shifting style brings in whole shifts of assumptions. In poems where one style is heavily dominant, the mixture is enough to comment on, but not enough to rival the dominant attitude; thus the touches of commonsensical humour in the *Knight's Tale*, the scrap of lyricism in the *Reeve's Tale*, and the formal rhetoric in the *Canon's Yeoman's Tale* are relatively minor in effect. The *Wife of Bath's Prologue* swallows up a great mass of learned doctrine without losing its dominantly naturalistic shape. But there are a number of tales in which, as in the *Parliament of Fowls* and the *Troilus*, the mixed style is on display and becomes part of the subject of the poem. These are the tales which seem most 'Chaucerian', comprehending in small space, as they do, so much of Chaucer's range.

The *Miller's Tale*

In the *Miller's Tale* the alien style contributes importantly to the realization of the theme, but it is not a central feature of the poem. That it is not accounts partly for the mixture's broadly comic effect. The tale does not have the pathos of a *Troilus* nor the bitterness of a *Merchant's Tale*, because the views it presents are so outrageously unbalanced. The courtliness in the *Miller's Tale* is never given full, traditional value. It is never a norm, always an idiosyncrasy; and it is juxtaposed to a naturalism of exceptional force and vitality.

The normal view is perhaps best apprehended in the fact that the Miller's 'noble tale' is fabliau at the stage of richest elaboration. All the fabliau features are here so completely realized that the genre is virtually made philosophical. The simple, sequential fabliau plot has become, in the lucidity of this complicated plot's arrangement, an assertion of the binding, practical sequentiality of all events. The pragmatic, prosaically solid imagery of fabliau is here built into an unbroken, unbreakable wall of accepted fact. The fabliau's preference for physical action becomes an ethical imperative. Even the stock triangle of fabliau – the lecherous young wife, the jealous husband, and the clever clerk (here two clerks) – is a self-assertive vehicle for the purest fabliau doctrine, the sovereignty of animal nature. So fully does the tale fulfill its fabliau entelechy that its working-out is attended, as Tillyard says, by 'feelings akin to those of religious wonder.'[1]

The poem's dominant style is of great intrinsic interest, and, having passed it by in my discussion of naturalism *per se*, I must notice it here in a rather elaborate preface to the main topic. Let me observe, then, that in no other naturalistic poem of Chaucer is practical circumstance so closely tended, and practical detail so closely accounted for. We are given the name of the town and of the neighbouring town, the names of all the characters (Nicholas, Absolon, Alisoun, John, Robyn, Gille, Gerveys) save one (the cloisterer, 3661), a close knowledge of the architecture and plan of the house:

And breke an hole an heigh, upon the gable,
Unto the gardyn-ward, over the stable . . .

(I 3571–2)

We have a scrupulous accounting of days of the week and of the hours of the crucial day. The description is rich with an expressive superfluity of specification:

'Clepe at his dore, or knokke *with a stoon*.'

(3432)

hente hym *by the sholdres* myghtily . . .

(3475)

1 E. M. W. Tillyard, *Poetry Direct and Oblique*, rev. edn., London, 1948, p. 92, in one of the few requisitely serious discussions of the poem.

His owene hand he made laddres thre,
To clymben *by the ronges and the stalkes*
Unto the tubbes *hangynge in the balkes* . . .
(3624–6)

The great mass of such given detail achieves an extraordinary solidity – beyond that of the *Reeve's Tale* or the *Wife of Bath's Prologue* – because so much of it is given specific antecedents or consequences. Where the typical fabliau brings in properties and explanations only as needed, the *Miller's Tale* seems to explain everything. That the town is Oxford explains – overpoweringly explains – the presence of a clever clerk. That Absolon is named Absolon 'explains' his blond beauty and his femininity. That John the carpenter is made a 'riche gnof' in the very first statement explains his securing a pretty, young wife. That Absolon offers her rich gifts, later on, is a link in this chain of explanations. That the carpenter 'gestes heeld to bord' in the second verse prepares for the boarder Nicholas in verse four. The boarder's two days' self-confinement is silently prepared for in the eighteenth verse (3204); he rooms 'allone, withouten any compaignye'. Before Robyn the knave can peek in through Nicholas' door we are told that

An hole he foond, ful lowe upon a bord,
Ther as the cat was wont in for to crepe . . .
(3440–41)

Besides generally poetic consequence on the one hand (the board and the cat for solidity and animality), and practical consequence on the other (the hole for Robyn to peek through), many details through sheer recurrence achieve what I can only call a psychological consequence. Nicholas' door is not only peeked through; it is first cried and knocked at, then heaved off its hinges, then prayed by, then shut fast. That this door is at best only a minor factor in the action is symptomatic of the care with which the 'naturalness' of the poem is contrived. The very smallest scraps of image and action are handled thus consequentially, even where they are entirely unnecessary to the gross plot. The cat image cited above is already the second such image in the poem. The hole image twice reappears later. The kinesthetic effect of its lowness is repeated with the carpenter's window

(3696). The whole denouement, coming when it does, is by virtue of a mass recurrence of images given an air of utter probability. The nocturnal visit of Absolon to the carpenter's house has first a dress rehearsal that seems inconsequential – 'This passeth forth; what wol ye bet than weel?' (3370) – except to familiarize us with this action, with such details as the wall and the hinged window, and with such minute facts as that the window can be heard through (cf. 3744). Similarly, the cockcrow, the knocking, the (sweet-smelling) mouth, the stone (I am citing items consecutively from verse 3675), the coal, the forge, the nobles, the cough, the knocking again, the haunch bone, the flatulence, bread and ale, the cry of 'out' and 'harrow', the neighbours, the carpenter's arm, the gaping and staring, the carpenter's madness – are all prepared for beforehand. The breath-taking effect of the poem's climax surely owes much to this process. The focal images – the flood, the carpenter in his tub, the axe and cord – are suddenly brought to our conscious attention, not from nowhere (with an effect of mere surprise and chance), but from the semi-conscious storage of previous acceptance, unanticipated, perhaps, but inevitable. It is this solidity of detail, along with the characterization interlaced intimately with it, that gives the ingenious plotting its overpowering substantiality.

In this remarkably self-contained world of facts, no room is left for abstract, *a priori* formulations. The humour of the poem arises from the unequal conflict between fact and the few illusions that unhappily insist on themselves. The devastating victory of the norm is supported, in the manner of comedy, by reducing the 'errors' to caricature. The error of religion – to pass over the error of not wedding one's 'simylitude' (3228) – is represented by the credulous, illiterate carpenter. His knowledge of Scripture is from mystery plays, seen 'ful yoore ago' (3537). Noe (Noah) for him is 'Nowel'. His piety is all spells and asseverations; he is of that self satisfied, unthinking persuasion that expresses itself in saws and goes by precedents:

'This world is now ful tikel, sikerly.
I saugh to-day a cors yborn to chirche
That now, on Monday last, I saugh hym wirche.'
                        (3428–30)

> 'Help us, seinte Frydeswyde!
> A man woot litel what hym shal bityde.
> This man is falle, with his astromye,
> In som woodnesse or in some agonye.
> I thoghte ay wel how that it sholde be!
> Men sholde nat knowe of Goddes pryvetee.
> Ye, blessed be alwey a lewed man
> That noght but oonly his bileve kan!
> So ferde another clerk with astromye;
> He walked in the feeldes, for to prye
> Upon the sterres, what ther sholde bifalle,
> Til he was in a marle-pit yfalle;
> He saugh nat that.'
>
> (3449–61)

He is gulled by a clerk, and by his belief in 'Goddes pryvetee'.

The error of clerk Nicholas is faith in intellect and in the sufficiency of wit:

> 'A clerk hadde litherly biset his whyle,
> But if he koude a carpenter bigyle.'
>
> (3299–300)

His quite enormous sufficiency, conveyed in the opening description (3199 ff.), is already touched with irony in the epithet 'hende'. It is fascinating to watch this term, which means 'gracious' and 'ready-handed' and 'clever' and 'comely' and 'near at hand', sharpen as the poem progresses. It becomes a signal of his defeat. He has already solved the ethic of the poem, assault, when his cleverness elaborately over-extends itself and leads to Absolon's assault on him.

Faith in Love is the heresy most elaborately dealt with in the poem, and it is most elaborately caricatured. Linguistic analysis has shown how much the Oxford idiom of love is the idiom of English rather than of French romance.[1] It is the native version of the imported heresy that is parodied here. More congenial to the setting, it is also funnier than Continental love would have been, for it is exposed to the laughter of the sophisticated, who know better, as well as of the

---

1 See E. T. Donaldson, 'Idiom of popular poetry in the *Miller's Tale*', in *English Institute Essays*, 1950 (New York, 1951), pp. 116–40.

Miller's kind, who know worse. But it remains crushingly conventional, and the stylistic vehicle for the comedy of love is the farrago of convention and naked instinct that is Absolon's courtship of Alisoun:

> '. . . I wol go slepe an houre or tweye,
> And al the nyght thanne wol I wake and pleye.'
> Whan that the firste cok hath crowe, anon
> Up rist this joly lovere Absolon,
> And hym arraieth gay, at poynt-devys.
> But first he cheweth greyn and lycorys,
> To smellen sweete, er he hadde kembd his heer.
> Under his tonge a trewe-love he beer,
> For thereby wende he to ben gracious.
> He rometh to the carpenteres hous,
> And stille he stant under the shot-wyndowe –
> Unto his brest it raughte, it was so lowe –
> And softe he cougheth with a semy soun:
> 'What do ye, hony-comb, sweete Alisoun,
> My faire bryd, my sweete cynamome?
> Awaketh, lemman myn, and speketh to me!
> Wel litel thynken ye upon my wo,
> That for youre love I swete ther I go.
> No wonder is thogh that I swelte and swete;
> I moorne as dooth a lamb after the tete.
> Ywis, lemman, I have swich love-longynge,
> That lik a turtel trewe is my moornynge.
> I may nat ete na moore than a mayde.'
> 'Go fro the wyndow, Jakke fool,' she sayde.
>
> (3685–708)

The French lover 'rometh' perhaps, but he does not 'swelte and swete', nor does he catch up on his sleep before a sleepless night. The courtly delicacy of speech and of toilette have become in this small-town, provincial version the anal-retentive, squeamish spotlessness registered in Absolon's portrait (3312 ff.) and punished with terrible aptness at the end.

The delectable Alisoun sets in motion the lovemaking of the poem, and her celebrated portrait answers to several versions:

Fair was this yonge wyf, and therwithal

As any wezele hir body gent and smal.
A ceynt she werede, barred al of silk,
A barmclooth eek as whit as morne milk
Upon hir lendes, ful of many a goore.
Whit was hir smok, and broyden al bifoore
And eek bihynde, on hir coler aboute,
Of col-blak silk, withinne and eek withoute.
The tapes of hir white voluper
Were of the same suyte of hir coler;
Hir filet brood of silk, and set ful hye.
And sikerly she hadde a likerous ye;
Ful smale ypulled were hire browes two,
And tho were bent and blake as any sloo.
She was ful moore blisful on to see
Than is the newe pere-jonette tree,
And softer than the wolle is of a wether.
And by hir girdel heeng a purs of lether,
Tasseled with silk, and perled with latoun.
In al this world, to seken up and doun,
There nys no man so wys that koude thenche
So gay a popelote or swich a wenche.
Ful brighter was the shynyng of hir hewe
Than in the Tour the noble yforged newe.
But of hir song, it was as loude and yerne
As any swalwe sittynge on a berne.
Therto she koude skippe and make game,
As any kyde or calf folwynge his dame.
Hir mouth was sweete as bragot or the meeth,
Or hoord of apples leyd in hey or heeth.
Wynsynge she was, as is a joly colt,
Long as a mast, and upright as a bolt.
A brooch she baar upon hir lowe coler,
As brood as is the boos of a bokeler.
Hir shoes were laced on hir legges hye.
She was a prymerole, a piggesnye,
For any lord to leggen in his bedde,
Or yet for any good yeman to wedde.

(3233–70)

This is not merely a dead convention vivified. So much has been said of the naturalness and realism of it that I may here speak one-sidedly for the effect of the convention itself. The form is still rhetorical *effictio*, and still preserves the convention of the inventory, disarrayed indeed, but listing at every turn the categories of the archetype: the fairness, the eye, the bent brows, the hue, the voice, the mouth, the carriage, the silken costume, the jewelry, the accomplishments. And each category is filled by a superlative. The similes are the similes that apply in the Oxford context, just as Absolon's gifts of spiced ale and piping hot waffles apply. In Oxford it is a brunette rather than a blonde, plucked brows rather than natural, embroidery of black silk rather than of gold, pearls of latten, not precious stones. The convention domesticated carries still some of its original idealizing power. Its function is manifold. I feel in this description, especially where it deals with such unsuspicious images as the 'newe pere-jonette tree', an outright, unqualified sympathy with the character, a response in the poet himself similar in some respects to his sympathy with the Wife of Bath. The literary effect is as if to present Alisoun as the one precious illusion in the poem. Here the milleresque philosophy finds its one ideal, and allows itself its one large formulation:

In al this world, to seken up and doun,
There nys no man so wys that koude thenche
So gay a popelote or swich a wenche.

(3252-4)

She was a prymerole, a piggesnye,
For any lord to leggen in his bedde,
Or yet for any good yeman to wedde.

(3268-70)

On another level the portrait is comic in the way that Absolon is comic. It matches perfectly (to the sophisticated audience) the gaucherie of his 'love-longynge'. This is a small-town heroine, whose brows *are* plucked, whose eye *is* lecherous, whose forehead shines – from washing after work (3310 f.). Finally, on the level of terms like 'weasel', 'loins', 'gore', 'colt', and 'pig's-eye', the portrait describes the delectable little animal who is not to be won by a protracted, artificial wooing.

The strands of imagery that I have rather painfully disentangled are of course twisted solidly together in the poetry. Images like 'morne milk', 'wolle . . . of a wether', 'hoord of apples', contribute to more than one strand. The silky black and white of Alisoun's ensemble, if it is not piquantly noncommittal, may contribute to all. 'Loins' and 'gore' in this context have literary-parodic as well as sexual associations. The humour of Absolon's discovery of the animal is prepared by his misguided attention to the ideal. For the Miller (whose views are presumably being reflected here, though the feeling is possibly too fine for him) the animalism and the ideality must be intertwined. As it does with the Carpenter's religion and Nicholas' cleverness, however, the poem's lusty naturalism bluntly triumphs over the illusion of Love, leaving Alisoun unscathed, perhaps, but not undiscovered.

There is nothing in the fabliau tradition that dictated the introduction of courtly conventionalism in the *Miller's Tale*. Chaucer had no need to encumber himself with the 'dreary', 'artificial', 'hackneyed' form, save the need of meaning. Here he actually realized a potency of the fabliau that is not quite realized in any fabliau of the French tradition. In *Du Clerc qui fu repus*, in *D'Aloul*, in the *Dit de la gageure*, the fragments of courtly convention are inoperative. In the *Miller's Tale* they serve perspective, affording the fabliau a mordantly pointed comment, from below, on the futility of love *paramours*.

(222-30)

Erich Auerbach

from *The Literary Language and its Public* 1958

A comparable alertness and racy wit are to be found in the fourteenth century in the literature of another country [besides Spain] on the fringe of Europe, namely, England; and here too they permit inferences as to the character and composition of the public. The early development of Anglo-Saxon culture had been interrupted by the superimposition of a new ruling class. But soon it became clear that the language of the thin Norman upper crust would not in the long run be the literary language of the country. In the course of the fourteenth century Anglo-Saxon, whose literary tradition had never entirely died out and which had meanwhile developed into Middle

English, attained a great literary flowering and with it the beginnings of standardization. And despite the medieval heritage common to all western Europe, despite the ancient, Christian, and French influences reflected in its themes, ideas, and forms of expression, a strong individuality and popular character are apparent from the first, owing perhaps to the fact that English had to assert itself not so much against Latin as against the French of the courts. Another factor is the political, religious, and economic awakening of the masses, which, if it did not occur earlier than elsewhere, was more thoroughgoing. Nowhere else during the Middle Ages are profound and varied social currents described with so much concrete truth, so much sympathy and humour as in fourteenth-century England. I am thinking of course of Chaucer's *Canterbury Tales*, which equal the *Decameron* in colour and are superior to the Italian work as a living picture of the times. The essential difference may be gathered from a comparison of the frames: Chaucer's narrators are pilgrims from all walks of life; they are sharply characterized, and the relations between them are vividly set forth. Thus the frame alone supplies a lively picture of the social scene in England. Boccaccio's narrators are a group of fashionable and cultivated young people who have fled to a country villa from the plague; they all belong to the same upper class of society and are only dimly characterized. Thus the *Decameron* conveys the atmosphere of a homogeneous culture, and its vulgar elements are absorbed into this cultivated medium. Medieval object lessons and compilations are almost entirely absent, and there is never any awkwardness or rupture of style. Chaucer, on the other hand, does not hesitate to employ as narrators persons such as Boccaccio uses only as characters *in* his stories. In thus representing much lower social classes as endowed with awareness and judgement, Chaucer communicates a much sharper and more political picture of the country. The style, indeed, is less homogeneous and sure, and there is hardly a sign of humanism. Chaucer still makes a considerable display of semi-erudite *exempla*, taken over from the earlier Middle Ages; the effect is often rather grotesque, as in the case of the misogynous tales which the Wife of Bath represents as the learned literary gleanings of her late fifth husband.

(324–6)

Paull F. Baum

from *Chaucer, A Critical Appreciation* 1958

The grounds for a proper criticism of Chaucer are, it seems to me, fairly simple: recognition of his position as court poet, with the limitations which that position implies; appreciation of his technique as prosodist (still neglected) and as narrative poet, with its ups and downs; and, negatively, avoidance of zealous effort to find in him aesthetic virtues which his kind of writing does not require or warrant. Such an approach is neither modern nor medieval but rests upon criteria by which all poets are judged. It admits the conventions of medieval rhetoric and of Courtly Love as he adapted it to his special purposes; it omits deliberately the medieval Four Levels of Meaning as inconsonant with his subjects and his ways of treating them. It sees him as a comic poet, whether by temperament or by the necessities of his milieu, and probably by both, endowed with very great gifts, and since poetry was his avocation, taking those gifts with a comfortable ease, untroubled by the severities which plague the dedicated artist; in two words, as *an amateur of genius*: a busy man of the world and very human who composed when it pleased him to do so poems which he thought would give pleasure to others. Yet even genius, the other side of the paradox, can be as fickle as Fortune, and we must accept its lapses. 'A healthy sagacious man of the world', as Bagehot calls him, 'has gone through the world; he loves it and knows it; he dwells on it with a fond appreciation.' This is what delights us and earns our praise. Be glad, he would say,

Be glad, thow redere, and thy sorwe of-caste.

Chaucer's art is pre-eminent in giving pleasure. He is companionable, our fellow man, sharing our whims and weaknesses, with no austere hatreds, no intense passions. It is his merit to be plain and earthy with our all-too-human earthiness, and we enjoy him for it; we even like to tolerate him when he is dull. Yet this is not to write him down as a mere entertainer. Comedy is never without its serious undertones, and if we sometimes deplore Chaucer's habit of seeming to laugh out of season, that is only to recognize a technical failure. *Seriousness*, in spite of Arnold, is not a word to conjure with; it is not a matter of subject but of treatment, of careful attention to getting the thing said in the best possible way. Has not Mr T. S. Eliot told us that Villon's *Testament* is more serious than *In Memoriam*? In the same sense the *Miller's Tale* is more serious than the *Knight's Tale*, the *Canon's Yeoman's* than the *Franklin's*.

At the same time, we cannot safely overlook his historical position, which gave him little incentive to exceed his grasp, or to forget the first audience for which he wrote, an audience which, enveloped as it was in social and political confusions and wishing to be entertained, was easily satisfied with what it could easily understand and would not greatly care for political, religious, or philosophical increments. He pleased them first with escape poetry from France and then, as his experience grew, with the comedy of low life, which also was remote from their personal concerns. His chosen models were Ovid and Boccaccio, and when he read the greater poets, Virgil and Dante, he used them for more stories and for fine phrases. All this is not to forget a few friends who would relish the philosophical increments; but even they encouraged him to no aspiration towards the highest levels of aesthetic experience which yield a sense of reality beyond the reality of appearance, which not only illuminate but enlarge the spirit. For Chaucer the word is *illuminates*. He had, as Mr Coghill says, 'an acute and questioning intelligence'. His observations of the world are clear and comprehensive, especially its common frailties, rarely its tragic flaws. His reporting of it is both brilliant and tolerant; but not hortative. *Swich is this world* is his theme, and there he rested.

I know I have been accus'd as an enemy of his writings but without any other reason than that I do not admire him blindly, and without looking into his imperfections. For why should he only be exempted from those frailties, from which *Homer* and *Virgil* are not free? . . . I admire and applaud him where I ought; those who do more do but value themselves in their admiration of him.

Thus Dryden on Ben Jonson. But it is not dispraise to seem to take away from Chaucer certain qualities which he never had. The aura of uncritical praise – sincere and often disguised as ingenious subtlety – can be rightly diminished without occultation or derogation from his genuine gifts as poet, story-teller, and humorist.

(ix–xi)

E. T. Donaldson

'Troilus and Criseyde', Chaucer's Poetry: An Anthology for the Modern Reader 1958

Chaucer's longest single poem is his greatest artistic achievement and one of the greatest in English literature. It possesses to the highest degree that quality, which characterizes most great poetry, of being always open to reinterpretation, of yielding different meanings to different generations and kinds of readers, who, no matter how they may disagree with one another on even its most important points, nevertheless agree in sharing the profoundly moving experience the poem offers them. Its highly elusive quality, which not only permits but encourages a multiplicity of interpretations, is in no way the result of incompetence on the part of the poet, but something carefully sought after as the best way of expressing a complex vision.

Chaucer is believed to have completed the work about 1385 or 1386, with some fifteen years of productivity remaining to him. Only extraordinary resourcefulness could bring it about that, having accomplished in *Troilus* what might well seem the principal work of his life, he was able to turn to other themes and other attitudes with undiminished energy and enthusiasm for experimentation. Readers occasionally wonder why romantic love – which is both a theme and an attitude – plays so little part in the *Canterbury Tales* that employed the last years of his life: the explanation lies in *Troilus*. Chaucer was apparently aware that he could not surpass his own treatment of this subject. And magnificent as the Canterbury collection is, both in the large conception and in the individual tales, *Troilus'* grandeur remains unsurpassed.

The source of the poem is one of Boccaccio's youthful works, the *Filostrato* (the Love-Stricken, according to Boccaccio's false etymology), a passionate narrative of 5700 lines in stanzaic Italian verse, completed before 1350, probably about 1340. Boccaccio's poem, in the original Italian and in a French translation, furnished Chaucer the essential plot, most of the narrative details – though Chaucer made a number of important additions – and even with a number of lines readily adapted to translation into English. Yet the qualities of the two poems are entirely different, and Chaucer's is, artistically speaking, by far the more original. In the clear, brilliant light of the Italian work everything seems fully realized, fully understood. One reads with interest, admiration, and excitement: the mind's eye is filled. Yet there is little in the poem that does not meet the eye, and the reader does not tend to re-create what he has seen after he no longer sees it. By contrast, Chaucer's poem is mist-enshrouded: the sun does, indeed, break through at times, but things are difficult to see steadily for more than a short period, reappear in changed shape, become illusory, vanish; as the poem progresses one finds oneself groping more and more in a world where forms are indistinct but have infinite suggestiveness; the mind creates and re-creates; and at the end one has not so much beheld an experience objectively as lived it in the emotions.

As in so many of Chaucer's poems, the guise of the narrator is important to an interpretation of the work. At the outset this seems to be the familiar one of the unloved servant of the God of Love, the man whose inexperience renders him singularly ill-fitted to write a romance, but who will nevertheless perform the pious act of translating – of all things! – an unhappy love story. As in the *Parliament of Fowls*, the value of love within the poem is heightened by the narrator's exclusion from it, his yearning toward it. But this lyrical function of the narrator is in *Troilus* less important than his dual, paradoxical function as a historian whose knowledge of the story is wholly book-derived and as an invisible yet omnipresent participant in the action. It is as a historian that he first presents himself – a rather fussy, nervous scholar who has got hold of some old books, particularly one by Lollius, that tell the story of the Trojan lovers. This he means to translate, although he complains that his sources fail to give as much information as they ought. Nevertheless, they present the essentials: the sorrow Troilus suffered before he won Criseyde, and how she forsook him in the end (1 55–6). Starting out with such inadequate and unpromising data, the historian proceeds to re-create the story as if he himself were living it without knowing its outcome. His second guise, that of the participant, unlike the guise of the historian, is largely implicit, a matter of the emotional intensity and lack of objectivity with which he approaches the characters. As the poem proceeds, the tension between the two attitudes, the historian dealing with incontrovertible fact, the participant speaking from

equally incontrovertible emotional experience, increases until it
becomes almost unendurable. By the beginning of Book IV (15-21)
the narrator's love for Criseyde has become such that when he finds
himself forced to face the issue of her perfidy he comes close to deny-
ing the truth of his old books. *For how Criseyde Troilus forsook*, he
begins, forthrightly enough; but reluctance to credit the bare statement causes him to soften it:

Or at the leeste, how that she was unkynde,
Moot hennesforth been matere of my book,
As writen folk thorugh which it is in mynde.
Allas! that they sholde evere cause fynde
To speke hire harm, and if they on hire lye,
Iwis, hemself sholde han the vilanye.

It is a strange historian who becomes so emotionally involved with
the personages of his history that he is willing to impugn the reliability
of the sources upon which his whole knowledge of those personages
presumably depends.

These two divergent attitudes of the narrator come to form an
image of the philosophical speculation that permeates much of the
poem: is it possible in this world to maintain a single firm idea of the
reality of any given human situation or character? This speculation
may be best illustrated in its bearing on Criseyde, upon whom so
much of the emotional force of the poem centres. History records
the literal fact that Criseyde proved, in the end, unworthy of the love
Troilus bore her. This is the flattest, most basic, and least assailable
of realities. (At the time Chaucer was writing, Criseyde's character
may not yet have suffered the deterioration that, by Shakespeare's
time, made her a kind of literary model of the unfaithful woman;
nevertheless Chaucer's method of handling her is essentially what it
would have been if the process had already taken place.) Despite our
knowledge of the ending, the narrator's loving presentation of
Criseyde in the course of the poem makes us feel the powerful
attraction that brought about Troilus's love; and we are even persuaded that she was worthy of it. Indeed, *Troilus* gains something of
the poignancy of the elegy by the very fact that we are aware of
Criseyde's eventual perfidy at the same time the narrator is depicting
the profound spell she casts – just as we know that Blanche, in the

Book of the Duchess, is dead even while the Black Knight describes the charm of her vitality. History tends to pronounce judgement on the final perfidy of Criseyde as effectively nullifying her positive worth as a human being; but the historical point of view does not exhaust the reality of Criseyde as the heroine of the poem.

It is true that at the end of the poem we are left with two widely different versions of Criseyde's reality, versions made mutually exclusive by the conventions of romance. These conventions make it impossible for a heroine worthy of love to prove faithless; and ultimately we must, of course, bow to the fact of her faithlessness. We must remember, however, that it was Chaucer's aim to make the reader suffer vicariously the experience of Troilus. The poet therefore creates in the person of Criseyde one of the most alluring of heroines; and more, he persuades us that her downfall does not so much falsify our first judgement of her as compel us to see the tragic nature of reality, in which the best so often becomes the worst.

Criseyde's most emphatically displayed characteristic is amiability – that is, lovability: she has almost all the qualities that men might hope to encounter in their first loves. This is perhaps the same as saying that she is above all feminine, suggesting for a young man like Troilus the compelling mystery and challenge of her sex. She is lovely in appearance, demure yet self-possessed, capable of both gaiety and gravity, glamorous in the truest sense of the word. Although she says nothing really witty, she responds to Pandarus's wit in such a way as to seem witty; her constant awareness of implications beneath the surface of the situation suggests, if it does not prove, intelligence. With her uncle and with Troilus she has the curiously endearing charm that arises from her consciousness, humorously and wryly expressed, of her own complicity in the events that befall her. The grace and tenderness with which she finally yields to Troilus (III 1210–71) are almost magically appealing.

But Chaucer did something more than present Criseyde as the completely agreeable heroine; he also suggested in her a really complex human being, filled with all sorts of latent qualities which are much more than mere enhancements of her magnetism. Chaucer's presentation, indeed, is so full as to invite his readers to find in Criseyde the seeds of her eventual falseness; but Criseyde's potentialities as a human being, so brilliantly sketched as partly to justify calling *Troilus* a psychological novel, elude us in the end. Several excellent critics have purported to find in this or that one of her qualities the definitive clue to her betrayal, but others continue to feel that the mainsprings of her action lie hidden. It seems to follow that if the poet were trying to make her motivation psychologically clear, he failed badly. It is, however, certain that this was not his purpose. Instead, he meant to present in Criseyde a broad range of the undefined but recognizable potentialities inherent in human nature.

Our longest and seemingly most penetrating view into Criseyde's character is afforded by Book II (596 ff.), when we are shown her reactions to the news her uncle brings her about Troilus's love. These reactions are filled with apparent clues to her basic character, but when analysed they lead to ambiguous conclusions. Criseyde is much concerned with Troilus's high estate as a prince of Troy, and this concern might be interpreted as indicative of opportunism; conversely, because her already precarious situation in the city might make it dangerous to refuse him, her concern might be interpreted as fearfulness. If the fact of her concern, regardless of what it springs from, is taken as an indication of an overcalculating nature, then the impression is counterbalanced by her involuntary moment of intoxication when she sees Troilus, in all his martial glory, riding homeward from battle. This incident in turn might suggest an oversensual nature; but the circumspection with which, a little later, she considers the whole affair might well reinforce an impression of her frigidity. Again, her inability to make up her mind might be taken to prove her indecisiveness and ineffectuality; on the other hand, since the problems she is facing are entirely realistic, it might be used to prove her native practicality.

The narrator is of singularly little assistance to the reader who is trying to solve the enigma. On every crucial psychological issue both he and his old books are silent. We do not know, though we may suspect, what Criseyde thought when Pandarus told her Troilus was out of town the day she came to dine. We never know to what extent she was influenced by her uncle's specious, often self-contradictory, arguments. And the narrator's explanations are even worse than his silences. For instance, just after Criseyde experiences the moment of intoxication mentioned above, the narrator pauses to consider the hypothetical objection of some envious person that she was falling in love too fast (II 666 ff.). With a fine show of indignation he protests that she did not fall in love immediately: she merely began to incline toward Troilus, who had to win her with long service. The effect of this kind of explanation – of which there are a number in the poem – is complex, not to say chaotic. The reader, who may never have thought that Criseyde is proceeding too fast, is suddenly encouraged to think she is by the narrator's gratuitous denial. The reader is made, as it were, an involuntary critic of the action instead of a mere spectator. Moreover, he is made to judge Criseyde according to a norm that the narrator's tone assumes to be well known but that is in fact undefined and totally unknown, namely, the decorous rate of speed with which a woman should fall in love. Finally, having cleared Criseyde of a charge which only he has made, the narrator asserts, in the very next stanza, that it was not her fault but Troilus's destiny that she should fall in love with him so soon. Analysed by the intellect alone, the passage seems to suggest that Criseyde did fall in love too quickly. Yet it precedes the far longer one in which she considers the whole matter so carefully that some critics have accused her of proceeding too deliberately!

The fact is that we do not read poetry with the intellect alone, and that when poetry makes two contradictory statements they do not cancel each other out. Both remain as part of the essential poetic truth, which is not the same thing at all as logic. There is surely no abstract, logical, ideal course of action for a woman falling in love, but we can recognize the process as being truly represented by Criseyde. Some parts of her nature are driving her forward with a speed that is utterly terrifying to the rest of her nature, and a bewildering variety of motives assert themselves in turn. But however we analyse these, in the long run we can say with assurance only that they are human. Any one of them, given a development which the poem resolutely refuses to permit, might become the reason for her eventual betrayal: mere timidity, mere opportunism, mere sensuality, mere inefficiency – even mere femininity. As it stands, however, we are emotionally no more prepared for the denouement than Troilus, though we have had one important advantage over him: we have been permitted to see, and have been disturbed by, suggestions of depths in Criseyde that her lover could not have seen. Our confidence in her is less serene, particularly as a result of the narrator's reassurances. It may be that her very elusiveness makes us nervous. If so, that is as it should be, since the only possible resolution of the two realities mentioned earlier lies in the unpredictability, the instability, of even the most lovely of mortal women.

Just as in later literature Criseyde was to become the type of a faithless woman, so her charming, witty, intelligent uncle Pandarus was, by a worse fate, to become the type of a pimp. In a long conversation in Book III (238–420) Pandarus and Troilus discuss, among other things, the implications of Pandarus's helping Troilus win Criseyde. The conclusion they come to is less than satisfactory: Pandarus's help is not the act of a procurer because he receives no reward for it. Thereafter the matter is not one of the overt issues of the poem, though in his last speech to Troilus (v 1734–6) Pandarus reverts to it almost as if he foresaw the deterioration of his name Pandar to pander. And while not overt, the issue once raised can never be wholly banished from the mind. Parallel to the question the poem raises about Criseyde, 'Is her reality that of a worthy lover or that of an unfaithful wench?' is the question it raises about Pandarus's assistance of Troilus: 'Is this the action of a loyal friend or of a mere pimp?'

History – in this case later literary history – has answered the question to the detriment of Pandarus, but the answer this poem gives is less absolute. The reader is assured by everyone – by Troilus, by Pandarus himself, by the narrator – that what Pandarus does is done wholly because of his devotion to Troilus, and surely the moralist must admit that human action is qualified by the motives of the agent. Yet, just as was the case with Criseyde, when we watch his character in action we seem to glimpse potentials – undefined, to be sure – that are not of a piece with the notion of a friend acting with entire altruism. In general he seems, like his niece, a person of great charm: gay, cheerful, witty, mocking and self-mocking, friendly, helpful, practical, intelligent, sympathetic, loyal – one could hardly wish for a better companion or friend. But despite these qualities, one's confidence in him does not remain altogether secure. Perhaps his pleasure in arranging this affair is too great. The brilliant comedy he performs at the lovers' bedside – a touch of the *Miller's Tale* – is perhaps suggestive of some vital flaw in his nature (and the narrator does nothing to improve the situation by failing to send Pandarus off to his own chamber). Even the delightful scene of Pandarus's visit to Criseyde's bedside after Troilus has departed is not without a hint of prurience. In the long run, it may be said of the complexity of Pandarus, as of the complexity of Criseyde, that it displays such a rich array of human qualities that we are at a loss in analysing his ultimate motives and character.

Pandarus bears a relation to the problem of reality – and hence to the philosophical speculation that is carried on in the poem – in another way. He is what would generally be called today a thorough-going realist. Paradoxically, this seems to mean that he has no respect for reality at all. For him, things are whatever one makes them. To accomplish a given action, all one has to do is manipulate the situation so as to produce the proper pressures on the actors. It does not matter in the least if these pressures are in reality nonexistent; it only matters that the actors should think them real. In putting his philosophy to work, Pandarus becomes the master-spinner of illusions. A persecutor from whom Criseyde needs protection is conjured up out of thin air. A dinner party is manipulated with excruciating attention to detail so that Criseyde may be introduced to Troilus under the most re-spectable of circumstances. When Criseyde must be induced to receive Troilus in her bedchamber, a rival lover named Horaste, whom Criseyde had never smiled upon and Troilus had never felt jealous of, emerges full-blown from Pandarus's fertile mind to produce the necessary pressure. And if Pandarus cannot actually produce rain, his foreknowledge that rain will come serves the magician's purpose of ensuring that his dinner guest will stay the night. The love affair itself seems to result largely from the illusions Pandarus creates for the paralysed Troilus and the passive Criseyde. One would not be surprised if he were to dictate Troilus's first letter to Criseyde and then to dictate her response, so close does he come to being the author of a living fiction.

Upon the significance of all this illusion-spinning the poem makes no overt comment. It even fails to distinguish clearly between real and illusory pressures exerted on Criseyde: for instance, we do not know whether Pandarus's account of his discovering Troilus's love-sicknesses (II 505–53) is in the realm of fact or merely a charming invention with which to please Criseyde. But in the poem's totality the implications of Pandarus's illusions cannot be avoided, because we know that in the end Criseyde's love for Troilus will prove to be a kind of illusion. Moreover, the dominant role the illusions play in the love affair, whether commented on or not, forces them on our consciousness, and once more we experience a sense of insecurity. This is embodied in the poem by the interchange between the lovers when their love is consummated (III 1338–52); both of them, especially Troilus, express uncertainty whether such bliss can in fact be true.

Pandarus continues a realist and a would-be manipulator of realities until the end, when reality defeats him. His first reaction on hearing that Criseyde must leave the city is that the love affair is finished. He tries to persuade Troilus to give her up (IV 380 ff.), to forget about her, and when that practical approach fails, as it is doomed to, he tries another equally practical one, equally doomed to fail: forcefully to prevent her going. When Troilus replies, with his usual integrity, that he cannot constrain Criseyde against her will, Pandarus observes that if Criseyde consents to leave Troy, Troilus must consider her false (IV 610–15). With this speech – which, incidentally, is the most strikingly revealing of several of Pandarus's reflections on Criseyde in the last two books – his effective role in the poem is completed. From then on all he can do is act as go-between. His efforts to rearrange reality in order to preserve the love affair are paltry and futile. After Criseyde's departure from Troy we see him upholding Troilus's hopes even when he himself recognizes their futility, and while in the earlier books Pandarus's attempts to uphold illusion did not seem offensive, now they seem the work of a half-hearted trickster. It is almost as if the reality he had tortured were having its revenge on him by redefining his actions as those of a mere procurer: for Criseyde, after all, becomes little better than a whore. In the end Pandarus – and Pandarus alone – accepts history's version of Criseyde: by saying, in his pathetic last speech (V 1731–43), that he hates her, he makes clear that for him any other value she may have seemed to possess has been cancelled out. He submits to the ultimate reality as Troilus, who can never 'unlove' Criseyde, refuses to do; yet one has felt that Pandarus's love for his niece was, in its way, as great as Troilus's.

Troilus, the hero of the poem and the most important of its personages, may seem in some respects less interesting than Pandarus or Criseyde. If, however, he lacks their human variety, his *trouthe*, his integrity, makes him in the long run a more fully realized person. This integrity, the quality that he will not surrender even to keep Criseyde with him, is the one human value the poem leaves entirely unquestioned: it is because of it that Troilus is granted his ultimate vision. It places him, of course, in sharp contrast with Criseyde and her *untrouthe*, and since one of the meanings of *trouthe* is reality, he emerges as more real than she. The sad fact that integrity does him no practical good does not in any way impair its value; indeed, its value seems enhanced by its preventing him, at least on one occasion, from attaining an apparent good. If he had been a different person – a Diomede, for instance – he might well have used force to stop Criseyde's exhange. This is what Pandarus advises and what both narrator and reader momentarily find themselves hoping for. But Troilus is acutely aware of both the public and the private implications of such an act. Criseyde's exchange had been legally determined by the parliament and duly ratified by King Priam, and to prevent it forcefully would be to substitute anarchy for law: the Trojan war had itself been caused by Paris's rape of Queen Helen, and to seize Criseyde would be once again to risk precipitating endless violent countermeasures. Furthermore, according to the medieval conventions of courtly love, the lover was the servant of his mistress – as the word *mistress* still suggests – and for the servant to overrule the mistress was unthinkable. As it frequently does, the courtly convention here merely articulates a real factor in the relationship of civilized men and women. A lover cannot impose his will upon his love, for unless she remains at all times possessed of free will, love itself becomes meaningless and the love affair vitiated. Similarly, to seize her would be inevitably to disclose their love affair and ruin her good name, which, according to the courtly code, he was sworn to protect. In view of these matters, for Troilus to 'ravish' Criseyde would be for him to violate his own nature, which, as Criseyde perceives, is one of moral virtue, grounded upon truth.

But if Troilus is the only unequivocally worthwhile person in the poem, why, one must ask, is he its principal sufferer? Troilus ascribes his misery to the operation of Fortune, or malevolent fate. A heavy atmosphere of fatality does, indeed, hang over the poem, so that even if the reader had not been told the outcome of the love affair he might feel it inevitable that Troilus should in the end fall, like Troy. Yet with one exception all the specific incidents, although the narrator may invoke for them the causality of the stars, seem equally attributable to the action of one of the three actors in the love tragedy. The exception is the intervention of Criseyde's forgotten father Calchas, an intervention that comes from his sure foreknowledge of the city's doom and that is beyond the control of Pandarus or the lovers. Elsewhere causality is ambiguous. For instance, the narrator ascribes to astrological influences entirely remote from Criseyde's control the rain which prevented Criseyde's leaving her uncle's house. On the other hand, we are aware that the rain had been foreseen by Pandarus, so that what may be deemed fate in its relation to Criseyde is at the same time mere machination on the part of Pandarus. Nor are we sure enough of Criseyde's state of mind in accepting her uncle's invitation – the narrator has been marvellously ambiguous about that too – clearly to exonerate her from an acquiescence in a foreseen fate so prompt as to make fate's role negligible. But here as elsewhere the impression of fatal influence is not cancelled out by the impression of human responsibility: both impressions remain and even unite into a single impression poetically truer than either by itself. Similarly, Troilus's failure to prevent Criseyde from leaving Troy, while it is the result of his own free will, might still be ascribed to fate, for in order to have stopped her Troilus would have had to be someone other than Troilus, and this he could not be.

In a more universal and more tragic sense, the impossibility of a human being's becoming anything but what he is is one of the principal points – perhaps the principal point – that the poem makes, and it is toward this point that the poem has been steadily moving. The form, as has been said above, is that of a history, the end of which is known, being lived by personages who do not know their end, and presented at times as if neither narrator nor reader knows it. Preoccupied constantly during the presentation with the charm and delight of humanity as represented by Criseyde and Pandarus, we can little more believe that things will turn out as they do than can Troilus. The fact that they turn out as they do almost seems, at times, a violation of our idea of reality; within the poem we are now and again apt to ascribe the ending to a malevolent fate which, in order to bring about what it foresees, contorts and constrains events and

persons from their natural course. This is the ultimate conclusion of
which Troilus is capable in his lifetime. His long soliloquy in Book IV
(958–1078) on predestination and free will comes in its tortured cir-
cularity to nothing more than a statement that what God has foreseen
must be – that free will does not exist. This soliloquy, of course,
precedes any suspicion on his part of Criseyde's infidelity, so that he is
not forced to consider the problem of her free will operating evilly.
When suspicions have once occurred, he is no longer able to think
even as clearly as he does here, but vacillates pathetically between the
two conflicting realities, Criseyde's apparently true love and Criseyde's
faithlessness. His still relatively happy ignorance stops him in his
soliloquy from going to the extreme of accusing his god of devising a
plot that does not fit its characters; but this is an accusation that
occasional readers have, with some reason, made against Chaucer the
poet, just as Chaucer the narrator comes close to making it against
his old books.

But to the profoundly medieval, profoundly Christian Chaucer
there could be no other plot because there could be no other characters.
According to some medieval thinkers, the whole duty of the historian
was to find in recorded history the image of instability: it is in this
sense that the *Monk's Tale* presents history, bad as the tale is. The
premise underlying such a definition of history is that natural, fallen
man is unstable. Chaucer, while surely not bound to any arbitrary
point of view, presents in *Troilus and Criseyde* a pattern of human
instability. Criseyde is its chief exponent in terms of human character;
Pandarus in terms of human action. Troilus comes, because of his
trouthe, as near to stability as man may come; but within a world
where mutation is the law – and in a world in which the stability of a
Christian God does not exist – it does him no good. Given Boethius
or Christian doctrine, Troilus might have progressed beyond the
point he does in his soliloquy on forcordination. As it is, he concludes
where Boethius began in his *Consolation of Philosophy*, before Philosophy had persuaded him that he must not commit himself wholly
and exclusively to this unstable world. Troilus's *trouthe* is, as has been
said above, a real value; but within the terms set by the poem, it
must remain only a moral value, imitating one aspect of God, who is
Trouthe, but hopelessly limited in other respects. Despite its alternate
meaning, reality, it cannot help Troilus perceive ultimate reality,

which only God can perceive; conversely, it cannot defend him
against illusion – the illusion of Criseyde's stability, of the enduring power of human love. It cannot, in short, enable him to see that
of all the conflicting realities the poem presents none is in the end real,
since compared to the reality of God no earthly substance has reality.

The poem comes to its tragic conclusion by no such bald statement
as the above. We have seen how in the ambiguity of the characterization of Criseyde and Pandarus there has been, since the beginning,
the potential of instability. One might say that in their very elusiveness, their unknowability, resides equally the image of unreality.
And we have since the beginning been fully aware of where the
story is leading, though our willingness to forget is the product of
Chaucer's art. As the poem approaches its climax – or anticlimax –
the poet so manipulates us that while we continue our intense involve-
ment with the characters, we begin to see them increasingly in the
light of historical generalization. Halfway through the fifth book
this manipulation appears most brilliantly. It is the ninth night after
Criseyde's departure, and we are taken to the Greek camp to see how
she is faring with her plots to return to Troy, as she had promised,
on the tenth day (v 686 ff.). Her pathetic soliloquy, so futile, so devoid
of resource, so spiritless, leaves us infinitely saddened. The narrator,
seemingly in hot pursuit of his story, turns quickly to Diomede, and
for a moment we enter that blunt, aggressive, unillusioned mind.
Diomede's interior monologue completed, the narrator, as if suddenly
recalling his own failure to characterize Diomede earlier, gives us a
one-stanza pen-portrait of him. And then, by a curious afterthought,
he gives a three-stanza description of Criseyde and a two-stanza
description of Troilus (v 806–40). The quality of these is, contextual-
ly, strange in the extreme: they are impersonal, trivial, oversimpli-
fied – as if a historian had collected all the information there was
about several persons of no special significance and were listing it,
not because of its inherent interest, but because the historian's duty is
to assemble and preserve any sort of scraps turned up during his
research. And indeed these scraps are in a very real sense the oldest
historical material relating to the story of Troilus and Criseyde, the
sparse material from which the full-grown story eventually sprang.
Chaucer's source for the portraits is not Boccaccio, but rather a sixth-
century narrative of the fall of Troy ascribed to Dares the Phrygian.

This book pads out its paltry fiction with brief descriptions of important people concerned with the Trojan war, among them Diomede, Troilus, and Criseyde, described just as Chaucer describes them in Book V but still some centuries removed from the relationship later writers were to give them. When, nearing the end of his poem, Chaucer saw that it was time to turn from the guise of the passionately committed participant to the guise of the objective, remote, detached historian, he did so with a vengeance. Perhaps nowhere else in the poem are the two conflicting versions of reality more boldly juxtaposed. Certainly nowhere else is the shock so great as when the historian, having listed a miscellany of Criseyde's attributes, some trivial but all agreeable enough, brings the portrait to the muted conclusion:

Tendre-herted, slydynge of corage;
But trewely, I kan nat telle hire age.

(v 825–6)

Slydynge of corage: the simple unemphatic statement of Criseyde's instability of heart is not even the climax of the portrait. From the point of view of the realistic historian, human nature is capable only of anticlimax.

The sudden re-emergence of the detached historian at this point in Book V provides a kind of foretaste of the dominant mood in which the poem concludes; but the narrator's other guise continues to reappear whenever Criseyde is mentioned. Indeed, Chaucer's manipulation of the two guises, and through them of the reader, is nowhere more adroit than in his handling of Criseyde's betrayal. Time and again while the narrative inexorably demonstrates the progress of her infidelity the narrator leaps to her defence, and by the very inadequacy of the defence reinforces the reader's condemnation of her. The most striking instance of this technique occurs after Diomede has visited Criseyde on the eleventh day, when she has already broken her promise to Troilus. The interview she has with Diomede is not described; instead the narrator rapidly summarizes all the later history of her amorous dealings with the Greek (v 1030–50). And then, having given to the whole history of her treachery the emotional impact of a single action committed in a day or two, he indignantly asserts that while his books are silent on this subject, all this successful wooing by Diomede must have taken a long time!

As if this were not enough, he carries us back to Troy to show us Troilus, standing on the walls, still scanning the outlying roads for his beloved. Months of action have rushed by in the Greek camp, but in Troy it is still only the tenth day, the day Criseyde is to return.

Thus the poem moves with mounting emotional force to its conclusion. The actual ending of the poem (v 1765 ff.) – generally though incorrectly called its epilogue – gathers up with extraordinary effectiveness the many moods and many attitudes which have alternated in the course of the narrative. There is both low and high comedy – and perhaps high truth, too – in the poet's prayer to 'every lady bright of hue' that she not blame him for Criseyde's faithlessness, and in his baldly illogical claim that he has told the story 'not only' that men should beware of women but 'mostly' that women should beware of men. There is comedy also in the poet's self-conscious fear that he has failed to make himself clear, that readers will mis-scan his lines and miss his meaning. The works of the great poets of the past with which he fears his 'little book' (of more than eight thousand lines) might be compared make him nervous. His successive echoes of the first line of the *Aeneid* (1765–6) and of the first line of the *Iliad* (1800) suggest that he is afraid he ought to have written not a love poem but a martial epic – if only he were up to it. In any case, may God give him power to write a comedy.

These outbursts of nervousness – which are perhaps a kind of mocking image of man's inability to make sense of the materials his own history provides him – intrude upon the story before it is actually finished, and almost by an afterthought the poet returns to it in order to tell the end of Troilus. Inevitably enough, history does not permit Troilus to kill Diomede or to be killed by him: even that meagre satisfaction is denied to our sense of the way things ought to be. Instead, Troilus is killed by Achilles. Only when he has been thus freed from his earthly misery is he rewarded for his earthly fidelity: he is admitted into heaven, a heaven that is physically pagan but theologically Christian. (It is not the first time in medieval literature that *trouthe* allows a non-Christian to enter into a Christian heaven, for according to both Langland and Dante the same quality had raised to heaven the Emperor Trajan.) From his remote sphere Troilus is granted that vision of the world he lately left which enables him to see in full perspective the pettiness and fragility to which he had committed his being: his *trouthe*, finally receiving its philosophic extension, is made whole. But Troilus's is not the ultimate vision in the poem. His could come only after his death, but to the Christian reader the vision is possible at all times during his life. In the last lines of the poem Chaucer gathers up all the flickering emotions, the flickering loves with which he has been dealing and unites them into the great harmony of the only true and perfect love. All the conflicting realities and illusions of the old story are subsumed under the one supreme reality.

Thus the conclusion asserts most solemnly the principle – towards which the poem has been steadily moving – that man's nature and his works are and must be unstable and unreal. Some readers are apt to feel, however, that the poet's final statement cancels all the human values which his own loving treatment has made real; that he is, in effect, saying either that he ought not to have written the poem or that the reader ought not to have read it. This feeling is natural enough in view of Chaucer's entirely specific condemnation of all things mortal except man's ability to love God. But it must be borne in mind that the ending is a part of the poem, and no matter how sincere a statement it is on the part of the poet, the ending combines with all the other parts of the poem to produce the poem's own ultimate meaning. As has been said before, nothing a poet writes is ever cancelled out by anything else he writes, and both the haunting loveliness of the story of Troilus and Criseyde and the necessity of rejecting it remain valid for the reader. And also, one may suppose, for Chaucer. For the lines in which he condemns the world –

... and thynketh al nys but a faire
This world, that passeth soone as floures faire –

(v 1840–41)

poignantly enhance the very thing that he is repudiating. It is in the quality of these lines, taken as an epitome of the quality of the whole poem, that the ultimate meaning of *Troilus* lies. The simultaneous awareness of the real validity of human values – and hence our need to commit ourselves to them – and of their inevitable transitoriness – and hence our need to remain uncommitted – represents a complex, mature, truly tragic vision of mankind. The prayer of the poem's last stanza suggests the poet's faith that his vision is also subsumed under the vision of the Author of all things.

(965–80)

Rosemary Woolf

'Chaucer as a Satirist in the *General Prologue* to the *Canterbury Tales*',
Critical Quarterly, vol. 1 1959

Many people nowadays acquire an early and excessive familiarity
with the *General Prologue* to the *Canterbury Tales*, which later blunts
their sharpness of perception. Since the *Prologue* is read at school,
necessarily out of its literary-historical context, its methods of satire
seem to have an inevitability and rightness which preclude either
surprise or analysis. This natural tendency to remain uncritically
appreciative of the *Prologue* has been partly confirmed by various
works of criticism, which, though admirable in many ways, effu-
sively reiterate that 'here is God's plenty': they thus awaken an
enthusiastic response to the vitality and variety of the characterization in the *Prologue*, at the cost of making the exact manner and tone
of Chaucer's satire quite indistinct. Despite the bulk of Chaucerian
criticism, there is still need for a detailed and disciplined examination
of Chaucer's style and methods of satire, which would include a
careful consideration of Chaucer's work against the background of
classical and medieval satire. Such a study would be of considerable
scholarship and length: it is the purpose of this short article only to
make a few general points about Chaucer's methods of satire.

It is sometimes taken for granted that the satirist speaks in his own
voice, and that any references to his opinions and feelings are a literal
record of his experience. This assumption perhaps requires testing
and reconsideration with reference to any satirist, but it is never more
dangerous than when it is accepted without limitation about Chaucer.
Chaucer was writing at a time when there was no tradition of personal poetry in a later Romantic sense: a poet never made his individual emotions the subject-matter of his poetry. Though the personal
pronoun 'I' is used frequently in medieval narrative and lyric poetry,
it is usually a dramatic 'I', that is the 'I' is a character in the poem,
bearing no different relation to the poet from that of the other charac-

ters, or it expresses moral judgements or proper emotions which belong, or should belong, to everybody. Chaucer's use of an 'I' character in his early poems belongs to the tradition of such characters in dream visions, but with an ingenious variation that the character appears naïve, well-meaning, and obtuse, and the joke thus depends on the discrepancy between this figure in the poetry and the poet of wit and intelligence who wrote the whole. Thus this treatment of the 'I' character is new in that it presupposes the poet in a way that the other characters do not.

It is well known that this character re-appears strikingly in the links of the *Canterbury Tales*, when he is rebuked for telling a dull story, but his presence in the *Prologue* has not been particularly stressed, yet it is through this character that both the apparently vivid individuality of the pilgrims and the satiric aim are achieved. Though there are various departures from consistency (to be noticed later), it is through the eyes of Chaucer the pilgrim, not Chaucer the poet, that the characters in the *Prologue* are chiefly presented. Obviously the choice of detail shows the sharp selectiveness of the satirist, but the friendly, enthusiastic, unsophisticated, unjudging tone is that of Chaucer the pilgrim.

From this invention there result two important advantages. Firstly by his fiction of having been a close companion of his characters, Chaucer suggests their reality and individuality, an individuality which is largely an illusion brought about by poetic skill. Chaucer makes us feel that we know them as individuals, though often, apart from physical description, they are simply representative portraits of various groups in society – friars, monks, summoners, nuns, etc. The same details of their tastes and behaviour can be found in any medieval moral denunciation of these people. Secondly, in his satiric character-sketches, Chaucer achieves a two-fold irony. He implies that most of the information which he gives us derives, not from a narrative writer's omniscience but from the characters' own conversation. In other words Chaucer unobtrusively uses a pointed satirical method, by which the characters are shown to have erred so far from the true moral order, that they are not ashamed to talk naturally and with self-satisfaction about their own inversion of a just and religiously-ordered way of life. At the same time Chaucer makes his response to this that of a man who accepts and repeats with enthusiasm, and without criticism, whatever he is told. It has been observed before how often Chaucer implies or states explicitly that each of his characters is an outstanding person (although a distinction should be made here between the statement when made of a virtuous character, such as the Parson, when it comes as the climax of a well-ordered enumeration of his virtues, and when it appears as a random remark in the sketches of the satirized characters). This has been explained as part of Chaucer's genial enthusiastic appreciation of all kinds of people or, in a manner less wildly wrong, as part of a literary convention of magnifying each character (Kemp Malone, *Chapters on Chaucer*, p. 167). But it is surely Chaucer the easily-impressed pilgrim who so indiscriminately praises the characters, sharing with them through an obtuse innocence the immoral premises from which they speak.

Chaucer the poet, for instance, must have shared the common knowledge and opinion in the late fourteenth century, that the friars, instead of serving all classes of men indifferently, though with a special tenderness for the poor who reflected the poverty of Christ, instead chiefly sought out the rich and those from whom they could make profit, and took the opportunity given by the privacy of the personal interview and confession for exploitation and unchastity. All this Chaucer could not have failed to have known to be an abuse, evil and widespread, of what had originally been a holy and noble conception. But Chaucer the character relates these details of his fellow pilgrims as though they were both inoffensive and idiosyncratic and in this way both the satiric point and the illusion of individuality are achieved. Similarly it was a common accusation that daughters of aristocratic households, who entered a convent, often did not discard their former manners and affectations. Genteel table manners, careful attention to dress, and a narrowly sentimental affection for pet animals might possibly in a noble household appear signs of a refined sensibility, but in a convent their worldliness would be plain. But of the distinction between the lady of the house and a nun Chaucer the pilgrim is ignorant, so he records all the details sweetly, as though there were no matter here for blame.

The clearest example, however, of this method is the account of the Monk. Just as in the description of the Friar Chaucer shows clearly by a sudden change to colloquial rhythms that he is ostensibly repeating the Friar's own arguments for not caring for the poor,

'It is nat honest, it may nat avaunce . . .', so in the account of the
Monk Chaucer repeats the Monk's arguments, and then even adds
a reply, 'And I seyde his opinion was good', supporting this by two
foolish rhetorical questions and a blustering retort 'Lat Austyn
have his swynk to hym reserved'. That Chaucer the poet would re-
ject the authority of St Augustine is as manifestly untrue as that he
had not the skill to tell an entertaining story. His protested sympathy
with the Monk is of the same kind as Juvenal's stated agreement
('you have just cause for bitterness') with the utterly debased and
contemptible Naevolus in the ninth satire. To suppose that Chaucer's
attitude here is ambivalent is to be deceived by the sweet blandness of
Chaucer's mask, just as to search for historical prototypes of the
characters is to be deceived by the brilliant accuracy of Chaucer's
sleight of hand, whereby he suggests an individuality which is not
there.

Amongst many other examples of the simplicity of Chaucer the
pilgrim may be noticed the frequent device of giving a false explanation of a statement – the Physician loved gold because it was of use
in medicine – and the making of absurd judgements: the remark that
the wives of the Guildsmen would be to blame if they did not support
and approve their husbands in their smug prosperity, or the query
of whether it was not 'by a full fair grace' that the Maunciple was
able to cheat and outwit his learned employers. It is in passages such
as the latter that the ironic tone of Chaucer the satirist can be most
clearly heard behind the blank wall of obtuseness of Chaucer the
pilgrim. Illustrations of the naïvete of Chaucer the character could be
multiplied to the point of tediousness, and so too there could be
laboured at length the demonstration that the substance of the description of each character consists solely of common medieval observation about the group to which he belongs. It should be added,
however, that the appearance of individuality is not achieved by the
intimate tone of Chaucer the character alone: at least equally important is the style. The neat grace of Chaucer's lines often deceptively
suggests that he has made a sharp and lucid observation, when in
fact it is but a commonplace, and the precision lies, not in its thought,
but in the style. Thus his method of pretending that the generalization about a group is the idiosyncrasy of an individual is given
persuasive force by his exact use of words and the shapeliness of his

couplets. There is an interesting contrast to this in the undisguisedly
generalized attack of Langland, the generality of which is driven home
by his swift but sometimes indiscriminate use of forceful words, and
his form of the alliterative metre, which has within the line a great
strength and impressive rhythm, but no larger pattern, so that there
seems to be no metrical reason why one line should not succeed
another without end.

The question to what extent we are aware of Chaucer the poet
in the *Prologue* is not easy to determine. Sometimes an example of
obtrusive poetic skill draws attention to him: it is Chaucer the pilgrim
who observes mildly of the unhealthy sore on the Cook's leg that it
was a pity, but the placing of this one line in the middle of the account
of the fine dishes made by the Cook exceeds the licence of poetic
cleverness which may by convention be allowed to a dull character
in poetry. Similarly the image which implies censure or ridicule is
self-evidently the satirist's: the Monk's bridle jingling like a chapel
bell, the Squire's coat so embroidered with flowers that it was like
a meadow, the snow-storm of food and drink in the Franklin's house,
the fiery-red cherubym's face of the Summoner, all undisguisedly
spring from the imagination of a satiric poet. Occasionally Chaucer
even speaks outright in his own voice, making a pointed exposure of
affectation or self-deception, which is in a quite different style of satire,
and provides an exception to the general truth that the characters are
not the result of actual observation. A well-known example is the
comment about the Lawyer:

Nowher so bisy a man as he ther nas,
And yet he semed bisier than he was.

(I 321–2)

This kind of remark shows the same mocking penetration into the
ridiculous complexities of human feeling and behaviour, as Chaucer
had already displayed in *Troilus and Criseyde*, from which one
striking example may be quoted: it was a commonplace in medieval
descriptions of a lover that by pining he grew pale and thin; but in
Chaucer's more subtle description, Troilus in the humourless self-
absorption of his love *imagines* that he has grown so pale and thin
that everybody notices and comments upon it. At first sight Chaucer
seems to be an exception to the general rule of the classical period and

eighteenth century that the satirist is to be feared. His disguise of Chaucer the pilgrim and elsewhere a sustained friendliness and moderation of tone imply that no man could be less alarming to those who knew him. But, whilst undoubtedly he was the less to be feared in that he did not make individual contemporaries the objects of his satire, as a century later Skelton was to do, yet only people free from all excesses of emotion and affectation could be sure that they would not be the source of some detail shrewdly observed in Chaucer's work.

Chaucer also speaks in his own voice in his occasional denunciation of evil in the descriptions of the Miller and the Pardoner, and most effectively in his descriptions of the virtuous characters, one drawn from each order of society with the addition of the Clerk. In these Chaucer establishes the true moral standard by which the topsy-turvyness of the rest may be measured. It was a tradition of satire to provide an ideal standard: some earlier medieval Latin satirists made use of the classical fable of the Golden Age, identifying it uneasily with the Garden of Eden: an example is the famous *De Contemptu Mundi* of Bernard of Cluny; Langland in a more complex and magnificent scheme makes his standard the pure charity of the Redemption of man by Christ. But Chaucer, lacking Langland's sublimity of imagination, but with a shrewd, clear thoughtfulness, gives a positive analysis of representative types of a well-ordered society, religious and secular. The detailed justice of these descriptions prevents the actual satire from seeming too mild or perhaps too pessimistic. Without them Chaucer's satire might seem to have too much detachment, too much ironic acquiescence. In Langland's angry denunciatory satire there is by implication a hope of reform; but in Chaucer's one feels the tone of a man who, aware of the incongruity between the gravity of the abuse and his own inability to help, is moved to an ironic and superficially good-humoured laughter. The virtuous characters, however, by their very presence imply a censure of the rest, which dispels any impression of over-sophisticated aloofness. The idea that Chaucer loved his satirized characters despite or including their faults is of course false, and springs from an imprecise consideration of Chaucer's methods of satire.

To what extent Chaucer was influenced by classical and medieval traditions of satire remains the final difficult but fascinating question. There is no incontrovertible evidence about his knowledge of classical satirists: Juvenal he quotes from and mentions by name, but the quotations he could very easily have gained at second hand; Horace he does not mention at all, but since, as other critics have pointed out, he does not mention Boccaccio either, this negative evidence is worthless. Juvenal had attacked with moral horror the widespread vices of his own time under the satiric disguise of describing historical personages of a previous age. This device was not imitated by the Fathers or the medieval satirists who were influenced by him, and the writers of the Middle Ages, with their preoccupation with what was common to all men rather than with what makes one man different from another, were not concerned to give any appearance of particularity to their satire. The result was either the blackened generalized picture of all men as totally corrupt, found in the *De Contemptu Mundi*, or the combination of allegory with satire, ingeniously used, though not invented, by Langland. But though the aim of Chaucer's satire is, like Langland's, the distinctive vices of people in various orders and occupations throughout society, he does not generalize but, like Juvenal, reduces the generalization to a description of particular characters. This, however, seems to be Chaucer's only resemblance to Juvenal, since self-evidently there could not be a greater difference of tone than there is between Juvenal's savage vehemence and Chaucer's specious mildness.

The resemblances between Chaucer and Horace are more subtle and more specific. The object of Horace's satire had been different from Juvenal's, in that Horace was chiefly concerned with those who disrupted the social harmony of life, the fool, the bore, the miser, and these he portrayed with a minute and particular observation of habit and conversation, which gives the impression that his description is of an individual, though by definition not unique, personality. His account, for instance, of the host who makes dinner intolerable for his guests by a tedious analysis of the sources and method of cooking of each dish, suggests a recognizable personality, not a moral generalization about excessive eating and drinking. The tone of Horace's satire is not designed to arouse horror or anger, but amused contempt for something worthless. It is obvious that this satiric manner required a sophistication not usually possessed in the Middle Ages, and a point of view less easily identifiable with the Christian than that of Juvenal. For, though evil was seen as a fit object for laughter in the Middle Ages, it was a strong laughter at the ugly and grotesque – the devils in the mystery plays, for example – rather than the slight ironic smile of the civilized man at those who deviate from reason and intelligence.

Chaucer shares some characteristics with Horace, though there is no certainty whether by influence, or by coincidence and some affinity of temper. He has in common with Horace the easy tone of a man talking to friends who share his assumptions and sympathies, though usually with a deceptive twist: for when Horace meets the characters in his satires, he expects his audience to sympathize with his misery, whereas Chaucer, as we have already seen, pretends that the situation was delightful and the characters to be admired. He shares with Horace too some other characteristics already noticed, such as the use of comic images, and, above all, the quick observation of human affectation, and the suggestion of a recognizable personality as in the lines quoted about the Lawyer. Chaucer, however, extends Horatian ridicule to the kind of objects satirized in the Juvenalian tradition, and modifies it by the tone of pretended naïvete, not found in Horace's style, but almost certainly learnt, at least in part, from Ovid, whose works Chaucer had undoubtedly read and who might indeed be called Chaucer's master.

The fact that it is relevant to ask the question, was Chaucer influenced by classical satirists, is in itself interesting, and throws light on Chaucer's distinctiveness. Though it cannot be answered definitely, his indebtedness to classical writers in general is indisputable, and is most interestingly noticeable in the fact that he thought of himself as a poet in a way that earlier medieval writers seem not to have done. He is the first English medieval poet explicitly to accept the permanent value of his work, and hence to care about the unsettled state of the language and its dialectal variety, the first to see himself as of the same kind as the classical poets. The writers of medieval lyrics, romances, plays, etc., almost certainly had a workaday conception of themselves, and did not think of a poet as a man of particular perception and judgement, but as a man who wrote verse in a craftsmanlike way for specific use. But Chaucer sees himself as a poet in the classical tradition, and it is for this reason that, despite the fact that the substance of his satiric portraits are medieval commonplaces, and despite his usual disguise of Chaucer the pilgrim, behind this disguise, and sometimes heard openly, is the truly personal tone of the satirist, which is quite un-medieval.

(150–57)

Bertrand H. Bronson

from *In Search of Chaucer* 1960

The evidence . . . seems to show that Chaucer and his contemporaries more frequently raised their eyes to the heavens than lowered them to the earth. The continual references in his work to the movements and positions of the heavenly bodies far outweigh his allusions to the natural scene as of significance to men's lives. A tree, a mountain, flowers – excepting symbolic daisies! – beasts and birds – unless they could talk! – had slight influence on man's conduct, his moral life, his spirit, otherwise than in generally increasing his seasonal enjoyment of living. Not for nothing, in his noble ballade on Truth, does Chaucer enjoin his friend

Know thy contree, look up! . . .
Hold the heye wey, and lat thy gost thee lede.
(*Truth*, 19–20)

His references, too, to natural objects are incidental and conveyed in simile or parenthesis, for the most part. They vivify our sense of appearances, or they serve to localize action, but they are seldom introduced for their own sake. When Arcite and Palamon engage each other in mortal combat,

Thou myghtest wene that this Palamon
In his fightyng were a wood leon,
And as a crueel tigre was Arcite;
As wilde bores gonne they to smyte,
That frothen whit as foom for ire wood.
(*Canterbury Tales*, 1 1655–9)

Again, the description of Alison in the *Miller's Tale* is full of natural comparisons: 'as any wezele hir body gent and smal'; her brows 'were bent and blake as any sloo';

She was ful moore blisful on to see
Than is the newe pere-jonette tree,
And softer than the wolle is of a wether;

(*Canterbury Tales*, I 3247-9)

her song 'was as loude and yerne | As any swalwe sittynge on a berne'; she could skip like any kid or calf following the mother;

Hir mouth was sweete as bragot or the meeth,
Or hoord of apples leyd in hey or heeth;

(I 3261-2)

she was as skittish as a pretty colt. Incidentally, again, sometimes a single natural detail will evoke a scene with marvellous effectiveness, as when Criseyde lies in bed savouring the first revelation that Prince Troilus is in love with her, and wondering how she shall respond:

A nyghtyngale, upon a cedir grene,
Under the chambre wal ther as she ley,
Ful loude song ayein the moone shene,
Peraunter, in his briddes wise, a lay
Of love, that made hire herte fressh and gay.

(*Troilus and Criseyde*, II 918-22)

With equal simplicity the poet suggests nightfall in two evocative lines of which the very absence of specific image constitutes the magic:

And white thynges wexen dymme and donne
For lak of lyght, and sterres for t'apere.

(*Troilus and Criseyde*, II 908-9)

In a poet with so keen an eye for the concretely telling detail, the avoidance in such passages of particular natural description is surprising. But I think it is also characteristic. The scenes that he gives us are suggestive, not usually specific: they are composed of generalized elements – of details, but of classes, without individualization;

rather identified than described. A memorable example, untypical in its fullness, occurs in the *Knight's Tale*:

The bisy larke, messager of day,
Salueth in hir song the morwe gray,
And firy Phebus riseth up so bright
That al the orient laugheth of the light,
And with his stremes dryeth in the greves
The silver dropes hangynge on the leves.

(*Canterbury Tales*, I 1491–6)

This is sheer legerdemain. We do not so much see, as experience, a country sunrise. The lark is not there to be seen, but only heard; the drying of the dews of night is not to be witnessed, but only its effects. The grey dawn disappears with the arrival of the fiery sun: truth is beauty, and we are completely satisfied. Arcite rises to enjoy the merry May morning, but he has missed the miracle of its coming.

Quite as surprising and miraculous are the eighteen lines that open the *Canterbury Tales*. So far as concerns the description of nature in pictorial detail, these lines are absolutely featureless: there is not a single visual image. Yet a profound realization of the stir and meaning of Spring's re-birth – of April to the end of time – has been implanted in our consciousness before the paragraph concludes. But when a detail of visible Spring flowers is later introduced, they are on the person of the Squire, in the embroidery of his gay clothing.

To us, nursed on the poetry of the last two centuries, on the small celandine, the primrose by the river's brim, the single flower in the crannied wall, this is a phenomenon well worthy of remark. The more so in that there is to be found in the lines quoted little or nothing of that conceptual abstraction characteristic of the eighteenth century, the merits of which also we are beginning to rediscover. Zephirus, to be sure, and perhaps *nature* ('so priketh hem nature in hir corages') are personifications, of a factual kind. Yet there is no *scene*. It is all generalized; and we return to the assertion that, in spite of his vividness and lack of abstraction, Chaucer seldom tries to describe an actual landscape or natural scene, or even to give us enough detail to enable us to compose one with any distinctness. It does not seem important to him to do so. What interests him on the surface of this earth is primarily man, not his physical environment.

All the important exceptions, all the more considerable landscape paintings, to be found in his work, occur in the dream-visions, and there is a significant reason, I believe, for this fact. It is that the dream scenery is not a picture of earthly nature but of idealized nature, a paradise not subject to chance or change, to decay or death.

Th'air of that place so attempre was
That nevere was ther grevaunce of hot ne cold;
There wex ek every holsom spice and gras;
No man may there waxe sek ne old;
Yit was there joye more a thousandfold
Than man can telle; ne nevere wolde it nyghte,
But ay cler day to any manes syghte.
                                        (*Parliament of Fowls*, 204–10)

It is a nature beyond time, and it is worth extended description just because it is unreal and unearthly in that sense.

For the last two centuries, at least, thoughts of the natural world have been involved, in greater or less degree, with the idea of divinity, of the imperishable and the sublime; of an immanent deity;

Of something far more deeply interfused,
Whose dwelling is the light of setting suns,
And the round ocean and the living air.

It is impossible for us to detach ourselves completely from these feelings and associations, no matter what the complexion of our religious beliefs. But, on the contrary, Chaucer was probably never much tempted to *attach* such sentiments to the visual scene. Although the 'noble goddesse Nature' is most beautiful, and, as 'the vicaire of the almighty Lord', acknowledged of all living creatures as in immediate command, she is rather familiar than awe-inspiring as Chaucer presents her – even in the *Parliament* especially designed to exalt her idea, while she administers the 'lawe of Kynde'. Things beneath the moon, apart from the soul of man, were of the earth, earthly, subject to time and fortune; things above the moon were timeless and eternal. And therefore – in the sense of my context – Chaucer was disposed to look up to the heavens and not down to earth. It is significant, I believe, that where he does make use in his poetry of natural scenes, he almost always emphasizes the most ethereal aspect of them, the least *embodied*, so to say: the qualities of light and shadow and colour, which borrow their attributes from above:

Bright was the day, and blew the firmament;
Phebus hath of gold his stremes doun ysent
To gladen every flour with his warmnesse. . . .

> (*Canterbury Tales*, IV 2219–21)

(16–20)

J. V. Cunningham

'Convention as Structure: The *Prologue* to the *Canterbury Tales*', *Tradition and Poetic Structure* 1960

A literary convention is obviously a principle of order in poetry. I shall maintain in this essay, against the consensus of scholarly opinion, that Chaucer derives the structure of the *Prologue* to the *Canterbury Tales* from one of the most common of the literary conventions of his time.

The *Prologue* is the only one of Chaucer's major works for which there is said to be no model, no genuine antecedents in the tradition. The *Book of the Duchess*, the *House of Fame*, the *Parliament of Fowls*, and the *Prologue* to the *Legend of Good Women*, for example, all belong to the well-recognized tradition of the dream vision, whose history and peculiar features have been described at length in a number of standard monographs. The antecedents of the *Troilus* are well known, and Chaucer himself assigns it to the medieval category of tragedy. The shorter complaints belong to a common literary type. But the most familiar of Chaucer's works and the one generally thought to be the best seems, as a whole, to be without literary predecessors, though there are, of course, sources for particular aspects and details. This circumstance has been construed by the literary historians in Chaucer's favour. They have seen in it the triumph of originality over convention and of realism over artifice. They have pictured Chaucer going directly to reality and reporting what he found. And so the defect of literary history becomes the glory of literary criticism.

The state of the question is summarized by one scholar: 'For the *Prologue*, as for the general device of the Canterbury pilgrimage, no real model has been found.'[1] Another remarks: 'There had never before . . . been the like of that singularly *modern* thing – to use our most complacent term of approbation – the *Prologue*.'[2] And a third: 'no source for' the *Prologue*, 'the most distinctive of Chaucer's works, has ever been discovered.'[3] The features which scholarship has particularly distinguished as unprecedented are the series of portraits in the *Prologue* and the device of a journey, and especially of a pilgrimage, as the frame for a series of stories. For example, the scholar continues in the passage just alluded to, 'No such series of descriptions [of characters] is to be found in any work of ancient or medieval literature which could have come to Chaucer's attention.'[4] It is recognized, of course, that 'individual sketches of knights or priests or peasants are common enough', that the 'allegorical writings of the age, both sacred and secular, abound in personified types . . . some of which Chaucer clearly imitates.' But the general conclusion is that 'in none of his predecessors has there been found a gallery of portraits like that in the *Prologue*, and there is very little that is comparable in later English poetry except in Chaucer's avowed imitators.'[5]

For the second feature – the general idea of a frame story – it is agreed that no particular model need be sought. Chaucer had already used it in the *Legend of Good Women*, and the idea was common in the tradition. For the device of a journey, and especially of a pilgrimage, there is a distant analogue in Boccaccio's *Decameron* and a closer one in a contemporary Italian work in which the tales are actually told by a single figure in the course of a journey. But the difficulty here has been that, though Chaucer could have been acquainted with these works, we have no evidence that he was. Furthermore, what has seemed to modern scholarship the special merit of Chaucer's device – the interplay of personalities on the journey – is only rudimentary in these possible models. The conclusion has been, as the latest writer on the subject puts it: 'There is really no necessity to search for the "source" of Chaucer's pilgrimage. It would, indeed, have been strange had there been no reflections in imaginative literature of the common medieval custom of going on a journey with a party of travellers.'[1] This is the general opinion. 'For his particular device of a group of persons on a pilgrimage to Canterbury on horseback,' we are told in the standard work, 'he needed only to draw on life about him. . . . Thus the device of a pilgrimage as a narrative framework was repeatedly presented to him in actual life, and he was at liberty to adopt it for his literary purpose with whatever degree of realism he found convenient.'[2]

It is noteworthy that this flight to reality on the part of eminent scholars is always subsequent to a search for an antecedent of the motif and a failure to find it. This is almost too obviously making a virtue of necessity and suggests that perhaps the search for antecedents has been misconducted. It has been a search for the prior appearance of the particular motif. And when this search fails, it has been felt that the only alternative is the recourse to reality. But the alternative is as unsatisfactory as the original undertaking, for it does not explain what it pretends to explain.

The pilgrimage was undoubtedly a common occurrence in Chaucer's day, and he had in all likelihood seen a good many groups of pilgrims among whom were to be found close analogues to the characters in the *Prologue*. Scholars have been concerned to establish that he lived in Greenwich on the Canterbury road, where he could have seen groups of pilgrims passing before his window, perhaps while he was writing the *Canterbury Tales*. Kittredge is willing to wager he had undertaken a Canterbury pilgrimage himself.[3] The argument is that what he found day after day in real life he needed no literary precedent to invent. But this is not so. It is not the direct observation of murders and of the process of detection that leads to the construction of a detective story. Nor was it the

1 W. W. Lawrence, *Chaucer and the Canterbury Tales*, New York, 1950, p. 38.
2 R. A. Pratt and K. Young in W. F. Bryan and G. Dempster (eds.), *Sources and Analogues of Chaucer's Canterbury Tales*, Chicago, 1941, p. 2.
3 'There is not one chance in a hundred that he had not gone on a Canterbury pilgrimage himself' (G. L. Kittredge, *Chaucer and his Poetry*, Cambridge, Mass., 1915, p. 149).

perception of violent death in high places that prompted the Elizabethan dramatist to compose a tragedy. What a writer finds in real life is to a large extent what his literary tradition enables him to see and to handle.

It may be conceded that experience is sometimes obtrusively at odds with tradition. We can see that it is, for we can see how tradition has been modified to render it more supple to experience. But the one term is always tradition, not unalterable but never abandoned, as, of course, the other term is always experience. The one is form, method, a way of apprehending; the other is matter, realization, and what is apprehended. What we should be concerned with, then, is to discover, if possible, a literary form extant in Chaucer's tradition of which the *Prologue* to the *Canterbury Tales* is a realization. It must be a form that will account not only for particular motifs, for the device of the journey or the series of portraits, but also for the other elements of the work and for their order and succession.

A literary form exists only in what I call a tradition. I use that word in the sense in which we speak of the tradition of the hard-boiled detective story or say that Shakespeare's sonnets are in the tradition of the *Astrophel and Stella* sequence or, more generally, in the Petrarchan tradition. A tradition is the body of texts and inter-pretations current among a group of writers at a given time and place. The description of literary traditions is a principal subject of literary history, and the nature of a tradition can be reconstructed only by the methods of literary history. If one were to construct, for example, the tradition of a number of contemporary poets in America, it could be described in terms of the poetry of Eliot, of Pound, Hopkins, Auden, and some fragments of Donne and Marvell, together with the associated body of commentary, the 'new criticism'. When a poet in this tradition undertakes what he has learned to distinguish as a metaphysical poem, the principles that determine the realization of what he regards as a particular literary form – the appropriate subject, devices and structure – are principles located in that tradition.

It follows from this that a literary form is not simply an external principle of classification of literary works, as is the Dewey Decimal System in the public library, nor is it an Idea. It is rather a principle operative in the production of works. It is a scheme of experience recognized in the tradition and derived from prior works and from the descriptions of those works extant in the tradition. It is, moreover, a scheme that directs the discovery of material and detail and that orders the disposition of the whole. If a literary form is an Idea, it is an idea only in the sense that it is the idea that the writer and reader have of the form. Thus a literary form may vary somewhat from work to work, since it is only a summary description of those elements of the tradition that entered into the conception and realization as into the appreciation by a qualified reader of the particular work.

I come now to my thesis, which may as well be stated clearly and simply at the start. The literary form to which the *Prologue* to the *Canterbury Tales* belongs and of which it is a special realization is the form of the dream-vision prologue in the tradition of the *Romance of the Rose* and of the associated French and English poems of the subsequent century and a half. This is certainly to find the answer in the most obvious place, to find it, like the purloined letter, in plain sight. For if one were to look for the source of anything in Chaucer, the first place an experienced scholar would look is in the *Romance of the Rose* and its tradition. The *Romance*, it has been said, 'probably exerted on Chaucer a more lasting and more important influence than any other work in the vernacular literature of either France or England.'[1] There are throughout Chaucer innumerable borrowings in detail from that work, and four of Chaucer's most extended poems are clearly in the form of the dream vision: one of them, indeed, is explicitly a prologue framing a series of tales, as is the masterwork of Chaucer's contemporary and friend, John Gower. If one asks why the similarity of the Canterbury *Prologue* to this well-known type has not been seen before, the answer lies in the method by which the form has been described in the scholarship on the subject. It has been described in terms of particular motifs, but the motifs have not been generalized and regarded as functional in a structure. One scholar, for example, enumerates 'the regular features of the love-vision': 'the introductory device of reading a book, the discussion of sleeplessness and dreams, the setting on May-day or in the springtime, the vision itself, the guide (who in many poems

1 Robinson, p. 663.

takes the form of a helpful animal), and personified abstractions, Love, Fortune, Nature, and the like.'[1] There is only one element in this description that is also to be found in the Canterbury *Prologue*, and that is the setting in spring, an element which is common to many other literary forms in the Middle Ages.

But if we describe the Canterbury *Prologue* in terms of the scheme of experience which orders it, in terms of its elements and their succession, we will find a striking similarity to – in fact, an identity with – the scheme of the dream vision. The *Prologue* can be described accurately enough in this fashion: at a certain time of the year – and the season is then described – the author comes to a place, to the 'Tabard' in Southwark. He there meets a company, who are then depicted, one after the other in panel fashion. After a brief digression, one of the company, not described so far (our host, Harry Bailly), is singled out as a master of ceremonies and proposes the device that orders the remainder of the poem, the telling of tales on the journey.

I shall now describe in the same fashion the opening of the *Romance of the Rose* and of a number of English poems in the same tradition. The *Romance* begins with some expository remarks on the truth of dreams, illustrated by the dream related in this book whose name is the *Romance of the Rose* and whose subject is an autobiographical account – for everything fell out just as this dream relates – containing the art of love. After a brief prayer and praise of the lady, the dream begins. It is May, and there is an extended description of the season. The author walks out into the fields, crosses a stream, and comes to a garden enclosed by a wall. He then describes, one after the other, a series of allegorical portraits painted on the wall, ten in number. He wants to enter the garden but can find no way in. Walking around the wall, he comes finally to a wicket gate and pounds on it. The porter Idleness opens the door, 'whose hair was as yellow of hue as any basin newly scoured', and leads him into the garden, which is described at length. He finds Sir Mirth dancing and singing there in company and depicts the company in a series of set portraits, fifteen in number. He then walks in the garden, followed by the God of Love with his arrows ready. The garden is leisurely described, including the well where Narcissus died, which leads to

1 Robinson, p. 315.

the interpolated tale of Narcissus. In the well he sees a rose bush full of roses; there is one bud in especial which he has a great longing to pluck. At this point the God of Love, who has been stalking him, looses an arrow, and the author is committed to the sentimental enterprise which directs the remainder of the poem.

These are the elements and their order: after the preliminary matter and the dream, at a given time of the year – and there is a description of the season – the author comes to a place where he sees a number of allegorical characters painted on a wall and describes them; a guide then appears and leads him to another place, where he sees a company in action, though the characters are personifications, and describes them in the same manner. There follows a framed tale, and then one of the characters initiates the action which leads to the remainder of the poem. This character is not strictly a master of ceremonies, but he might in another poem and in other hands develop into one. The form is clearly not too unlike the form of the Canterbury *Prologue*, particularly if we collapse into one movement the two instances of an author's coming to a place and substitute for allegorical characters and personifications realistic portraits of representative members of society.

In other poems of this tradition the dream-vision prologue appears now as a separable and independent form, now as an element and sometimes a repeatable element in a work of larger scope, and most commonly as an introduction to a poem that continues now in one way, now in another. It is so used in the *Confessio Amantis*. In this poem, after a discursive and sententious preface, similar to, but more extensive than, the one in the *Romance of the Rose*, the author comes to his *matere*. He walks out in May and comes to a wood, where he begins to complain of his woe and falls into a swoon. On recovering, he utters a prayer to Cupid and Venus, whereupon he sees both of them come by. The King of Love, as he passes, throws an arrow through his heart, but the Queen pauses and speaks to him. On hearing what he has to say, she proposes the device: he shall confess to her priest, Genius. The essential structure of the *Romance* is here preserved, though in summary fashion. The nature description is quite brief, as are the descriptions of the characters. A swoon supplants the dream, and the interpolated prayer, an element in the opening of the *Romance*, occasions the appearance of the figures.

Nevertheless, the author goes out at a certain time of the year and comes to a place where he sees figures riding by, one of whom proposes the device that directs the remainder of the poem.

The scheme of the vision is repeated, this time without the dream, in the course of one of the tales that form the bulk of Gower's work. This is the tale of Rosiphelee (IV 1245 ff.). Before dawn on a May morning she walks out in a park through which runs a great river. She bids her women withdraw. She sees the flowers blooming, hears the birds singing, and sees all the animals, male paired with the female. As she looks around, she sees a company of ladies riding by, whose dress is then described. She wonders who they are and then sees a woman on a horse, who is described at length. She questions her about the company of ladies and receives the answer which changes the course of her life. Here is the typical nature description, the character who comes to a place where he sees a company, and, finally, the master of ceremonies, who disposes the particular device of this poem. And in this case it is no dream.

So much for Gower. Chaucer himself had written, if we allow the accepted chronology of his work, four dream visions by the time he undertook the *Prologue* to the *Canterbury Tales*; indeed, while he was engaged in the composition of the *Tales*, he rewrote with considerable thoroughness the last of these, the *Prologue* to the *Legend*. The earliest, the *Book of the Duchess*, begins with preliminary matter on the melancholy and sleeplessness of the author, who reads a book to pass the time, the tale of Ceyx and Alcyone. At one point in the tale Alcyone prays Juno for sleep and a dream, and the author decides to try the same method, whereupon he falls asleep and dreams. It is a May morning, with birds singing. He finds himself in a room with glass windows and full of pictures depicting the whole story of Troy and the whole *Romance of the Rose*, both text and gloss. He hears the sound of hunters, rises, takes his horse, and comes to a field where he overtakes a great company of hunters. He inquires of one of them, 'Who is hunting here?' and is told the Emperor Octavian. He follows the chase. When the hunt ends, he walks from a tree and follows a whelp into a field full of flowers, where he becomes aware of a man in black. This is the figure that introduces the device of the poem.

The *House of Fame* is a poem in the same tradition. It begins with preliminary matter similar to that in the *Romance* and the *Book o the Duchess*, a proem on dreams and an invocation. It continues with the dream. Exactly on the tenth of December – there is in this case no description of the season – the author falls asleep and in a dream finds himself in a temple made of glass. There are many images there, finely wrought portraits, among them one of Venus, 'naked fleeting in a sea', of Cupid, and of Vulcan, 'that in his face was full brown'. As the dreamer walks about, he sees on the wall the story of the *Aeneid*, portrayed in a series of panels. These are described at length, one after the other – 'There saw I', 'There saw I' – in a manner and in a position in the scheme of the poem analogous to the portraits on the wall in the *Romance* or the portraits of the pilgrims at the Tabard. The author then leaves the temple, finds himself in a barren desert, looks up to heaven in prayer, and becomes aware of an eagle larger than any he has ever seen. The eagle is the figure who disposes the device which accounts for the remainder of the poem.

I come now to the *Prologue* to the *Legend of Good Women*. The later of the two versions is more relevant to our purpose, since it is closer in form to the scheme of the Canterbury *Prologue*, though the differences between the versions are not sufficient to call for separate treatment. The poem begins with preliminary matter, in this case of exceptional distinction, and then the poet late in the month of May falls asleep and dreams. He finds himself in a field – 'With floures sote enbrouded was it al' – where 'The smale foules, of the seson fayn' sing a hymn to St Valentine. There appear the God of Love and his Queen, Alceste, whose dress in particular is described at some length. Behind the god the author sees nineteen ladies in royal dress, and after them an extraordinary number of women. There follows the action which leads to the device: the King and especially the Queen as masters of ceremonies impose on the author the task of writing a series of tales of true lovers as penance for his heresy in love.

The underlying scheme of the dream-vision prologue should now be clear. If we set aside the preliminary matter as not relevant to the form of the Canterbury *Prologue* and begin, as it does, after the dream, we will find the following elements in this order. The poem is set at a given time of the year, generally in May, but perhaps exactly on the tenth of December, or sometime in the latter part of April, as the astrology of the Canterbury *Prologue* indicates. The time of the year leads in many cases to a description of the season, which may be brief or leisurely, simple or, as in the case of the Canterbury *Prologue*, ornate, with elements drawn from the introductory nature descriptions of other literary forms. The author, usually as the dreamer, is a character in his own poem, though when the scheme is used in a narrative, as in the tale of Rosiphelee, the principal character takes the place of the author. He comes to a place, usually a field, but sometimes a chamber or temple of glass, and in one case the Tabard in Southwark. He sees there a company, or occasionally one or two persons, and sometimes some birds who are treated as characters. Or he sees a number of portraits depicted on a wall, or incidents in a famous story, and then, after another journey, comes to a company. These may be described at length, one after another, in panel fashion, or they may, especially if the material is common in the tradition, be briefly and summarily denominated. At this point, or after another journey, or, as in the case of the Canterbury *Prologue*, after a brief digression, one of the company or another character who is now met, the man in black or Harry Bailly, initiates the action of the poem. This may consist, as in the *Prologue* to the *Legend* and the *Prologue* to the *Canterbury Tales*, in proposing the relation of a series of tales.

But the *Canterbury Tales* extend beyond the *Prologue*. Is there any precedent in the tradition for the particular way in which Chaucer proceeds to develop the poem? Of course, there is precedent in the *Legend* and in Gower for the framed tales, but I have in mind something more definite and limited than this. I have in mind the problem of the principles of order in the work as a whole, of which the idea of the frame story is only one. I have in mind a very restricted question: is there in the tradition or in those realizations of the tradition that Chaucer had already accomplished any scheme of development from the dream-vision prologue that is similar to the development in the *Canterbury Tales?*

The whole problem of the construction of the *Canterbury Tales* is a vexed and difficult one. The work as it has come down to us consists of a number of fragments, each disjoined from the others and each consisting of several tales and of the prologues to and links between the tales. The *General Prologue*, for instance, is followed by three tales with the links between them and breaks off abruptly, shortly after the beginning of a fourth tale. This section is usually called the 'A Fragment'. I will concern myself only with this.

It is clear from the state of the manuscripts, then, that the project was never one that was complete in design though incomplete in execution. The design itself was in a fluid state. The general outlines of the framework were perhaps clear: it would involve a pilgrimage, and the completion of the journey would coincide with the completion of the design. The characters of most of the pilgrims, at least, were determined. There was to be a leader of the party, the Host, whose word was law. Each pilgrim was to tell a given number of tales, and the tales he told were to accord with his rank and nature according to the ancient principles of decorum. But within what was already determined there was much that was indeterminate, especially the principle or congeries of principles that would determine the succession of speakers and tales.

What principles had Chaucer? He begins with the principle of lots which could have served to order the whole, but he uses it only to determine the first speaker. Again, the principle of lots, whether by chance or by Providence guiding chance or by the manipulation of the Host, serves to pick out the man of highest rank in the company as the first to speak. This again would have served as a sufficient principle; the order of precedence in society could have determined the order of precedence in the telling of tales, and the Host, who was a proper man to be a marshal in a hall, could easily have settled the questions of etiquette. But this principle breaks down immediately after the Knight's tale. The Host calls on the Monk, who would probably be considered next in social rank, to relate something that will fit in with the Knight's tale. But the Miller, who is a churl and will abide no man for courtesy, cries out in Pilate's voice, 'I know a noble tale with which I will repay the Knight's.' His tale, of course, is just the opposite: it is an ignoble tale of churls and obscenity rather than a noble tale of princes and high love.

Is there any precedent for this in the tradition? There is, in the scheme of experience of a dream vision which Chaucer wrote some years before this, the *Parliament of Fowls*.[1] In that poem, after the

1 Suggested by Émile Legouis (*Geoffrey Chaucer*, trans. L. Lailavoix, London 1928, pp. 85–6).

customary preliminary matter, the author falls asleep and dreams. A guide leads him to a spring scene, a garden full of birds and trees, where he sees Cupid and Will, his daughter, and many other allegorical figures and a temple of brass with more figures inside it and the story of many famous lovers painted on the wall. He walks forth again from this place and comes on the figure who disposes the device that orders the rest of the poem. This is Nature, who is holding a parliament of birds on St Valentine's Day. The birds are then summarily described. Nature opens the parliament and stipulates that the birds shall speak in order of rank; and so they do until suddenly the lower orders break out, crying, 'Have don, and lat us wende! . . . Whan shal youre cursede pletynge have an ende?' (492–5). The subject has been high courtly love, and now the vulgar point of view is urged by a vigorous churlish personality amid a certain amount of general uproar.

Obviously, the scheme of progression at the beginning of the *Canterbury Tales* is similar in these general respects t the scheme of the *Parliament of Fowls*. It is not only the form of the *Prologue* that derives from the dream vision, but from the particular scheme of a particular dream vision which Chaucer had written some time before derives the underlying principle of order of the A Fragment as a whole. In both, the master of ceremonies, by stipulation and by lot, appoints the highest in rank to speak first. The discourse is on high courtly love. It is interrupted by the lower orders of society who urge a vulgar point of view, and there follows strife among the churls. This is developed in the A Fragment by a new principle, the principle of retaliation. The Miller tells a tale about a carpenter, and the Reeve, who had been a carpenter, answers with a tale about a miller. The Cook offers to go on in this vein, begins, and the fragment breaks off. It is open to question whether or not in this instance the form of the dream vision itself broke down, whether or not it was inadequate to handle the material which Chaucer wished to explore by its means. But it does not seem to me open to question that the form of the *Prologue* and indeed of the A Fragment is, if we understand by a 'literary form' the method by which material is discovered and ordered, the form of the dream vision in whose terms Chaucer himself had learned to feel and think through many years of love and apprenticeship.

The identity of the literary form of the *Prologue* to the *Canterbury Tales* with the conventional form of the dream-vision prologue can be regarded as established. It may be felt, however, that the distinctive feature of the Canterbury *Prologue* – the series of portraits – has not adequately been accounted for. No one, I trust, will ask one to account for the greatness of Chaucer's portraits, for his peculiar skill in writing. If such matters can be explained, certainly they lie outside the scope and method of this chapter. The question is rather, I should say, is the technique of portraiture in the dream-vision convention of the same kind as Chaucer's technique in the *Prologue*? It is. The model in the tradition – and the model to which Chaucer recurred here – is the double series of portraits at the opening of the *Romance of the Rose*, the portraits that occupy the same place in the scheme of that poem as Chaucer's do in the scheme of his.[1]

I would distinguish several points of similarity of technique in the portraits themselves and two further points in their connexion with the remainder of the poem. The portraits are given in succession in both poems, without transition or with the most summary form of transition: 'And next was peynted Coveitise', 'Elde was paynted after this', 'And alderlast of everychon | Was peynted Povert al aloon', 'And next hir wente, on hir other side', 'Love hadde with hym a bacheler'. Chaucer's technique is similar: 'With hym there was his sone, a yong Squier, | A lovyere and a lusty bacheler', 'A Monk ther was'. There are a number of such portraits, a group of ten and of fifteen in the *Romance* and twenty-one in the *Prologue*, plus the five guildsmen who are treated as a unit and several others who are just named. The portraits are of varying length, but they vary roughly within the same range: in the *Romance* they run from four to ninety-six lines, averaging around thirty-two; in the *Prologue* they run from nine to sixty-two lines, averaging around thirty-one. The peculiar coincidence in the averages, of course, is of no significance. The portraits in each are introduced by brief critical remarks in which the terms derive from the medieval arts of poetry. The second series in the *Romance* begins (I quote the medieval translation of the poem which is often ascribed to Chaucer):

1 H. R. Patch, 'Chaucer in medieval literature', *MLN*, vol. 40 (1925), pp. 1–14.

Thanne gan I loken ofte sithe
The shap, the bodies, and the cheres,
The countenaunce and the maneres
Of all the folk that daunced there,
And I shal telle you what they were.

(812–16)[1]

Chaucer begins with an explicit remark, 'Me thynketh it acordaunt
to resoun', that is, *secundum rationem*, in accordance with the law of
the kind. He begins the *Complaint of Mars* with a similar remark,
indicating an awareness of the requirements of a literary kind:

The ordre of compleynt requireth skylfully.

(155)

He proceeds:

Me thynketh it acordaunt to resoun
To telle yow al the condicioun
Of ech of hem, so as it semed me,
And whiche they weren, and of what degree,
And eek in what array that they were inne . . .

(*Canterbury Tales*, I 37–41)

These are the principal technical correspondences. But one might
observe further that the method in both poems is one that allows
not only objective presentation and analysis but also author's comment and that the portraits in both contain a good deal of sharp
realistic detail of the same type. For example, of Hate:

Hir heed ywrithen was, ywis,
Ful grymly with a greet towayle . . .

(*Romance of the Rose*, 160–61;
original, 150–51)

Avarice is clad

Al in an old torn courtepy,
As she were al with doggis torn.

(220–21; original, 208–9)

There are two further points that concern the relation of the portraits
to the remainder of the poem. The first is that some at least of the

1 Lines 796–800 in the original (*Roman de la Rose*, ed. E. Langlois, Paris,
1920, vol. 2).

characters described act and interact as the poem goes on – this is obvious in the *Canterbury Tales* but is also true in some measure of the *Romance*. The second is that the author who describes these characters as an external observer becomes involved in action with them.

In brief, the technical features of the portraits in the Canterbury *Prologue* have exact analogues in the portraits of the *Romance*. There are in each a number of portraits of moderate length, containing realistic detail, introduced by critical remarks, described by the author in his own person, and presented one after another with the minimum of transition, as in the description of a panel of portraits on a wall. If a composition instructor were to assign the portraits in the *Romance* as a model for imitation and stipulate that the method there exhibited be applied to a range of figures from contemporary society, his better students would produce a series of characters not too unlike the series in the *Prologue*. And if he should extend his assignment to the whole scheme of the opening portion of the *Romance* and of the associated poems in the tradition, the result could well be the *Prologue* to the *Canterbury Tales*.

In these terms the development of Chaucer's career becomes intelligible. We must give up the naïve conclusion of literary criticism and literary scholarship that in his earlier work Chaucer had yielded 'with docility to medieval schematism' and then suddenly broke 'with all such rigid notions of order'.[1] We can no longer say, as the latest writer on the subject does, that 'one of the most astonishing things about the *Canterbury Tales* is that Chaucer, a courtly artist, steeped in French, Latin, and Italian models, chose as a framework a direct departure from them. He did not have to go to sleep and dream in order to get started . . .'.[2] For Chaucer did not simply go to reality; he apprehended reality by the means he had learned and cultivated. He was original and traditional at the same time, and his originality lay in the application to fresh material of the old method – new wine in the old bottle. He brought to life a tradition that had grown, perhaps, too contrived, though the *Prologue* to the *Legend* is an exquisite thing of its kind. But he brought it to life within the framework of the tradition. He was an artist, and he worked by artifice, for he knew that realism is artifice.

(59–75)

1 Kittredge, p. 166. 2 Lawrence, p. 30.

R. E. Kaske

from 'Patristic Exegesis: The Defence', in D. Bethurum (ed.),
Critical Approaches to Medieval Literature 1960

Chaucer was capable of using exegetical allusion in ways hitherto
little recognized, and . . . we will be wise to explore his work
further in this direction. Especially provocative examples are the
theme of the Scriptural eunuch and the Pauline 'Old Man' in the
Pardoner's Tale, analysed by Robert P. Miller;[1] and the echoes from
the Canticle of Canticles in the *Merchant's Tale* and the *Miller's
Tale*. Robertson has offered what seems to me a correct interpretation of these echoes in the *Merchant's Tale* (IV 2138-48).[2] In the
Miller's Tale, the allusions to Canticles are organized around a
broadly comic association of Absolon with the bridegroom and
of Alisoun with the bride. Let us first recapture the major echoes
themselves, beginning with the most obvious.

Absolon's fateful second arrival beneath Alisoun's window is
self-heralded by a baroque plea, stylistically rather unlike anything
else in the tale:

'What do ye, hony-comb, sweete Alisoun,
My faire bryd, my sweete cynamome?
Awaketh, lemman myn, and speketh to me!
Wel litel thynken ye upon my wo,
That for youre love I swete ther I go.
No wonder is thogh that I swelte and swete;
I moorne as dooth a lamb after the tete.
Ywis, lemman, I have swich love-longynge,
That lik a turtel trewe is my moornynge.
I may nat ete na moore than a mayde.'

(*Canterbury Tales*, I 3698-707)

The situation here, with the lover pleading outside the chamber of
his beloved, parallels generally that in the second and fifth chapters

1 'Chaucer's Pardoner, the Scriptural Eunuch, and the *Pardoner's Tale*',
Speculum, vol. 30 (1955), pp. 180-99.
2 'The doctrine of Charity in medieval literary gardens', *Speculum*, vol. 26
(1951), p. 45.

of Canticles; more important, however, are a number of detailed correspondences between Absolon's plea itself and these same two general parts of Canticles. His first two lines, for example, contain three echoes from near the end of Chapter 4:

Thy lips, *my bride*, [are] as a dropping *honeycomb*;
honey and milk [are] under thy tongue. . . .
Spikenard and saffron, sweet cane and *cinnamon*,
with all the trees of Libanus. . . .

(Cant. iv 11, 14)

While Absolon's ambiguous 'my faire bryd' (able to mean either a bride, woman, or bird) is in itself no novelty in Middle English love poetry, I know of no comparable and straightforward uses of 'honycomb' or 'cynamome'; the latter seems pointedly to echo the *cinnamomum* of the Vulgate, since the much more usual word for cinnamon in Middle English is 'canel'. Absolon's third line,

'Awaketh, lemman myn, and speketh to me!'

is a paraphrase of Canticles ii 13, 14 –

Awake, my love . . .
let thy voice sound in my ears. . . .

Having established his reference to Canticles by concentrating four recognizable echoes into these first three lines, Chaucer proceeds to fill the rest of Absolon's plea with comic variations on the theme. Time will not permit a detailed exposition; but by way of example, we may notice the bridgroom's beautiful love-plaint –

. . . my head is full of dew,
and my locks [are full of] the drops of the nights

(v 2)

– which degenerates soggily into

'That for youre love I swete ther I go.'

Again, in this frame of reference Absolon's 'love-longynge' suggests the famous *Quia amore langueo*[1] of Canticles ii 5 and v 8; while his reference to the mourning turtle, besides its non-biblical associa-

1 For I am sick from love. [Ed.]

tions, can recall the voice of the turtle in Canticles ii 12 – interpreted
in medieval commentary as the mourning of the devout soul over
the slowness of earthly life, which keeps it from its heavenly reward.

These echoes in Absolon's plea inevitably colour the events which
follow. One is led to think, for example, of the sensuous dignity
of the bride's response in Canticles:

I arose that I might open to my beloved;
my hands dropped myrrh,
and my fingers [were] full of the choicest myrrh.
(v 5)

Alisoun's reply gains in economy what it loses in elegance:

'Go fro the wyndow, Jakke fool,' she sayde.
(*Canterbury Tales*, 1 3708)

Or there is the stately and repeated request in Canticles, interpreted
by commentators as loving solicitude on the part of the bridegroom –

I adjure you, daughters of Jerusalem,
by the rocs and harts of the fields,
that you stir not up, nor make [my] beloved to waken,
until she please.
(Cant. ii 7; iii 5; viii 4)

– and against it, Alisoun's self-solicitous yell:

'Go forth thy wey, or I wol caste a ston,
And lat me slepe, a twenty devel way!'
(*Canterbury Tales*, 1 3712–13)

Once aware of these echoes in and around Absolon's plea, we
may find ourselves taking a fresh look also at Chaucer's introductory
portraits of Alisoun and Absolon. The first long *effictio* of Alisoun
includes the lines,

Hir mouth was sweete as bragot or the meeth,
Or hoord of apples leyd in hey or heeth.
(3261–2)

These two details clearly echo a description of the bride in Canticles:

... the odour of thy mouth [is] like apples.
Thy throat [is] like the best wine. ...

(vii 8–9)

In addition, the pictures of the two women are full of tantalizing
half-correspondences, which cumulatively suggest a naturalistic re-
working of the exotic imagery of Canticles by Chaucer. At the
risk one always runs by quoting such parallels in isolation, I call
your attention to Alisoun's brooch as broad as the boss of a buckler
(3265–6) and the 'thousand bucklers' that make up the necklace of
the bride in Canticles iv 4 – two rather unusual figures, used in
approximately corresponding parts of the two portraits. Or there is
the description of Alisoun's frisking –

Therto she koude skippe and make game ...
Wynsynge she was ...
Hir shoes were laced on hir legges hye ...

(3259, 3263, 3267)

– and the famous Canticles vii 1:

How beautiful are thy steps in shoes, O prince's daughter!

A little later in the tale, Absolon is described:

Crul was his heer, and as the gold it shoon,
And strouted as a fanne large and brode;
Ful streight and evene lay his joly shode.
His rode was reed, his eyen greye as goos.

(3314–17)

In Canticles, our basic reference in chapters iv and v is followed at
no great distance by a description of the bridegroom:

My beloved [is] white and ruddy,
chosen out of thousands.
His head [is as] the finest gold.
His locks [are] as the upright branches of palm trees. ...
His eyes [are] as doves upon brooks of waters. ...

(v 10–12)

Though Absolon's golden hair and fresh complexion clearly have their origin in a medieval *effictio* of the biblical Absalom, I am not sure that this disqualifies them as echoes also of the bridegroom's golden head and of his white and ruddy complexion. The essential picture in the bridegroom's hair like standing palm-fronds is caught, but comically, by Absolon's hair that 'strouted as a fanne large and brode'. The dove in this passage, according to medieval commentators, signifies wisdom; the goose who is substituted in the description of Absolon seems clearly to suggest folly, a significance she bears consistently in Chaucer as elsewhere. Finally, the description of the bridegroom in Canticles continues:

His cheeks [are] as beds of aromatic spices,
set by the perfumers.
His lips [are] lilies,
dropping choice myrrh. . . .
His throat [is] most sweet,
and [he is] wholly desirable. . . .

(v 13, 16)

One recalls Absolon's preparations a few lines before his plea:

But first he cheweth greyn and lycorys,
To smellen sweete, er he hadde kembd his heer.
Under his tonge a trewe-love he beer,
For therby wende he to ben gracious.

(3690–93)

Several further correspondences can be found, including a probable outrageous connexion between Absolon's kiss and the famous opening verse of Canticles. Whether one accepts all of my proposed examples or not, I suppose that any serious disagreement about this series of echoes would centre not so much on its existence as on its degree of meaningfulness. Without invoking complex external arguments from the nature of medieval thought and poetic expression, it seems to me that within the tale itself everything is against our reading these parallels as superficial verbal borrowings. First, there is the pattern of increasing elaborateness and perceptibility into which they fall: the single distinct allusion and the probable surrounding hints in the description of Alisoun; the more concentrated echoes in the description of Absolon; and finally the full expansion of the parodic theme in the situation and the series of allusions in and around Absolon's plea. Second, there are the other obvious strains of biblical allusion in the *Miller's Tale* – one embracing Absolon's name and his biblical hair, medieval exegeses of which have been conveniently assembled by Father Beichner;[1] and another the pervasive theme of Noe and the Deluge. And third, there is the indicative fact that Chaucer has seen fit to attach echoes of Canticles to precisely two such futile lovers as Absolon and January.

So far, I have said almost nothing about medieval commentary on Canticles. Its controlling ideas can be stated briefly: the bridegroom signifies Christ; his bride is the Church or the individual Christian soul; the love of the bridegroom for the bride, and the sexual love to which he exhorts her, is the spiritual perfection of charity. To whatever extent our pattern of allusions may be admitted in the *Miller's Tale*, their common significances seem to me fairly clear. On the simplest level of comedy there is the very incongruity of Canticles and its mystical associations set into the fabliau context, plus the inversions and other comic variations performed on individual verses. Only slightly more complex is the picture of the foolish and effeminate Absolon, his fate as a lover, and his ungallant concept of revenge, beside the elevated and successful love of the bridegroom; and along with it the shrill vulgarity of Alisoun – a side of her that comes out only in her dealings with Absolon, and consistently there – beside the gracious compliance of the bride. Underlying the whole series of allusions, however, is a more important contrast between the carnality of Absolon and Alisoun, and the charity of bridegroom and bride. As divine charity is fitly portrayed through the exalted imagery of Canticles, so carnal cupidity is not only dramatically presented but in part also figuratively defined in the hopeless folly of Absolon, the sluttish action and speech of Alisoun, and the inexorable obscenity of the carnal lover's reward.

For the attachment of this biblical and exegetical theme to a character obviously suggesting the biblical Absalom, there is an immediate basis in the medieval identification of the author and literal bridegroom of Canticles as Solomon, together with the natural parallel between Solomon and Absalom as sons of David and their

1 'Absolon's hair', *Medieval Studies*, vol. 12 (1950), pp. 222-33.

traditional contrasts in other respects. Medieval interpretations of Absalom consistently oppose him to precisely the perfections of the bridegroom – either identifying him with various arch-enemies of Christ or associating him with the negation or perversion of charity, very often by way of carnal desire. Through such channels he sometimes finds his way into the commentaries on Canticles itself. In the *Miller's Tale*, the whole comic association between Absolon and the divine bridegroom seems subtly reinforced shortly after Absolon's plea, by a pair of juxtapositions which for simple expletive have always struck me as rather oddly fashioned:

'I love another – and elles I were to blame –
Wel bet than thee, *by Jhesu, Absolon.*'

'Thanne kysse me, syn it may be no bet,
For Jhesus love, and for the love of me.'

(3710–11, 3716–17)

(52–60)

John Stevens

from 'The "Game of Love"', *Music and Poetry in the Early Tudor Court* 1961

Among the pleasures of his youth at Windsor which Surrey recalled in a poem written during his imprisonment, are (my italics)

The statelye sales: the ladyes bright of ewe;
The daunces short; *long tales of great delight.*

The reading of 'long tales' was a favourite courtly pastime for centuries before Surrey. What we think of now as a solitary pursuit was, in the days before printing, a social recreation. A well-known manuscript of Chaucer's *Troilus and Criseyde* shows the poet reading from a sort of pulpit to a courtly gathering which consists mostly, though not entirely, of ladies.[1] Occasions of this sort must have been

1 Chaucer illumination: Cambridge, Corpus Christi College M S. 61 [see Plate 1].

frequent and of varied kinds. Perhaps the illumination just referred to shows a 'command performance'. Court-servants other than Chaucer were called upon to show their prowess by reading in public. Hawes is said to have had a reputation for being able to recite long passages from the early English poets, particularly Lydgate, by heart. Skelton's *Garland of Laurel*, too, seems to reflect a society of which the Countess of Surrey was the hub: its members are bent to 'work' him a 'chaplet'; in return he is devising a 'goodly conceit'. Froissart, while in Orthez, had to read each night after supper to Gaston de Foix from a book of love-poems.

More informal occasions are suggested by the passage in *Troilus and Criseyde* where Pandarus goes to call on Criseyde,

And fond two othere ladys sete, and she,
Withinne a paved parlour, and they thre
Herden a mayden reden hem the geste
Of the siege of Thebes, while hem leste;

(II 81–4)

Gower's Lover, too, pleading 'not guilty' to the sin of Somnolence, points out that he is always ready

. . . on the Dees to caste chaunce
Or axe of love som demande
Or elles that hir list comaunde
To *rede and here of Troilus*.

(*Confessio Amantis*, IV 2792;
my italics)

These two passages are interesting not so much as evidence (of which there is plenty) that reading was a social rather than a solitary activity, as because they both show that such an activity could be part of the 'game' of courtly love. The Lover, in Gower, does not think of *Troilus* as literature; he associates it with such things as 'questions of love' and dice-play with amorous stakes. Pandarus, too, has one idea in his head:

'But I am sory that I have yow let
To herken of youre book ye preysen thus.
For Goddes love, what seith it? telle it us!

Is it of love? O, som good ye me leere!'
'Uncle,' quod she, 'youre maistresse is nat here.'

(*Troilus and Criseyde*, II 94–8)

Romance-reading upon the book was a fine opportunity for
'dalliance'. 'Dalliance' is a word which has lost some of its meaning.
There is little or no flirtatious undertone to the word as used of the
conversation between Sir Gawayne and the Lady of the Castle: 'her
dere dalyaunce of her derne wordez'.[1] The word describes the by-
play of courtly conversation, though it is easy to see how the purely
amorous implications developed (the talk was private, 'derne').
Reading of love in the right company gives the courtier an opportunity to display the finesse of his approach to the opposite sex and
the delicacy of his understanding.

There was perhaps a general expectation of 'dalliance' before,
after, and perhaps even during, a reading of a love-poem (the
illumination already mentioned shows one couple 'commoning' as
Chaucer reads). It is one of the subtleties of Chaucer's poetic art that
he so nicely conveys this atmosphere and uses it. Whatever else its
implications, the *Parliament of Fowls* has this atmosphere. The closing
lines, which have often been taken as an appeal for royal favour,
are surely a gambit in the 'game' of love – what one might call a
'dally':

I hope, ywis, to rede so som day
That I shal mete som thyng for to fare
The bet, and thus to rede I nyl nat spare.

(697–9)

This perfectly rounds off a poem which began with a playful twisting
of the age-old aphorism, *Ars longa vita brevis* – 'Al this mene I by
Love . . .' [declare in respect of] – and with an equally playful claim,
'I knowe nat Love in dede'. It may be that Chaucer's favourite
dramatic pose of himself as an unsuccessful, or inexperienced, lover,
one who serves the servants of Love (as he says in *Troilus*) but is
not quite 'up to it' himself, is a deferential recognition of the com-

---

1 *Gawayne and the Green Knight*, 1012; her = their.

paratively lowly place he himself occupied in the high society of Richard's court. However this may be, that Chaucer 'dallies' in his more courtly poems with the 'gentils' of his audience is undeniable. The *Prologue* to the *Legend of Good Women* is a long semi-flirtation, a piece of gallantry, directed at the ladies of the Court. And to describe the subtlety of his dramatization of himself as the poet of Love in *Troilus and Criseyde* would require a whole essay. Chaucer plays to his gallery of lovers. Other poets did the same, though with less subtlety. It was partly the expectation of this play which gave a spice to the reading of books of love and made such occasions as much social as literary.

(156–8)

R. Neuse

'The Knight: The First Mover in Chaucer's Human Comedy', *University of Toronto Quarterly*, vol. 31 1962

In recent years there seems to have been general agreement that the *Knight's Tale* is a 'philosophical romance'[1]* which raises the problem of an apparently unjust and disorderly universe. By this reading the Tale emerges as a philosophic theodicy culminating in Theseus's speech on cosmic order. The latter implicitly denies the final reality or rule of an arbitrary Fortune, but at the same time stoically accepts the inscrutable workings 'in this wrecched world adoun' of an eternal cause. The Tale is thus seen as the Knight's – and Theseus's – somewhat wistful 'consolation of philosophy', the affirmation of an ultimate order that actual experience seems, often sadly, to deny.

Quite recently a study has suggested that the Tale 'depicts its human world in a more critical light' than has hitherto been acknowledged.[2] The author challenges the view that Theseus is the spokesman for the poem's concept of order by pointing to the problematic nature of Theseus's actions and to the inadequacies of his philosophic outlook. None the less he continues to regard the Tale's central theme

---

* The superior figures in this extract refer to the notes which appear at the end of the extract.

as the assertion of a divine order; but instead of finding this theme directly figured forth by Theseus, he sees it embodied in the symmetrical structure of the Tale itself. The poetic form is thought to be the vehicle for a philosophic idea.[3]

At first glance, it seems surprising that either the Knight or Theseus, both successful men of action, should feel in need of philosophic consolation. Indeed, the Tale could be considered as Theseus's success story: it begins with his triumphant campaign and ends with his plan to have Palamon marry Emily brought to a successful conclusion. It may be objected that Theseus is not the real focus of attention, and that the problem arises from the unequal fates of Palamon and Arcite. Again, however, the story begins with the rescue of these two from almost certain death – a stroke of singularly good fortune – and both get precisely what they asked for. Arcite has his victory and 'finest hour'; Palamon and Emily live happily ever after.

What is left of the dark fatality that has been found lurking in the Tale? And what of the philosophical problem? With respect to Palamon and Arcite, it is contended, character-differentiation has been deliberately underplayed so that the question of justice in the world must be confronted: when two equally deserving men strive for the same goal, why should one succeed while the other is killed?

'What is this world? What asketh men to have?' the dying Arcite is led to ask, and his question is indeed tragic in suggesting a fatal gap between human expectation and the apparently arbitrary ways of the world. Theseus's final oration only underscores this gap in terms of a theoretical reason and a practical unreason. As it images a world order governed by the Prime Mover, it holds out to man no more than the certainty of death. The human spirit has no discernible place in this cosmos, and yet it is subjected to the corruption of matter. If man is no longer the fool of fortune, he is the victim of necessity.

But Theseus here not only 'fails to see the crux of the human situation'[4] philosophically; he also appears as the spokesman and representative of a world-view which the entire narrative places in an ambiguous light. To show how this is so, I shall propose a different view of the *Knight's Tale*, with respect to the kind of poem it is, and its place in the scheme of the *Canterbury Tales*, both as the beginning of its human comedy and as the imaginative act of the Knight-narrator.

Like many of the other tales, the *Knight's Tale* reveals a teller self-consciously engaged in reshaping (and adapting) an 'olde storie' for the audience and the occasion.[5] This much is clear. But it does not seem to have been argued hitherto that the Knight's approach is basically comic and ironic. We see him in an unbuttoned, holiday mood. Repeatedly, he places his narrative and his audience in a comic light: interrupting his tale in the manner of the *demande d'amour:*

Yow loveres axe I now this questioun:
Who hath the worse, Arcite or Palamoun? . . .
                    (*Canterbury Tales,* I 1347–8)

delivering a witty comment on the situation in the grove when Palamon overhears Arcite,[6] or on the behaviour of lovers:

Into a studie he [Arcite] fil sodeynly,
As doon thise loveres in hir queynte geres,
Now in the crope, now doun in the breres,
Now up, now doun, as boket in a welle. . . .
                    (I 1530–33)

At first glance, indeed, there seems to be an inconsistency between this playful narrator and the imposing figure of the *General Prologue* who is yet 'as meeke as is a mayde'. But we must not be misled by the method of the *General Prologue:* there it is mainly external 'identity' that counts.[7] The pilgrims appear as self-sufficient 'concrete universals' while their potentialities – the incompleteness of their natures – remain largely hidden until they enter upon the stage of action.

Accordingly, the *Prologue* gives us not so much an abstract chivalric ideal as clues for understanding a character conceived in its human complexity. 'He loved chivalrie', we are told about the Knight; and this chivalry is intimately linked with the Christian faith, for all the Knight's campaigns involved the cause of religion. It has been plausibly suggested that 'in his lordes werre' (47) refers to his warfare in the service of God.

If it is scarcely surprising that the *Knight's Tale* deals with chivalry, it does seem significant that it deals with a chivalry lacking a Christian basis. Indeed, it is here that the Tale's central irony develops: a chivalric romance is placed within the framework of the classical epic. The characters act by the conventions of courtly love and medieval chivalry, but over all preside the antique gods.

From the fusion of these two motifs, classical and medieval, there results the Tale's double view of pagan epic sans legendary heroes (if we discount 'duc' Theseus) and mythic exploits; and of the chivalric romance shorn of its metaphysically inspired idealism. What the consequences of this central irony are, the following discussion hopes to make clear. At this point we may state by way of anticipation some of the Knight's concerns as they emerge from the Tale. What, first, becomes of chivalry (and chivalric action) without its religious rationale? What of courtly love without the same transcendental dimension? What are these codes of conduct in themselves? Finally, what are the implications – humanly, socially, politically – of a whole-hearted commitment to this world, to things as they are?[8]

It is the specifically pagan elements that become the source of much of the poem's comedy. The Knight has his fun imagining Emily's rites in the temple of Diana, a matter he won't go into, 'And yet it were a game to heeren al' (2286). There is the burlesque scene in which the wood-nymphs and other forest deities are unhoused and sent scurrying about when the trees of the grove are cut down for Arcite's pyre (2925 ff.). And a kind of Homeric comedy plays around the epic machinery of the gods, whose role at times borders on farce.

As in the classical epic there is in the *Knight's Tale* a consistent counterpointing of human and divine, earthly and celestial action. Human agents do and suffer in the consciousness or name of cosmic forces that further or thwart their desires, and the conflict of human passions finds its counterpart in the conflicting wills of the gods.[9] Specifically, there are three deities that mirror the Tale's love-triangle and, beyond that, figure forth its fictive macrocosm. These two functions can be seen fully conjoined in the central symbolic *locus* of the poem, the building of the lists and temples for the great tournament. The stadium is the artistic microcosm within which is to be performed the central ritual of chivalry, the tournament 'for

love and for encrees of chivalrye' (2184). Surrounding the lists and
defining in a precise way the limits of this little world are the temples
of the gods.

The two-hundred-odd lines that describe the temples (and constitute a kind of epic catalogue) serve to extend the audience's
awareness of the gods' significance in the poem. Encyclopaedic and
monumental both in a rhetorical and substantive sense, this passage
recreates the world as its inhabitants experience it. The baleful
influence of the gods is much in evidence, confirming the pessimism
voiced by most of the characters at some point in the story. The
temple of Venus contains a good gloss on the love action. There
'maystow se'

Wroght on the wal, ful pitous to biholde,
The broken slepes, and the sikes colde, . . .
The firy strokes of the desirynge
That loves servantz in this lyf enduren; . . .
Despense, Bisynesse, and Jalousye. . . .

(*Canterbury Tales*, 1 1919–28)

But the goddess's temple presents a mixture of love's pleasures and
woes; thus it is not as bleak as that of Mars, which portrays every
form of violence and brutality:

The crueel Ire, reed as any gleede; . . .
The smylere with the knyf under the cloke;
The shepne brennynge with the blake smoke. . . .

(1997–2000)

At the same time, the gruesomeness is relieved by considerable
comedy, as in the juxtaposition of epic catastrophes and trivial
accidents (e.g., 2016–20); and in the deliberate anachronisms:

Depeynted was the slaughtre of Julius,
Of grete Nero, and of Antonius;
Al be that thilke tyme they were unborn,
Yet was hir deth depeynted ther-biforn.

(2031–4)

In the temple of Diana there is a similarly jocular tone – as when the
Knight carefully spells out the difference between Da(ph)ne and

Diana (2063-4) – though here again the disastrous and painful aspects of the goddess's domain are stressed.

In the first place, therefore, the gods stand for things as they are, *moira*. The artists who have adorned the temple walls see no chasm between earthly reality and the divinities that rule over it. Second, the divine presences sum up certain ways of life to which men dedicate themselves. In another sense, they have a *psychological* function: the god a person serves is his ruling passion. The gods are men's wills or appetites writ large.[10]

It is the narrator himself who suggests this identification. 'For certeinly,' he says,

> oure appetites heer,
> Be it of werre, or pees, or hate, or love,
> Al is this reuled by the sighte above.
>
> (1670-72)

And he goes on to speak of Theseus, who

> in his huntyng hath . . . swich delit
> That it is al his joye and appetit
> To been hymself the grete hertes bane,
> For after Mars he serveth now Dyane.
>
> (1679-82)

Theseus successfully combines the service of Venus, Mars, and Diana, whereas Palamon, Arcite, and Emily are committed exclusively to one deity embodying their appetite and destiny. 'I kepe noght of armes for to yelpe,' says Palamon to Venus before the tournament, 'Ne I ne axe nat tomorwe to have victorie,'

> But I wolde have fully possessioun
> Of Emelye, and dye in thy servyse.
>
> (2242-3)

Arcite, convinced that Emily is indifferent and must be conquered anyway, asks Mars for victory and promises to 'ben thy trewe servant whil I lyve' (2418). Emily prays in vain. She is a pawn in the chivalric game of love, just as Diana must submit to the wills of her fellow deities.

Between the latter a 'theomachia' breaks out, for in granting their votaries' prayers Venus and Mars have created a celestial impos-

sibility. Jupiter, father of the gods, is helpless to settle their strife
until grandfather Saturn intervenes, who, because of his age and
experience, we are told, is well qualified to solve such conflicts of
interest (2443-6). 'As sooth is seyd,' the Knight observes with sublime
irony,

> elde hath greet avantage;
> In elde is bothe wysdom and usage;
> Men may the olde atrenne, and noght atrede.
>
> (2447-9)

For to make peace – 'Al be it that it is agayn his kynde' (2451) –
Saturn delivers an idiotic speech to Venus that catalogues his 'olde
experience', a series of natural and historic disasters caused by his
malign planetary influence. He concludes by reassuring her:

> 'I am thyn aiel, redy at thy *wille;*
> Weep now namoore, I wol thy lust fulfille.'
>
> (2477-8)[11]

The tournament on earth over, the celestial comedy resumes.
Venus is disconsolate and weeps 'for wantynge of hir *wille,* | Til
that hir teeres in the lystes fille' (2665-6). Again Saturn consoles
her:

> 'Doghter, hoold thy pees!
> Mars hath his *wille,* his knyght hath al his boone,
> And, by myn heed, thow shalt been esed soone.'
>
> (2668-70)

And his 'solution' has the lack of subtlety we have come to expect
from the 'aiel' of the gods.

The divine-human parallelism in the poem may be represented
schematically:

Saturn	Egeus
Jupiter	Theseus
Mars – Venus – Diana	Arcite – Palamon – Emily

It underscores the Tale's comic structure, which doubles the absurdity
of the earthly action with that of the celestial. For the conduct of the
two young knights is at bottom as laughable as that of their divine
counterparts. Similarly, Egeus's platitudinous garrulity follows in

Saturn's rhetorical footsteps. His age and experience are also stressed (2839–41), and they have led to no more than the Saturnian wisdom:

'Right as ther dyed nevere man,' quod he,
'That he ne lyvede in erthe in some degree,
Right so ther lyvede never man,' he seyde,
'In al this world, that som tyme he ne deyde. . . .'
And over al this yet seyde he muchel moore
To this effect . . .
(2843–51)

Like Jupiter, Theseus is momentarily helpless after Arcite's death, until Egeus's 'consolation' brings him relief. After a gesture of mourning, Theseus becomes again the human figure in the Tale that most clearly resembles the Jupiter of his own speech, a mover of the destiny of men and nations. He proceeds to order a burial for Arcite as sumptuous as had been the tournament. Finally, after the Greeks have stopped mourning, he convenes his parliament at Athens, on which occasion are discussed certain matters of Athenian foreign policy: 'To have with certein contrees alliaunce | And have fully of Thebans obeisaunce' (2973–4). Theseus knows exactly how to accomplish this submission for the sake of international 'order':

For which this noble Theseus anon
Leet senden after gentil Palamon,
Unwist of hym what was the cause and why;
But in his blake clothes sorwefully
He cam at his comandement in hye.
Tho sente Theseus for Emelye.
(2975–80)

With his hands firmly on the ropes, he goes on to employ his best oratorical skill:

Whan they were set, and hust was al the place,
And Theseus abiden hadde a space
Er any word cam fram his wise brest,
His eyen sette he ther as was his lest.

And with a sad visage he siked stille,
And after that right thus he seyde his wille.

(2981–6)

Given this setting, should we still expect a statement of deeply considered conclusions? Mr Underwood has noted that the human level is absent from Theseus's speech,[12] without, however, drawing any conclusions from this for the rest of the speech. What for instance, becomes of the 'cheyne of love'? Divorced from its relevance to human beings, it assumes the scientific neutrality of gravitational force (note the wording, 2991–3). Even the rhetorical question,

What maketh this but Juppiter, the kyng,
That is prince and cause of alle thyng,
Convertynge al unto his propre welle
From which it is dirryved, sooth to telle?

(3035–8)

views the first cause purely *sub specie naturae*.[13] It does not lead to a spiritual vision but merely to the tyrant's plea, 'To maken vertu of necessitee' (3042).

The fact is that Theseus does not need to relate the principle of a First Cause to the human realm simply because in this realm he *is* the 'prime mover' responsible for almost all its weal and woe. For the successful prince, problems of responsibility, free will, or Fortune's cruelty never really arise. And his watchword is: politics as usual. Hence his philosophical reflections are enlisted rhetorically in the service of his marriage plans for Palamon and Emily. And he has his will with such promptness that the bereaved Palamon does not even have time to change his suit of mourning (3094–6)! Thus, far from being an account of Theseus's attempts to preserve or impose order in the face of Fortune's chaos, the poem shows us a brilliant political opportunist who at the outset mounts to the pinnacle of success – in love and war – by one clean stroke. 'He conquered al the regne of Femenye' (866) literally and metaphorically: right after the conquest there ensues his marriage to Hippolyta.

There is an element of 'wit' in such skill, and this is characteristic of the poem. Throughout, there are no half-measures, everything – events, situations, actions – being doubled or even tripled. And this massive coincidence (in every sense) is counterbalanced by rhetorical amplification and reduplication. A sense of friction between economy of action and verbal exuberance heightens the impression of a wilful incongruity between literary 'form' and 'content'. The geometric design of the *Knight's Tale* functions more as a comic 'mechanism' than as a means for expressing a concept of order.

At the same time the character of Theseus is consistently made to appear in a very ambiguous light. For example, when he discovers Palamon and Arcite duelling in the grove, his first reaction is to have them killed – until the ladies of the court intercede (1760–61). But it is clear that his pity is no instinctive matter of the gentle heart. He enjoys feminine supplications (cf. 952–64); and he must *reason* his pity (in a kind of interior monologue):

> . . . although that his ire hir gilt accused,
> Yet in his resoun he hem bothe excused,
> As thus: he thoghte wel that every man
> Wol helpe hymself in love, if that he kan,
> And eek delivere hymself out of prisoun.
> And eek his herte hadde compassioun
> Of wommen, for *they wepen evere in oon;*
> And in his gentil herte he thoughte anon,
> And softe unto hymself he seyde, 'Fy
> Upon a lord that wol have no mercy,
> But been a leon, bothe in word and dede,
> To hem that been in repentaunce and drede,
> As wel as to a proud despitous man
> That wol mayntene that he first bigan.
> That lord hath litel of *discrecioun*,
> That in swich cas kan no divisioun,
> But weyeth pride and humblesse after oon.
>
> (1765–81; my italics)

The irony here as elsewhere derives from the judicious blend of motives reconciled on the ground of reason – which is as much *raison d'état* (the lord's discretion) as a rather comical understanding of women's and love's irrational ways.

Theseus proceeds to settle the lovers' destiny (in effect) by commanding a tournament for Emily's hand (1842 ff.). His later decision to make it a bloodless tournament proves a move well calculated to gain the increased enthusiasm of the populace which has been pushing to see him 'at a wyndow set, | Arrayed right as he were a god in trone' (2528-9).[14] And so, throughout the poem, Theseus fairly dazzles the beholder with his skill. Yet as we move back and forth from inner to outer man, the ironic disparity between the two ever obtrudes itself. In his world Theseus is a Jovian prime mover, with many of the characteristics of the Renaissance machiavel, as H. J. Webb's indictment of his conduct in the poem strongly suggests.[15] If it is possible to sum up the mainspring of his actions, I would call it the will to power, the determination to 'have his world as in his time'.

Outwardly, indeed, it seems as though agents and events in the *Knight's Tale* are under the governance of supra-human forces. It has often been noted that the gods double as planets whose conjunctions form a web of astrological fate controlling the events of the Tale. But despite appearances, it may be argued that the real causality of events lies in the human will or appetite. As we have seen, the gods ultimately function as metaphors of man's will, which (we conclude), instead of being powerless over against Fate, *is* his fate.[16] Hence derives a major irony of the poem, an irony at once tragic and comic, namely that everyone gets precisely what he desires.

Confirmation of this point comes from the Miller, who tells his tale to 'quite the Knyghtes tale', as he drunkenly proclaims.[17] In the triangle of Nicholas, Absolon, and Alisoun, each likewise gets what he desires: Absolon his kiss, Nicholas the enjoyment of Alisoun, and John the carpenter gets at the least the cuckolding he expected. But in the *Miller's Tale* the conventions of courtly love that play such an important role in the *Knight's Tale* burst like a bubble as love is reduced to its most basic terms. Rhetoric, for Nicholas, comes after the act, instead of being a prologue or a substitute for it. And physical nearness is all, whereas in the *Knight's Tale* it counts for nothing.[18] Hence 'Absolon may blowe the bukkes horn'[19] while Nicholas has his way.

Of course, Nicholas himself constructs a gigantic trick to achieve his desire. But here again the joke is on the *Knight's Tale* with its apparent suggestion that the planet-gods shape the outcome of events. Nicholas, we are told, is an expert in astrology (3208 ff.), and he will *use* astrology to bring about the desired end. The carpenter, with the practical man's sense of superiority to 'clerks', ridicules 'astromye' (3451; 3457 ff.) but becomes himself the simple-witted dupe of Nicholas's fantastic astrological joke. He falls – in every sense – because of his belief in the stars,[20] but by their means hende Nicholas achieves his will.

In this sense, the *Miller's Tale* is certainly a parody of the Knight's. It bluntly manifests desire or will as the source of action, which in the other tale seems to be concealed under the drift of events or happenstance. Just as the lovers of the *Knight's Tale* 'suffer' their love, so they seem to be the passive agents of a superior destiny. Actually, however, the Tale constantly reveals that the Knight, though no reductionist like the Miller, has a perspective very similar to the Miller's.

The terminology of will and appetite in the *Knight's Tale* supports this idea. In Palamon's lament to the gods the will is linked with animal impulse in a way that foreshadows the Miller's use of animal imagery:

What is mankynde moore unto you holde
Than is the sheep that rouketh in the folde?
For slayn is man right as another beest,
And dwelleth eek in prison and arreest. . . .
(1307–10)

What governance is in this prescience,
That giltelees tormenteth innocence?
And yet encresseth this al my penaunce,
That man is bounden to his observaunce,
For Goddes sake, to letten of his wille,
Ther as a beest may al his lust fulfille.
(1313–18)

The tragic element here is reduced by the terms of the lament and by the divorce between will and reason[21] that it implies. Life, seen as a process of restless and blind willing, is felt to be dominated by an irrational fate. The pathos as well as the absurdity of Palamon and Arcite lies in their acceptance of the view that man is ruled by his animal will but at the same time bound to act by certain conventions.

Even love in the Tale is a blind appetite, though its formal expression is in the style of courtly love.[22] The result is an essentially loveless love-story. In the name of that love, the sworn blood-brotherhood of Palamon and Arcite is soon destroyed,[23] and the theme of broken friendship and a disruptive Cupid runs through the poem. Shortly after the quarrel between the former friends, the audience is reminded of another kind of friendship more ideal and durable, the love between Theseus and Perotheus:

So wel they lovede, as olde bookes sayn
That 'whan that oon was deed, soothly to telle,
His felawe wente and soughte hym doun in helle, –
But of that storie list me nat to write.

(1198–1201)[24]

This love is also a direct commentary on the following action. While Palamon remains in the hell of his prison tower, Arcite wanders about preoccupied with his own lot. In a later scene Palamon accuses Arcite of treachery for loving his lady, bejaping Theseus, and changing his name! He declares his mortal enmity (1580–95), and, despite the violence of feeling, they arrange a duel for the next day. At the agreed time they fight like wild beasts, though they are careful to do it according to the book (of chivalry): 'Everich of hem heelp for to armen oother | As freendly as he were his owene brother' (1651–2). When Theseus arrives on the scene, Palamon (again) makes an immediate confession and asks for death. Moreover, he does not hesitate to reveal Arcite's identity and goes on to request that Arcite be executed first. There is a certain grim comedy in Palamon's wavering as to who should be killed first.

As has often been asserted, the reader's sympathies remain, at length, evenly divided between the two men. Both are seen to behave equally absurdly, badly, and nobly. The truth is that we are not permitted to care greatly about either, and this allows us to appreciate the comic element in the poetic justice meted out to Arcite. For even the 'accident' that leads to his death was no divine or demonic 'miracle' (2675), but rather his own fault. He wasn't looking where he was going:

This fierse Arcite hath of his helm ydon,
And on a courser, for to shewe his face,

He priketh endelong the large place
Lokynge upward upon this Emelye;
And she agayn hym caste a freendlich ye
(For wommen, as to speken in comune,
Thei folwen alle the favour of Fortune)
And was al his chiere, as in his herte.

                    (2676–83)

With the co-operation of Emily and the jubilant applause of an equally fickle plebs[25] ringing in his ears, Arcite's excitement sets the scene for a mishap that scarcely needs the *diabolus ex machina* of 'a furie infernal' (2684). Despite the undeniable pathos of Arcite's death-bed lament,[26] the Knight, who dislikes tragedy,[27] consistently presents his story in such a way as to make genuine tragedy impossible.

Similarly, Emily's character is hardly the kind to inspire a noble passion. She is lovely, no doubt, but not much more than that.[28] This is not altogether her fault, since she is after all merely the prize for which men fight. But, as the tournament scene shows, she plays the part expected of her, and her passivity fits well with the passive role that the society assigns her.

Love in the Tale is an essentially amoral and self-regarding passion. Theseus views it chiefly as folly, though with a tolerant irony:

'The god of love, a, *benedicite!*
How myghty and how greet a lord is he!
Ayeyns his myght ther gayneth none obstacles.
He may be cleped a god for his myracles;
For he kan maken, at his owene gyse,
Of everich herte as that hym list divyse.'

                    (1785 90)

He admires Cupid as an image of his own ideal of (complete) lordship. At the same time, Cupid's power illustrates for him the folly of letting passion triumph over reason. How could 'love, maugree hir eyen two' (1796) lead Palamon and Arcite to risk death and fight over one totally ignorant of their existence?

After the latter have decided to duel to the death, the Knight is similarly prompted to exclaim:

O Cupide, out of alle charitee!
O regne, that wolt no felawe have with thee!
Ful sooth is seyd that love ne lordshipe
Wol noght, his thankes, have no felaweshipe.

(1623–6)

But the difference in outlook here between the Knight and Theseus defines the distance between the teller and his tale. By paralleling love and lordship in this fashion, the Knight hints at the major themes of his unfolding Tale. This love is the disrupter of 'felaweshipe' and also the will to sexual 'lordshipe' analogous to the will to power or political lordship.

Finally, there is a punning comment on this kind of love in the Knight's exclamation. 'Out of alle charitee' is first of all a colloquial tag; as such it is applied to the Wife of Bath in the *General Prologue*, also in a mildly punning form.[29] In addition, 'charitee' denotes the religious *caritas* that in the *Prologue* is explicitly exemplified by the Plowman (1 531–5), and in a general way forms the backdrop (so to speak) against which are played the endless metamorphoses of human love that we find in the Canterbury pilgrims.

In the *General Prologue*, that is, each pilgrim is ruled by a specific *eros* that defines the centre of his being. These loves vary from the most intense self-love to the most ideal and selfless, but they all (it seems to be suggested) participate, however obscurely, in the transcendent-immanent love of the Creator for his creation. At the least, each love is capable of conversion towards that which is at once the motive power and goal of the human pilgrimage. Hence the latter is not to eradicate the 'love of the creature', but to purify it by showing its dependence upon the divine.

Put in another way, the comedy of the *Canterbury Tales* sees no real discontinuity between matter and spirit. The wind that 'inspires' the 'tendre croppes' also inspires folk to make their pilgrimages. It stirs to life the hidden seeds of perfection everywhere, so that the human desire for regeneration is an extension, as it were, of the miracle of spring, ascending by imperceptible degrees from vegetable to rational nature, from matter to spirit.[30] By a happy etymological providence, 'spirit' proceeds from 'breath'.

Man, though he has the freedom to pervert the natural intention

(Boethius) of creation, still finds himself caught in its *élan vital*. Hence we discover in the pilgrims a group representative of the spectrum of human nature; saint-like and depraved, they combine to form a society moving towards a goal which, whether they are aware of it or not, represents the ultimate fulfilment of their earthly destiny. This movement towards transcendence is not always apparent in the poem. Certain pilgrims with their full-blown individuality practically burst the bounds of their fictive-symbolic framework. Nor is it difficult to see in the *General Prologue* lineaments of a larger social order in crisis (as evidenced, for instance, by a thoroughly corrupt clergy),[31] indices of that waning of the Middle Ages historians have taught us to look for.

Over against the symptoms of disorder, however, there emerges from the *Canterbury Tales* the idea of what I would call a 'comic society', whose order is not so much conceptual as it is pragmatic, being rooted (as it were) in the nature of things.[32] In such a society the control or order arises from below, we might say, because nature is a function of (the comic) spirit. Men have the freedom to follow their natural inclinations, because by doing so they imitate the inner drive in all things towards their full being or perfection. But in so far as they deviate drastically from the norms of a publicly defined good, they are exposed to the censorship of laughter.

The society that meets at the inn in Southwark is not so much a perfect counterpart as a prototype of the larger society from which it derives. The pilgrims re-enact the fundamental rite on which all community life is based: the being together of people in 'sociability'.[33] The perfect setting for such sociability is the tavern, which, with the fellowship engendered there by drinking together (*symposion*), has sometimes been thought to be the true place of origin of human society.[34] Sociability, moreover, manifests itself in the sense of freedom and play which is so prominent in the *Canterbury Tales* that we might almost speak of the poem as viewing not only society but the world itself *sub specie ludi* (to adopt a phrase of Huizinga's).

The world of the *Canterbury Tales*, then, is in a constant process of becoming. The portrait 'stills' of the *General Prologue* are a momentary illusion: their subjects are poised to leap out of their frames into a fuller existence, and the road to Canterbury is the stage on which the *dramatis personae* act out their natures. The tales themselves are part of the progressive unfolding of the pilgrims' selves, and thus a way to new insights and a means of communication strengthening the bonds of community implicit in the pilgrimage. Finally, the self-knowledge gained is a stage in the journey of self-transcendence, a step towards the perfection of the individual.[35]

It is part of Chaucer's brilliant subtlety that the reader remains legitimately in doubt as to the Knight's full understanding of this basic motion towards a higher fulfilment. But it appears that as narrator the Knight becomes increasingly aware of the kind of world his story presents, so that the ambiguity of 'Cupid, out of alle charitee!' serves as a reminder or invitation to judge this world by a standard that lies outside it and within the world of the pilgrims at whose head the Knight appears.

In a variety of ways, the Knight is able to suggest an alternative manner of looking at man and society, not least by the comedy of his Tale. It is he rather than Theseus who resolves the problem of a seemingly unjust world by reminding his audience that Fortuna with her outrageous coincidences is both comic and subject to

> The destinee, ministre general,
> That executeth in the world over al
> The purveiaunce that God hath seyn biforn,
> So strong it is that, though the world had sworn
> The contrarie of a thyng by ye or nay,
> Yet somtyme it shal fallen on a day
> That falleth nat eft withinne a thousand yeer.
> For certeinly, oure appetites heer, . . .
> Al is this reuled by the sighte above.
>
> (1663–72)

This conception differs crucially from Theseus's First Mover, who

> 'Hath stablissed in this wrecched world adoun
> Certeyne dayes and duracioun
> To al that is engendred in this place,
> Over the whiche day they may nat pace,
> Al mowe they yet tho dayes wel abregge.'
>
> (2995–9)

And significantly, the Knight ends, not here, but with the wedding of Emily and Palamon, as well as a final ambiguity: 'And God, that al this wyde world hath wroght, | Sende hym his love that hath it deere aboght' (3099-100).[36]

Palamon and Emily live happily ever after, and as the Knight steps out of their world into his wider world his optimism asserts itself triumphantly to encompass 'al this faire compaignye'. But it does so only after he has, through his Tale, confronted some of life's baffling complexities. For the price of this comic outlook is a steady vigilance; in short, it requires the qualities that the *Prologue* tells us the Knight possesses: 'And though that he were worthy, he was wys' (68).

This wisdom involves a prudent circumspectness, keeping one's eyes open and being prepared for eventualities. For life always has more in store for man than he bargained for, so that it is likely to make him look foolish if not worse. And from this point of view the 'heathens' and their gods in the Tale are after all metaphors for the human condition at large, in so far as we all share in that more than partial blindness of a Palamon and Arcite, and hence in their possibilities for appearing tragic, absurd, wicked, and innocent. That, it would seem, is one crux of the human situation.

The other crux is perhaps that of action and commitment, in short, of being 'worthy' as well as 'wys'. And here the missing transcendental link of the *Knight's Tale* is of crucial importance. This link is man himself in the cosmic 'cheyne of love'. For it is only by placing his actions and aspirations within that context, that man raises them above the level of mere Will and Self.

Is there an element of *paideia* in all this? We have noted that the Tale presents an image of different generations, and we can now add to our earlier scheme:

	Saturn	Egeus
Knight	Jupiter	Theseus
Squire	Mars, etc.	Arcite, etc.

Included in the Knight's audience is his son, the very type of a courtly lover. In the *General Prologue*, moreover, their portraits suggest two stages of the chivalric life, the father furnishing the model for the 'bachelour' who 'carf biforn his fader at the table' (100).

The Tale, then, deals precisely with those themes that most nearly concern the Knight. Yet it appears that the latter casts an ironic eye at the relationship between the generations. Man in the Tale does not learn much by age and experience. What wisdom can the older transmit to the younger generation? The *Knight's Tale* is a testimony to the insufficiency of human wisdom at the same time that it transcends it.

1. See the commentary on the *Knight's Tale* in E. T. Donaldson, *Chaucer's Poetry: An Anthology for the Modern Reader* (New York, 1958), p. 901. Recent critical views are represented preeminently by Mr Donaldson, C. Muscatine ('Form, texture, and meaning in Chaucer's *Knight's Tale*', *PMLA*, vol. 65 [1950], pp. 911–29), and W. Frost ('An interpretation of Chaucer's *Knight's Tale*', *RES*, vol. 25 [1949], pp. 289–304). Though I dispute what I believe to be a central point of their interpretations, my own analysis is of course greatly indebted to these and other writers on the Tale.

2. Dale Underwood, 'The first of the *Canterbury Tales*', *ELH*, vol.26 (1959), p. 455. Paull F. Baum's *Chaucer, A Critical Appreciation* (Durham, North Carolina, 1958), pp. 84–104, with its valuable emphasis on the comic elements and the mixture of styles in the *Knight's Tale*, anticipates some of my argument in this paper. But in the end Baum regards these features as more or less serious blemishes (pp. 90, 95, 96, 101). In what follows I shall try to show that they serve, rather, as an index of the narrator's outlook.

3. See Underwood, *passim*. Underwood here goes back to the view most fully stated by Muscatine.

4. Underwood, p. 466.

5. Note, e.g., his recurrent use of *occupatio*; see note to line 884, F. N. Robinson (ed.), *The Complete Works of Geoffrey Chaucer* (Cambridge, Mass., 1957), pp. 670–1.

6. Lines 1521–4. See Donaldson's excellent paraphrase (p. 905): 'One is constantly keeping appointments one never made.'

7. The Knight's later conduct does not exactly suggest a virginal modesty (cf., e.g., VI 960 ff.; VII 2767 ff.).

8. An interesting point is the relation of the Knight (and his Tale) to contemporary historical realities; namely, the notorious decay of chivalry in the fourteenth century, its degeneration into a military instrument of power politics. An article by H. J. Webb ('A reinterpretation of Chaucer's Theseus', *RES*, vol. 23 [1947], pp. 289–96), is very suggestive in this respect. Cf. J. Huizinga, 'The political and military significance of chivalric ideas in the late Middle Ages', *Men and Ideas* (New York, 1959), pp. 196–206.

9. For the Homeric prototype, see C. Whitman, *Homer and the Heroic Tradition* (Cambridge, Mass., 1958), chap. 10, 'Fate, time, and the gods', esp. pp. 221–34. I am not suggesting that Chaucer had any direct knowledge of Greek literature, but Homer's practice in this as in other respects

influenced the later Roman epic with which Chaucer was undoubtedly acquainted.

10. For the suggestion that already in the *Thebaid* the gods perform such a double function, see Willy Schetter, *Untersuchungen zur Epischen Kunst des Statius* (Wiesbaden, 1960), pp. 5–29.

11. Here and in the following two quotations I have italicized the terms reflecting the gods' will-psychology.

12. Underwood, pp. 465–6.

13. Compare Nature's speech at the end of the Mutability Cantos.

14. See also 2561–4. Even wartime tournaments between knights of opposing armies, Webb points out ('A reinterpretation of Chaucer's Theseus', p. 295), were seldom allowed to result in death. He concludes that there was nothing unusual in Theseus's decision, 'unless it were a strange mildness in an otherwise rather harsh character', and also suggests that it was prompted by desire to curry favour with the crowd.

15. Webb's main contention is that the Tale shows us a Theseus who even at his most chivalrous displayed the ignoble traits that in later life led to his damnation (p. 289). He cites four acts of Theseus in support of his contention, such as the injustice he commits in freeing Arcite and keeping Palamon imprisoned, commenting that 'from the standpoint of medieval ethics (particularly as applied to rulers) he was something less than "noble"' in doing so (p. 294). For medieval concern with the noble ruler, see L. K. Born, 'The perfect prince: a study in thirteenth- and fourteenth-century ideals', *Speculum*, vol. 3 (1928), pp. 470–504.

16. Except that the consequences of his willing may altogether surpass his expectations. The fact that man's will is often thwarted by others – as is Arcite's and Palamon's in the tower – is no serious objection here. In their laments (1223 ff.; 1281 ff.) it never occurs to Palamon or Arcite to question Theseus's responsibility for their hapless circumstances.

17. The *Miller's Prologue*, I 3127. Donaldson (pp. 906–9) has an excellent discussion of the relation between the two tales.

18. For seven years Arcite is close to Emily, but no nearer than Palamon to making his love known to her.

19. Cf. Theseus's statement, I 1838. The *Miller's Tale* contains a number of verbal allusions back to the *Knight's Tale*. Nicholas lives in the carpenter's house 'Allone, withouten any compaignye', echoing the most pathos-filled line of the *Knight's Tale* (2779).

20. See also J. J. O'Connor, 'The astrological background of the *Miller's Tale*', *Speculum*, vol. 31 (1956), pp. 120–5.

21. For the medieval idea of conflict between 'will' and 'wit', see J. A. W. Bennett, *The Parlement of Foules: An Interpretation* (Oxford, 1957), p. 85 and references.

22. For a survey of the two traditions of love, see Maurice Valency, *In Praise of Love: An Introduction to the Love-Poetry of the Renaissance* (New York, 1958).

23. Arcite first abjures friendship on the ground that love is a greater law which ordains that each man look out for himself (1165–86).

24. The last word is Chaucer's slip, but the line is none the less significant. Note also that this friendship is placed in a future remote from the time of the Tale. We seem to have in these lines a reference to the later damnation of Theseus.

25. We are made aware of the populace at various points in the Tale, usually in a comic way. E.g., the reaction to Arcite's death: ' "Why woldestow be deed," thise wommen crye, | "And haddest gold ynough, and Emelye?" ' (2835–6). And compare the Knight's request for silence from the pilgrims (2674) to the herald's attempt to silence the crowd at the tournament (2533–5).

26. Even this is counteracted by the excessively scientific account of his malady (2743–60) and the incongruously cavalier tone of its concluding lines (2759–60). Further, there is the Knight's cryptic comment (2809–14), in which he places a great distance between himself and the narrative (Arcite's death); 'His spirit chaunged hous and wente ther, | As I cam nevere, I kan nat tellen wher. . . .'

27. He (somewhat rudely) cuts short the Monk's recital of 'tragedies' and exclaims that he prefers the Horatio Alger type of story. See the *Prologue* to the *Nun's Priest's Tale*, VII 2767ff.

28. For ways in which Chaucer has adapted and consistently flattened Emily from her counterpart in the *Teseida*, as well as reducing her role in the narrative, see W. G. Dodd, *Courtly Love in Chaucer and Gower* (Harvard Studies in English, vol. 1, 1913), pp. 239–45.

29. She was 'out of alle charitee' (452) whenever she was preceded at the offering in church; 'put out', that is, but also 'not inclined to gifts of charity'.

30. For a good recent account of Chaucer's concept of Nature (and Eros), see Dorothy Bethurum, 'Chaucer's point of view in the love poems', *PMLA*, vol. 74 (1959), pp. 511–20. See especially pp. 512–15, and 519 for her discussion of the idea that natural eros leads to divine eros.

31. See Muriel Bowden, *A Commentary on the General Prologue to the Canterbury Tales* (New York, 1948), pp. 1–18, for a sketch of the social and political conditions in England during the 1380s.

32. Compare Swift's rejection of a rational–utopian conception of society as represented by the Houyhnhnms, in favour of the pragmatic Yahoo society which hyperbolically and comically mirrors the actual society of his (and our) time.

A conclusion by two historians of medieval politics may also be cited here: 'The life of the Middle Ages was turbulent, disorderly, often almost anarchic, but they found the remedy for this not in submission to an irrational despotism, but in the recognition of the supreme authority of law, a law not external or mechanical, but the expression and embodiment of the life of the community' (R. W. and A. J. Carlyle, *A History of Medieval Political Theory in the West*, vol. 5, p. 474).

33. See H. D. Duncan, 'Simmel's image of society', *Georg Simmel, 1858–1918: A Collection of Essays* (Columbus, 1959), pp. 100–18.
34. Compare the social and political significance of the mead-hall in *Beowulf*.
35. Cf. E. Gilson on 'Christian Socratism', *The Spirit of Medieval Philosophy* (New York, 1940), pp. 225 ff.
36. The 'hym' and 'his' of the second line refer ostensibly to Palamon (did he buy his love so dearly?). But the phrasing also suggests the usual religious meaning, in which case 'it' would refer back to 'this wyde world'.

(299–315)

Wolfgang Clemen

from *Chaucer's Early Poetry*   1963

We can now do justice at more than one level to Chaucer's 'art' in these early poems; we can, indeed, appreciate his skill in expression and portrayal, in combination and transition, in veiled reference and subtle allusion. It is just this subtlety, however, which often conceals Chaucer's art that may present itself in an artless guise. Especially in the early poems he frequently expresses something 'by implication', making the sense he intended reveal itself without the need of words, and keeping silent where others would have spoken out plainly. Today we see all this as an indication of a great degree of artistic skill; and it is by precisely these features (which are not found in this form in any of his contemporaries or immediate successors) that Chaucer anticipates developments not carried through in English poetry until very much later.

In general, new traits can only come to the fore when other and opposing tendencies recede. In Chaucer's case a strongly didactic basic tendency had to make way before any new qualities could emerge. Didacticism had been very largely dominant in the literature of the thirteenth and fourteenth centuries. Even those Middle-English rhymed romances (now toned down to middle-class proportions), which seem at first glance to aim purely at 'entertainment', seek to edify and bring home some practical moral by means of a tale skilfully told. Their endeavour to make the story easier to follow and thereby to point the moral more clearly may be the reason for the lack of vivid description of milieu and for the very simplified action in these works.

Later generations praised Chaucer as a 'moral poet', and his work certainly contains didactic elements; but these are introduced in a subtle, unobtrusive fashion which exactly matches the form in which they are presented. He has achieved a new way of uniting entertainment with instruction. But the blending of the two is not always the same; for at times the didactic element is entirely absorbed in the delight at telling a story, while at other times it may emerge more clearly. We may note this in the range of the *Canterbury Tales* from 'moral' tales to rollicking farces – although in the *moral tales*, delicate irony and skill in delineating characters and types not only balances the didactic element but often exposes it in a different light. What characterized didactic poetry at that time was that everything was expressly stated and made plain. The reader was very seldom indeed left in any doubt, he always knew what this or that 'meant' and he was always told what precisely was the point in question. This same endeavour to 'make things plain' is also present in allegorical poetry, for in spite of all the disguise allegory uses we find the significance of what is portrayed yet more strongly emphasized and expounded. Yet though he interposes as narrator, commenting and taking sides, we do not find Chaucer expressly stating the essential point in his early poems. Not that we get anything in Chaucer comparable to the obscurity of modern poetry. On the contrary, Chaucer almost invariably speaks clearly and plainly. But in regard to the significance of whole sections or poems, he developed a new art of silence, of reserve, of cautious suggestion, unique in his own age. His silence even amounts at times to what might be called mystifying the reader; and there are endless puzzles especially in the *House of Fame* and the *Parliament*. The individual themes and vivid scenes seem for the most part understandable, and yet it is a hard matter to discover what Chaucer means to convey by their sequence and by the essential relationship in which the individual parts of a poem are placed. Chaucer has clearly evolved a novel process to impart the significance of his poems – a process indeed that strikes us as almost modern. By putting different elements together without comment, simply by the sequence or juxtaposition of his episodes or symbols, he can convey a definite way of interpretation, a train of possibilities, a line of choice. The reader is always left to draw his own conclusions. The 'significance' however lies in the realm of imaginative, poetic logic, in the 'logic of imagination' rather than on the plane of mere logical deduction. And this makes things more difficult for any literary critic intent upon discovering some conclusive formula and significance. Chaucer cannot be tied down like this; and in the early poems there are many juxtapositions and sequences which still leave scope for new interpretations in the future. We ought to admit these ambiguities and open questions and we should not feel limited to one meaning alone where Chaucer had so clearly avoided this. Chaucer did not want to present his reader with a complete answer and dismiss him, accurately primed, at the end of the poem; what he was seeking to do was rather to induce in him a state of questioning disquiet, of 'wonderment', to awaken his faculty of imagination and in this way to set him thinking. When we read Chaucer's early poems we feel the author's awareness of how complex and involved the events and circumstances of life are, of how they defy any single interpretation.

(9–11)

A. C. Spearing

'Criseyde's Dream', *Criticism and Medieval Poetry* 1964

The first episode occurs about halfway through Book II, and it concerns a dream dreamt by Criseyde. Because this dream seems to sum up a whole situation, to mark a watershed in the poem, it will be necessary to look first at the events which lead up to it. It occurs after the first meeting between Pandarus and Criseyde, at which Criseyde has been told that Troilus is in love with her, indeed, is dying of love for her. After this, Criseyde sees Troilus from her window, as he rides past from a skirmish against the Greeks. He is a romantic, battle-scarred figure, with his helmet dinted in twenty places, and even his horse wounded and bleeding. And yet he is also described as vulnerable in an almost feminine way. He rides along blushing, with his eyes downcast, as the crowd press forward to catch a glimpse of him; and Criseyde's heart is touched. 'Who yaf me drynke?' (II 651), she murmurs to herself, thinking of those magic love-potions so common in medieval romance. The narrator emphasizes that this is a turning-point in his story. Someone in his audience, he says, might complain, 'This was a sodeyn love . . .' (667), but, he explains,

. . . I sey nought that she so sodeynly
Yaf hym hire love, but that she gan enclyne
To like hym first . . .

(673–5)

After Troilus has passed by, Criseyde has a long (and formalized) debate with herself about what her feelings towards him are, and what attitude she ought to take up in the future. The debate ends inconclusively:

Than slepeth hope, and after drede awaketh;
Now hoot, now cold; but thus, bitwixen tweye,
She rist hire up, and wente here for to pleye.

(810–12)

Now begins the episode with which we are mainly concerned.

Criseyde goes out into the garden with her three nieces, attended by other women, and they wander up and down talking. One of the three nieces, Antigone, sings a song in praise of love and of an ideal lover. Criseyde first inquires who wrote the song, and then she asks with a sigh,

'Lord, is ther swych blisse among
Thise loveres, as they konne faire endite?'

(885–6)

Antigone answers that only those who are themselves in love can tell of the 'blisse' of lovers:

'Men mosten axe at seyntes if it is
Aught fair in hevene (why? for they kan telle),
And axen fendes is it foul in helle.'

(894–6)

The state of love is thus left as equivocal as ever – heaven or hell – and Criseyde does not pursue her question any further:

Criseyde unto that purpos naught answerde,
But seyde, 'Ywys, it wol be nyght as faste.'
But every word which that she of hire herde,
She gan to prenten in hire herte faste,
And ay gan love hire lasse for t'agaste
Than it dide erst, and synken in hire herte,
That she wex somwhat able to converte.

(897–903)

Criseyde's abrupt change of subject reveals beautifully how difficult
she has found it to retain her self-possession during Antigone's song.
She has been affected deeply and personally by the subject of 'love',
although this is a subject which in her society (seen by Chaucer as a
medieval courtly society, like Camelot in *Sir Gawain and the Green
Knight*) forms a normal and rather abstract topic of conversation.
Again the subject to which she switches, apparently at random, is
revealing. When she says 'it wol be nyght as faste', she means simply
that it is time to go indoors, but the phrase seems to contain a deeper
ominousness – a threat held in suspense, and as yet undirected, as she
passes into a new phase of experience, which may be heaven or may
be hell. Criseyde, then, while she is still awake, is in a state of mind in
which she is tending to disclose her hidden motives without being
conscious of doing so. Thus we are prepared for her to do the same
thing when she is asleep. Chaucer describes the descent of night with
an unparticularized but evocative brevity – 'And white thynges
wexen dymme and donne' (908) – and then Criseyde goes to bed.
Once in bed,

Whan al was hust, than lay she stille and thoughte
Of al this thing; the manere and the wise
Reherce it nedeth nought, for ye ben wise.

(915–17)

This enigmatic statement is rather typical of Chaucer's presentation
of Criseyde. The responsibility for interpretation is thrown entirely
on the audience, and yet we feel that we are far from being wise
enough to understand Criseyde's 'real' motives and thoughts. We
can reasonably guess, I suppose, that she is thinking of love, and that
her thoughts are tinged with anticipation and foreboding. Whatever
they are, her thoughts are merged into the song of a nightingale

which is singing on a cedar outside her window: singing perhaps, the narrator says, 'in his briddes wise, a lay | Of love' (921-2). Criseyde's love, then, springs from an impulse common to the whole of nature. The idea is similar to that expressed in the opening lines of the *General Prologue* to the *Canterbury Tales*, where the same impulse makes birds want to sing at night and people want to go on pilgrimages. Now at last Criseyde falls asleep. The actual phrase used is 'the dede slep hire hente' (924); she does not simply fall, she is seized by a sleep which is hovering on the edge of personification, she is drawn into the whole movement of descending night as it completes itself. And there is perhaps a touch of the sinister in this line: the active verb given to sleep has an unusual force, and the effect of the adjective 'dede' is disturbing as well as soothing. Finally, after all this careful preparation, we have the dream itself. In it, these hints from the preceding stanzas of the ominous and the sinister are brought into sharper focus in a symbolic form.

And as she slep, anonright tho hire mette
How that an egle, fethered whit as bon,
Under hire brest his longe clawes sette,
And out hire herte he rente, and that anon,
And dide his herte into hire brest to gon,
Of which she nought agroos, ne nothyng smerte;
And forth he fleigh, with herte left for herte.

(925-31)

Unquestionably, I think, this has the authentic strangeness of a dream experience. It seems to be saturated with a meaning that demands to be interpreted; but Chaucer offers no interpretation whatever. Having described the dream in the stanza quoted, he leaves the whole subject, and turns to tell us about Troilus instead. The dream has in fact more than one meaning, and in order to make its ambiguity clear we shall have to embark on a short excursion into medieval ideas about dreams.

Dreams were a subject of great interest in the Middle Ages, and there developed around them a large body of theory, with a proliferation of technical terms.[1] They came within the purview of theologians,

1 Much of the following account is based on W. C. Curry, *Chaucer and the Medieval Sciences*, 2nd edn (London, 1960), chapters 8 and 9.

physicians, astrologers, moralists, and other experts, and almost
every writer on the subject had his own bias and his own vagaries of
classification. The consensus of medical opinion, however, was that
dreams might be caused in three distinct ways, two natural and one
supernatural. The type of dream that was thought to have some
supernatural cause, whether astrological or theological, may be
called the *somnium coeleste*, and was also often thought to be prophetic – to give a genuine insight into the future. A second type of
dream, the *somnium animale*, had natural causes of a psychological
kind: it reflected the preoccupations of the dreamer's waking life,
so that, on the simplest level,

The wery huntere, slepynge in his bed,
To wode ayeyn his mynde goth anon;
The juge dremeth how his plees been sped;
The cartere dremeth how his cartes gon;
The riche, of golde; the knyght fyght with his fon;
The syke met he drynketh of the tonne;
The lovere met he hath his lady wonne.
(Parliament of Fowls, 99–105)

This is how Chaucer puts it in one of his own dream-poems; and
in fact in many medieval dream-poems there is a deliberate link
between what the narrator has been thinking or reading before
falling asleep and what he dreams about afterwards. The third, and
lowest, type of dream is the *somnium naturale*, which again has
natural causes, but of a merely physical kind. It occurs because the
sleeper is hungry, or has indigestion, or is suffering from some
disturbance of the 'humours' that in medieval physiology form the
body's make-up. Chaucer himself was particularly interested in
dreams and dream-theories, and later in *Troilus and Criseyde* he
makes Pandarus give a lucid though sceptical summary of the three
types mentioned: dreams may be 'revelaciouns', they may be caused
by psychological 'impressiouns', or they may come from physical
'complexiouns' (v 365–78). Pandarus's scepticism arises from the
fact that any dream can be put into any category according to the
classifier: priests will say one thing, doctors another, and so on. There
is nothing in a dream itself to indicate the type to which it belongs,
and thus the meaning of dreams usually remains doubtful despite

the elaborate medieval theories of interpretation. Chaucer makes use of this doubtfulness elsewhere in his work. It is a central issue in the *Nun's Priest's Tale*. There, it will be remembered, the cock Chauntecleer has had a terrifying dream about a dog-like creature, coloured 'bitwixe yelow and reed' (*Canterbury Tales*, VII 2902), but with its tail and ears tipped with black. His wife Pertelote is sure that this is a *somnium naturale*, for the very good reason that she is sure that *all* dreams are *somnia naturalia*, occurring 'Whan humours been to habundant in a wight' (2925). A superfluity of the red humour, choler, causes people to dream of red things, and a superfluity of the black humour, melancholy, causes people to dream of black things. Chauntecleer has dreamt of a red and black creature, therefore he is suffering from a superfluity of both humours, and the remedy is to 'taak som laxatyf' (2943). Chauntecleer, on the other hand, is convinced that dreams usually are prophetic, *somnia coelestia*, and he tells a whole string of stories to illustrate this view. So far as his own dream is concerned, he is proved right, for the red and black creature materializes in the form of a fox, who carries him off and nearly succeeds in killing him. But the general question about the nature of dreams is never settled, nor does it seem capable of settlement.

We can now return to Criseyde's dream and its ambiguity. We can exclude, I think, the possibility of its being a *somnium naturale*, for we are told nothing of her physiological state. But it might well be either a *somnium animale* or a *somnium coeleste*. The *somnium animale* view is of particular interest, since clearly more than one psychological explanation is possible for the same dream. Thinking of the dream's symbolism in medieval terms, we can easily see how it reflects Criseyde's mental and emotional state when she is confronted with the possibility of taking Troilus as her lover. The exchange of hearts in the dream obviously reflects Criseyde's preoccupation with love in general. Moreover, the eagle, a royal bird, would seem quite naturally to a medieval writer and his audience to stand for Troilus, who is a king's son. The general outline of the dream's symbolism, then, is fairly obvious; but we have still not accounted for the strange details that give it its peculiarly dream-like quality – in particular, for the lack of pain and fear felt by Criseyde. To account for this, we may turn to speculations of a more modern kind. The medieval view, expressed in the *Parliament of Fowls*, that all dreams are *somnia animalia*, is roughly equivalent to the twentieth-century psychoanalytic view of dreams. For Freud,[1] all dreams have their origins in the individual's psychology, but he distinguishes between a dream's manifest content and its latent content. The manifest content of a dream is the form in which the latent content expresses itself – the form into which it has had to be changed in order to evade the censorship imposed by the higher layers of the mind. We do not have to accept Freud's suggestion that 'every dream [is] linked in its manifest content with recent experiences and in its latent content with the most ancient experiences' (Freud, p. 218), to see the value of this distinction as a means of explaining the anomalies and contradictions that are so common in dreams. Freud also claims that 'in every dream it is possible to find a point of contact with the experiences of the previous day' (p. 165). Now we may suggest that the latent content of Criseyde's dream is a secret wish to give herself to Troilus – the wish that has caused her to blush as she murmurs 'Who yaf me drynke?' Her wish indeed may have been to be seized by Troilus, to have her mind made up for her, since she is presented elsewhere in the poem as a rather passive creature, always at the mercy of events. This at least is what her passivity before the eagle in the dream suggests. But the form in which her wish-fulfilment expresses itself – the encounter with the eagle – has been moulded by her experience immediately before going to sleep. The nightingale which she had heard singing outside her window re-appears in her dream, but it is now transformed into a bird of a different kind. The connexion between the nightingale and the thoughts of love that had been preoccupying her is of course traditional, and is in any case made explicit in the narrator's suggestion that the nightingale was singing of love 'in his briddes wise'. This interpretation of Criseyde's dream will also serve to explain the odd fact that she felt no terror or pain when her heart was seized from her breast. Freud points out that 'In a dream I may be in a horrible, dangerous and disgusting situation without feeling any fear or repulsion' (p. 460). He explains this fact by arguing that while the original 'ideational' material of a dream will have been changed so

1 The views put forward here are those expressed in Sigmund Freud, *The Interpretation of Dreams*, trans. James Strachey (London, 1954).

that it may become manifest, the 'affective' shading that goes with it will remain that of the dream's latent content. Thus Troilus (with the help of the nightingale) is transformed into an eagle, of terrifying appearance and savage action; but the desirability to Criseyde of being seized by Troilus is not changed, and so in the dream she feels no fear or pain.

An interpretation of this kind cannot, of course, be more than suggestive. Even if Freud had happened to hit on the one right explanation of how dreams are caused (which seems unlikely), it would still not be possible to carry out an accurate analysis of Criseyde's dream without having Criseyde herself present to answer questions about the associations the various dream-elements had for her. When one attempts to apply a psychoanalytic interpretation to a medieval dream, one is probably doing no more than to trans-late its symbolism into other terms. But these terms seem acceptable and relevant; and that this should be so is not surprising. Chaucer, of course, can have known nothing of a psychology that was not evolved until five hundred years after his death, but his subject was human nature, and so was Freud's. In so far as Chaucer has successfully explored human nature in his poem, we should expect it to be open to interpretation in terms of the psychology of any age.

So far as Criseyde's dream is concerned, however, a psychological explanation will be possible only so long as we assume that it is a *somnium animale*. In fact, it may, as we said, be a *somnium coeleste*, and in this case its function in the poem will not be to probe Criseyde's secret motivation, but to hint in a more impersonal way at the future course of the poem. Love is the theme of *Troilus and Criseyde*, but so far we have seen only the more attractive aspects of love. The dream seems to suggest that it has more sinister and savage aspects, which will emerge when Criseyde does take Troilus as her lover. The early effects of courtly love are delightful and admirable; the lover becomes gay and gentle, and is purged even of those faults of character that Christianity sees as sins:

Thus wolde Love, yheried be his grace,
That Pride, Envye, and Ire, and Avarice
He gan to fle, and everich other vice.

(III 1804–6)

But in its ultimate effect this merely human love is bitterly destructive, and by the end of the poem we are prepared emotionally, if not logically, for a complete change in our attitude towards it. The narrator, who in Book III can write of the lovers' first going to bed together,

> O blisful nyght, of hem so longe isought,
> How blithe unto hem bothe two thow weere!
> Why nad I swich oon with my soule ybought,
> Ye, or the leeste joie that was theere?
>
> (III 1317–20)

by the end of the poem offers the love of God as a substitute for earthly love. Human love had seemed to be one with that universal divine love 'that of erthe and se hath governaunce' (III 1744), but by the end it is revealed to be the very reverse of an ordering force. A medieval listener, knowing the story in advance, gets a glimpse of this ultimate vision of human love in the long-clawed eagle of Criseyde's dream. But at the time when she has the dream, it is still possible that it is only a *somnium animale*, revealing her own wishes rather than the predestined future. The possible and the predestined are held in balance; or, we may say, they are superimposed one on the other in this ambiguous dream, with no clue given to the relationship between them. This is a common effect in *Troilus and Criseyde*, and the source of much of its power to move us, as we watch human beings acting for all the world as if their future were not inevitable. For the moment, offering no gloss on the dream, Chaucer allows the matter to remain ambiguous.

(100–108)

F. W. Bateson

from *A Guide to English Literature* 1965

Broadly speaking, up to 1350 or even later, the ruling class spoke and wrote in French, while the country's official and intellectual life was conducted in Latin. English, the speech of the middle and lower classes, was hardly ever *written* at all, except for purposes of religious edification. But in the second half of the fourteenth century English began to displace French and Latin more or less everywhere. (The non-literary evidence of this linguistic revolution is summarized in G. G. Coulton's *Chaucer and His England* [1908].) Inevitably, however, because of the suddenness with which English rose in the social scale, it retained – even in the hands of courtiers such as Chaucer and Gower, or intellectuals such as Wycliffe and Hilton – much of its popular nature. An important literary consequence is that Middle English poetry – unlike Old English poetry – has almost no conventional 'poetic diction' until the fifteenth century. The most disconcerting characteristic, however, of fourteenth- and fifteenth-century Middle English for the modern reader is its plethora of varying forms and pronunciations. Those simple outlines of Chaucer's English that are obligingly provided in modern editions of his poems are always tiresomely peppered with qualifications – 'sometimes', 'often', 'usually', 'occasionally'. There *was* no standard or King's English in the fourteenth century, largely because until Henry IV no King of England had spoken English as his native tongue since Harold. Instead there were dozens of overlapping regional dialects, each as 'correct' as the next. The immediate literary effect of the dialectal differences in pronouns, inflectional endings, pronunciation and vocabulary was to make stylistic finish, 'the best words in the best order', an ideal almost impossible to attain. Even in London no two speakers could be counted on to agree which the best words, word form and word order were. One must not, therefore, expect a Middle English equivalent either of *la poésie pure*, with its 'vowel music' and elaborate repetitive patterns, or of the delicate linguistic precision that almost any eighteenth-century satirist seems to exhibit. It is true Chaucer's early poems are full of the rhetorical figures that Geoffrey de Vinsauf, Matthieu de Vendôme and the others had codified, but he was never able to maintain this artificial elegance for more than a few lines at a time. The commentators are fond of pointing out the *interpretatio* (variations) – complete with *sententia* (moral generalization), *contentio* (antithesis), *circumlocutio*, oxymoron, chiasmus, and suspension – of the opening lines of the *Parliament of Fowls*:

The lyf so short, the craft so long to lerne,

Th' assay so hard, so sharp the conquerynge,
The dredful joye, alwey that slit so yerne . . .

But they all omit the rest of the stanza, in which Chaucer gets off the
rhetorical high horse with an almost ludicrous haste:

Al this mene I by Love, that my felynge
Astonyeth with his wonderful werkynge
So sore, iwis, that whan I on hym thynke,
Nat wot I wel wher that I flete or synke.

Instead of a climax in the same resounding end-stopped iambics, the
rhythm has suddenly become that of common speech:

Al this mene I . . .

(That is, four stressed syllables in a row.) The 'iwis' of the last line
but one is also the merest padding, and the stanza ends with a
grotesque image, apparently, of Chaucer bathing.

　　The *Parliament* is one of Chaucer's earlier poems, and the lapse from
decorum was perhaps unintentional. Later, however, a playing off of
the low with the high style became one of his regular devices. He
even evolved a sort of 'low' rhetoric of his own, with the popular
proverb displacing the *sententia* and such phrases as 'shortly for to
telle' and 'nevere was ther seyn with mannes ye|So noble array'
displacing respectively *occupatio* (the continued refusal to describe
this or that – a device by which this or that is in fact described) and
hyperbole. Chaucer is noticeably more comfortable in these native
and colloquial figures of speech than in the 'colours of rethoryk'. The
English language was clearly not ripe as yet for a Milton or a
Mallarmé. The fact that Lydgate, Chaucer's most indefatigable
disciple, keeps on eulogizing his master's 'flowers of rethorick
eloquence' only confirms the doubts everybody has always had
about Lydgate's literary sense.[1] Even in the fifteenth century, though
English had by then largely lost its semi-servile status, the problem
of linguistic 'correctness' had not been consciously realized.

(22–3)

[1] Lydgate's real point – which is echoed in most of the fifteenth-century
compliments to Chaucer – is that with Chaucer English poetry becomes a
conscious art comparable to that of the Greeks, Romans, Italians, and French.
It is in this sense that he is the 'Father' of our poetry.

P. G. Ruggiers

from 'The *Franklin's Tale*', *The Art of the Canterbury Tales* 1967

The opening of the tale describes the relations of Arveragus and Dorigen in terms familiar to any reader of medieval love poetry. These terms are romantic and courtly: a lover serves his lady, they are both of high estate, the lover suffers pain and distress for his lady. She is inspired with pity to love him, but not in the special way of *amour courtois*: these lovers marry and in marrying define the terms of their mutually held contract; that is, he will never assume mastery against her will nor play the jealous lover. He will, nevertheless, pledge his obedience. She, for her part, responds with equally generous terms. He will have no cause for quarrelling with her: as a counter to his obedience she pledges humility and fidelity. The husband wishes only to retain the appearance, the name or reputation, of mastery; 'the name of soveraynetee, / That wolde he have for shame of his degree' (v 751–2). And with this sly comment Chaucer makes an immediate line in our minds with the previous exploration of the mastery theme.

His unusual sanity now offers a common-sense solution to the bitter extremes posed by the *Wife of Bath's Prologue* and by the *Clerk's Tale*. The relationship of lovers in the matrimonial bond is that of mutually tolerant, trusting friends, neither of whom acquires mastery over the other:

Love wol nat been constreyned by maistrye.
Whan maistrie comth, the God of Love anon
Beteth his wynges, and farewel, he is gon!
(v 764–66)

Patience, endurance, temperance, self-control, discretion, self-knowledge are infinitely to be preferred to high-handedness in human relations, as Arveragus the wise man knows. The result is a marriage of the ideal sort, described in terms of a delicate mixture and balance of service and lordship, a marriage in which Dorigen is both the beloved of courtly tradition and the wife of acceptable theological doctrine. In Chaucer's terms,

Thus hath she take hir servant and hir lord, –
Servant in love, and lord in mariage,
Thanne was he bothe in lordshipe and servage.
Servage? nay, but in lordshipe above,
Sith he hath bothe his lady and his love;
His lady, certes, and his wyf also,
The which that lawe of love acordeth to.

(v 792–8)

This attitude marks a considerable advance over any purely courtly love tradition inasmuch as it reconciles the role of women in the courtly love code with their role in marriage, presenting to Chaucer's sophisticated audience a truly Christian relationship justifiable on the grounds of mature common sense, and perhaps more importantly, on the grounds of that higher love which Boethius celebrates in the *Consolatio* at the close of the second book. It is a paradox that the law of love, while a guise for a kind of necessity that rules the universe, yet assures to man his freedom throughout the moral realm. If our practical common sense demurs that marriage surely brings with it restriction and limitation, this story nevertheless insists upon the terrible burden of freedom, which takes precedence over even the terms of the contract. And love, while it liberates, carries with it grave responsibilities not only of being free, but of assuring, nay, guaranteeing, the freedom of one's contractual partner. Thus, while the friends in marriage are debtors, as the Wife of Bath and the old knight January would have us remember, their relationship is the delicate one of a rewarding liberty, a relationship conducive to virtue both ethically in the relation of friends and neighbours and morally in clarifying the relation of creature to creator.

When Arveragus departs from his castle home at Penmarch, embarking upon his quest for fame and reputation, he leaves behind a loving wife vulnerable to fears. Her ceaseless weeping gives grave concern to friends, who persuade her eventually to come disport with them. But her fears persist, and these are given philosophical and appealing utterance in one of the few Chaucerian loci to deal with the problem of evil (v 865–94). Her prayer is Boethian in tone and asserts much the same basic premises that are to be found in the *Consolatio*, namely that the world is governed ultimately by the providence of God; that nothing in it was made without a use or function. But the black rocks on which her husband may founder, she opines, seem to be anything but the beautiful and useful parts of a good creation, especially since they have been a means of man's destruction. Is it possible that a good creator has wrought such means to destroy man, who is created in God's image?

The extravagance of her outburst is a measure of the distress underlying her longing for her husband. But this speech is something more than the expression of an overwrought mind or the indication of a poignantly feminine perturbation. It is more too than a mere indication of the range of interests attributable to the teller of the tale, although this does add a cubit to his stature.

What this 'more' is becomes discernible as the larger landscape of God's world with its problems of conflicting freedoms and functions gives way to the smaller, man-made pleasure garden with its inevitable, gentle tempter, where the problem of evil, of personal freedom and responsibility will be put to the test.

The Franklin's middle class morality notwithstanding,[1] we are back in the milieu and intellectual ambience of a courtly love code, with its subtle attack on the integrity of marriage, a code consciously opposed to the ideal clearly stated in the *Merchant's Tale* as 'that hooly boond |With which that first God man and womman bond' (IV 1261–2). And just as we may suppose Arveragus acted in his courting days – but with the goal of marriage – so now we see Aurelius enduring the role of the romantic, suffering lover: despairing of the goal, hinting at his love in poetry, looking meaningfully at Dorigen in social gatherings, and finally by a gradual process revealing his affection for her.

Dorigen is faithful to her husband, swearing by God that she will never by word or deed betray him; in the next breath, in jest, she makes way for the trap in which she is subsequently ensnared, setting the terms of an 'impossible', the removal of those rocks along the coast. In a sense she offers an impossible for an impossible: I will love you best if by the removal of the rocks you allow the man I love best to return to me. A delicate irony! In short, she requires a miracle, the only solution to the problem of evil as stated in her long exclamation

1 Walter Morris Hart, 'The *Franklin's Tale*', *Haverford Essays* (Haverford, Pa., 1909), p. 186.

about the relative functions – and freedoms – of created things. Indeed the only way in which the collision of freedoms may be prevented is by a suspension of the laws of the universe so that one freedom may prevail. This miracle may be performed only by God – or by magical illusion, wherein only the surface appearance of nature and life, not its essential reality, is affected.

And so out of the garden has come the first assault upon the marriage, one which opposes the ideal of adulterous persuasion to the ideal of marital fidelity. Aurelius has his good features; the conventions he lives by are as valid for his actions as those by which Dorigen and Arveragus abide. The lines which assure us of Dorigen's scorn must indeed have sounded, as Hart reminds us, very strange in his ears:

'What deyntee sholde a man han in his lyf
For to go love another mannes wyf,
That hath hir body whan so that hym liketh?'
(v 1003–5)

But they serve their purpose in widening the difference in convention and attitude between them and assuring us of Dorigen's fidelity in the 'paradox of married lovers'. Moreover, when Aurelius has successfully brought about the illusion of removed rocks, Dorigen's extravagant complaint rings in our ears both as the natural demonstration of her character and femininity and as a further exploration of the theme of freedom. First stated on the larger scale in the bitter contemplation of the black rocks, it is now reduced to the purely human consideration of possible moral choices arising out of the garden in which Dorigen, however jestingly, toyed with the impossible.

Aurelius in his dismay appeals to the pagan gods for the miracle of the sustained opposition of sun and moon so that the rocks will in actuality be submerged for a period of two years. He recognizes that only a miracle will accomplish the goal; in his heartfelt prayer addressed to the pagan gods (Apollo to intercede on his behalf with Lucina) Chaucer opposes conventions once again: the courtly lover prays to gods; Dorigen appeals to the one God. And as we later see, Aurelius uses the offices of magic, in a sense an emulation of God's power, to which the Franklin will oppose the tradition and weight of Holy Church. At any rate, for the price of a thousand pounds, he has his sham miracle, not for two years as he hoped, but for a week or two.

When Dorigen is confronted in a temple with the unforeseen threat of the loss of honour – Aurelius is still the gentle, amiable lover as he presents her with the consequences of her joking bargain – she sees the choice before her as one between death and dishonour, maintaining that she would rather die than be a faithless wife sullying her reputation. In her long outbursts she cites instances of many women, both wives and virgins, who chose death over dishonour; and, running out of such examples as chose self-slaughter, she cites others who, when their husbands died, refused second marriages and so constitute exemplars of uxorial chastity and fidelity.[1]

The whole complaint does give the impression of an emotionally distressed woman contemplating the choice of death or dishonour, dwelling upon certain of the examples among those who made the fatal choice, then widening the range of association and self-reproach to examples of continent and faithful wifehood, which she seems on the verge of violating. The gradually increased tempo, the variety of rhetorical pattern, and towards the end, the cramming of illustrations into few lines, manage to say, whether or not the list is precisely apt, that these wives provide models of chastity such as Dorigen would emulate if she could. Chaucer has felt no need to reiterate Jerome's view here that the virtue of women is purity. In the light of the sanity and good-natured seriousness of the first sixty lines of the tale, none of us can doubt that gentilesse as the bond of perfection precludes any active moral defection in Dorigen. But love has made her free, and it is this terrible freedom to choose between dishonour and life with truth that the complaint spells out and foreshadows for the remainder of the tale.

It would be ridiculous for us to entertain even for a moment the possibility of either death or dishonour as the solution to the problem. The sanguine nature of the teller of the tale prevents it, the literary type opposes it, the intellectual tone precludes anything but a witty

1 The dynamics of the complaint have been evaluated by Germaine Dempster, 'Chaucer at work on the complaint in the *Franklin's Tale*', *MLN*, vol. 52 (1937), pp. 16–23, and 'A further note on Dorigen's exempla', *MLN*, vol. 54 (1939), pp. 137–8, and by James Sledd, 'Dorigen's complaint', *SP*, vol. 45 (1947), pp. 36–45. More recently the subject has been reopened by Donald C. Baker, 'A crux in Chaucer's *Franklin's Tale*: Dorigen's complaint', *JEGP*, vol. 60 (1960), pp. 56–64.

conclusion or answer to the riddle it has posed. We cannot say even that the solution grows out of the character of the agents, though there are some who would see the triple generosity as an outgrowth of the character of Arveragus. But the plot seems rather situational than an expression or outgrowth of character, and all of the male agents must exemplify in one way or another the principles of honour and generosity. Their willingness to conform to the principles, or at the very least to emulate at whatever personal cost a precedent action, lends to the tale its note of moral romance and the tone of a Christian comedy.

Dorigen must keep her word since in Arveragus's opinion, 'Trouthe is the hyeste thyng that man may kepe' (v 1479), an irony no less than the irony of being trapped by a sham miracle as a consequence of what was thought to be a sham bargain in the first place. For the reader asks, what of the obligations of the marital contract wherein alone the convention of *amour courtois* and that of Christian marriage have been accommodated to each other? But firmly Dorigen is sent out to take the consequences of her promise; and Aurelius releases her from her bargain rather than commit a dishonour 'Agayns franchise and alle gentillesse' (v 1524), commending the love of man and wife and hailing her as the truest and best wife he has ever seen. In his turn the magician, seeing in Aurelius honour and in Arveragus true nobility, releases the squire from his indebtedness.

The two acts of generosity succeeding that of Arveragus are slowly developed by Chaucer. He will make his point, but by demonstration as much as by overt statement; for although the reader thinks the story has reached its proper close in the restoration of the wife to her husband and of the stability of the marriage to its original state, Chaucer has yet to dispose of the bargain between his cheated squire and the almost cheated magician. Far from being a blemish upon the structure of the tale, the elaboration of magnanimity in Aurelius and the magician, cycles of generosity set in motion by Arveragus's devotion to an ideal of behaviour, seems the necessary demonstration of the theme in as concrete a way as possible. Is this a weakness in execution?[1] Or is it rather concern with the working out of the plot even at the risk of psychological credibility? A concern for demonstrating rather than merely stating the theme? It is, to my

1 See Hart, *Haverford Essays*, p. 201.

mind, in the successive acts of charity and mutual forbearance that one point, perhaps *the* point, of the tale is made in an inevitable idealistic solution to the plot. It is, too, this repeated action of generosity which rouses in us a sense of approbation, of mellow feeling, of almost-laughter touched by reflection.

Tatlock has written most persuasively of the character and performance of the magician in the tale; he has noted that the magician is 'the most subtly interesting person of the tale', that he has sagacity and tact, that he is proficient in business as well as in his science, that he is humorously sympathetic towards Aurelius, in short that he is a 'business-like man of science who is a gentleman as well.'[1]

The complexity of his character is, we may note further, a clue to the supernatural, to the final poetic meaning of the story. It is, after all, the illusion he creates which supplies the answer to the demand for a miracle implicit in the lament of Dorigen. The setting side by side of Dorigen's plea to God, which only a miracle can solve, with the plea uttered by Aurelius to the magician implies a sly metaphorical *rapprochement* between the magician and God Himself. The mixture of aloofness with kindness, the pleasantly masculine evocation of a springtime world of hunting and hawking and jousting in the midst of December, his anticipation of the needs of the young squire ('I knowe the cause of youre comyng'), his judicious dissipation of the obligation at the close of the story – all stir the imagination. He seems more than the businessman-magician; he verges upon the creator-poet shaping the stuff of dreams and mere appearance to create a reality. Although he lacks what Dante, in speaking of the virtuous heathen, calls the 'good of the intellect', he is capable of the warmer traits of humanity; more noteworthy, and crucial in the tale, the illusion of reality which he creates sets in motion the widening circles of selfless charity, the last act of which he himself performs, participating so to speak in the miracle which his 'poetry' has been enabled to imitate.

'But God forbede, for his blisful myght,
But if a clerk koude doon a gentil dede
As wel as any of yow, it is no drede!'

(v 1610–12)

1 J. S. P. Tatlock, 'Astrology and magic in Chaucer's *Franklin's Tale*', *Anniversary Papers* [for] *George Lyman Kittredge* (Boston, 1913), pp. 340–41.

We can consider then in this state of mind how much Chaucer has risked for the sake of so delicate and poignant a theme: an Arveragus, who seems at first glance – and sometimes at second – a fool to risk so much for an ideal of truth; a promise made by a distraught wife in a moment of jest, a promise which is as binding as a contract; a miracle which is only an illusion; a deliberate collision between conventions; a magician with a shrewd sense of business who gives up his claim to a thousand pounds. The risk is eminently worthwhile. If we have had for the moment to suspend our disbelief, poetic faith has led inevitably to another kind of faith.

Seen in the light of the spiritual revolution which Christianity effected in the history of the world, what we witness is the inevitable impingement of the spiritual order upon the sensual nature of man and upon the social and mundane spheres. It is not strange that the Fall in the Garden should become for Chaucer the basis for commentary upon a subsequent fall in a garden both here and in the *Merchant's Tale*. It seems worth noting that in the Merchant's garden, with its temptations and its resultant fall, the emphasis rests upon a kind of successful evil, an insistence upon the attraction of youth to youth as a retaliation for the blind lust of a duped old man. But here and in the other marriage tales, the relationship of equal to equal becomes, if not sacramental, at least symbolic of larger meaning spreading beyond the social unit of marriage into other spheres. The garden here produces only a semblance of a fall, and out of the semblance arises a generous vindication of the rule of love.[1]

In terms of the problem of evil and of the necessity of making choices, a Christian rather than a purely Boethian construction casts a good deal of light. The departure from the Garden imposed upon our first parents the necessity of using the will forever to make moral choices, a new way of accommodating creature to Creator. The soliloquy uttered by Dorigen voicing the frightening possibility of collision between the freedoms of created things is in a sense a

1 Cf. Malcolm Mackenzie Ross, *Poetry and Dogma* (Rutgers University Press, 1954), p. 196. 'The grace of charity is the lifeblood of the Mystical Body, the living energy of the Christ symbol. It is Love who bids the tortured George Herbert to sit and taste His meat. It is the same Christian charity that in Chaucer's *Franklin's Tale* transcends the logic of courtly love dissolving in a single mercy the plight of the wife and the sensuality of the lover.'

lamentation that the departure from the Garden deprived men of a continuously miraculous life in which no conflicts or catastrophes could exist, a co-operation with God. But man wished to be free, and he must accept the consequences of being free, working out as best he can, in the sight of a watchful God, his own destiny. Dorigen in her subsequent complaint suggests fallen humanity under the painful necessity of making choices, while Arveragus's restraint from disturbing Dorigen's freedom reflects, at however distant a remove, the restraint of God from interfering in men's choices. Arveragus's condition as a purely human agent is profoundly affecting.[1] In even a faintly allegorical light, however, we understand the function he performs of focusing attention on primal obligations.

Dorigen may not know the difference between illusion and reality, may be ignorant of magic, but more important for Chaucer's moral purpose, she does not realize the enormities to which love has liberated her in the delicate balance between self-control and obedience. She must bear the consequences of her freedom, and out of this exploration of her freedom grows the consummate artistry of the tale. From it flows the translation of gentilesse out of the abstract regard for truth into pity, and finally into generous action.

Any attempt to answer the final question of the tale clarifies its poetical bearings: worldly attitudes distress and strain its intentions. From the point of view of any possessive husband, Arveragus is a fool for setting aside his prior marital rights for the sake of his wife's integrity and 'franchise'. From the point of view of the callous amatory man, the squire is a fool, amiable though he be, for not taking Dorigen against her will and against any law of love. From the point of view of the practical man of the business world, the magician is a fool for not insisting upon the obligations of the bargain Aurelius has made with him. The absurdity of straining for what the literary type cannot countenance makes it equally obvious that Chaucer intends a balanced *jeu* in which any of the candidates may be defended as generous beyond all others. Indeed the posing of the question

1 Percy Van Dyke Shelly, *The Living Chaucer*, p. 283: '. . . Chaucer, or the Franklin, . . . is giving his views on the subject of human relationships in general, stressing the necessity of patience and tolerance and of our recognizing that at one time or another we are all guilty of offence.'

at all forces us to set against each other the practical considerations of selfish action against those more charitable actions which the story has presented to us. In fine the tale seems a vindication by the higher imagination of a poetically realized comic, Christian truth opposing the 'practical' facts of a lower mode of comic statement. Weighing the one against the other, we tend to see in the opposition of the *Merchant's Tale* to the *Franklin's Tale* the same antithesis that exists between the bitterly, unassailably true, and that more harmonious and optimistic vision which qualifies as a higher kind of truth.

(229–37)

Gervase Mathew

from 'The International Court Culture', *The Court of Richard II* 1968

Court life was a factor in the society of western Europe from the late fourteenth until the early twentieth century. It died during the 1914 war but it was already sickening; the last court in England was that of Edward VII. Throughout its history it possessed a number of characteristics that differentiated it from the *Curia Regis* of the early medieval kings. There was the presence of women of influence and standing. There was a strict ceremonial that merged into an elaborate etiquette. There was an intricate system of patronage often exercised in the disposal of quite minor sinecures. There was the tendency for courtiers to form distinct groupings and this in turn could lead to a web of court intrigues. There were at least elements of luxury. And perhaps most significant of all there was the conception of fashion. Fashion was shown both in clothes and in food and drink. It could also affect manners. It brought with it a new form of values in which contemporaneity was prized. It is likely that in 1390 in several English magnates' households, old fashions in dress, food, drink and manners were valued because they were old-fashioned. At the court to be old-fashioned was simply to be unfashionable. Changing fashions reflected the tastes of the King. It was perhaps the mark of the new courts that they centred not so much on the power as on the preferences of the monarch.

Aspects of this vanished court culture have been described by two writers of genius, Saint Simon and Stendhal. There were to be differing nuances in different periods and at times it would develop a Baroque façade, but its essential structure remained unaltered and it derived from the international court culture of the late fourteenth and early fifteenth century.

This can be traced first in Naples during the reign of King Robert of Anjou from 1309 to 1343. His Neapolitan dynasty was a younger branch of the royal house of France and still intermarried with it. There was always to be a North French element in their court. This is apparent in the delight in tournaments – there were six tourneys held at Naples between January and May 1331 – and in their predilection for the Gothic, so marked in architecture and latent in the work of court painters like Simone Martini. A Provençal element was also strong and was being perpetually reinforced from the wide lands that the Angevins held along the Rhone, and all this was set in an essentially south Italian milieu; there were great Court families like the San Severini who had held high office under the Emperor Frederick II and the relatively elaborate civil service was ultimately derived from the half Byzantine, half Arabic administration of the Norman Kings of Sicily. It forms a clear example of cross fertilization.

There was also an external factor; the Angevin dynasty was oriented to the Byzantine sphere. The founder, Charles of Anjou, had planned the conquest of the Eastern empire. Their possession of the Duchy of Durazzo in Albania kept open the road to Constantinople. There were close contacts of intimate enmity with the Imperial house of the Palaeologoi. It would be a mistake to emphasize Byzantine influences on the creation of the western court culture. There was never to be a western equivalent to the stiff décor of the Byzantine court, its distaste for novelty and the rhythms of its court ceremonial conceived as a liturgy of an imperial sovereignty. Yet in the western courts there were always to be some Byzantine echoes, however transmuted and remote, and it seems likely that these had passed through Naples.

But the immediate and moulding cause of Neapolitan court culture were the tastes and personality of Robert of Anjou. He was a great 'clerk', a learned man, and this gave his court its civilian character and led to his patronage of 'good letters', even in the vernacular. He was patron both to Petrarch and to the young Boccaccio – and it is significant that Chaucer's *Knight's Tale* and his *Troilus and Criseyde* had their origins in Angevin Naples and that at the end of the century court painters like Stefano da Verona still clearly derive from Simone Martini. The characteristics of the court cultures of 1400 were all apparent under Robert of Anjou: the presence of the sovereign and the possibility of close personal contact with him; the use of sinecures and high honorary office as a reward; the presence of luxury and the possibility of credit, both perhaps feasible because of the neighbourhood of a great city – Naples or Paris or London. The presence of women and their easy relationship with men led inevitably to the cultivation of sensibility.

There was also the new fashion for good letters. This was to have a transforming effect on the vernacular literature of Europe; it brought a new social prestige to the poet, but while he wrote in the vernacular for his court public, fashion demanded that he should show a close knowledge of the classics and be prized primarily as a rhetorician. Chaucer is characteristic when he writes 'and kis the steppes where as thow seest pace | Virgile, Ovide, Omer, Lucan, and Stace'. Fashion demanded that the vernacular should be used in two styles, in a 'curial' mode fertile with literary allusions, or frivolously in what would be judged amusingly commonplace language. This was Boccaccio's distinction between writings in the 'volgare illustre' and in the 'Fiorentino di mercato vecchio'. Chaucer was to be a master of both. His use of an English variant of the 'Fiorentino di mercato vecchio' is sufficiently well known from the *Canterbury Tales*, but he could also compose the Ballade which he presented to Queen Anne at Court, possibly about 1390.

Hyd, Absolon, thy gilte tresses clere;
Ester, ley thou thy mekuesse al adown;
Hyd, Jonathas, al thy frendly manere;
Penalopee and Marcia Catoun,
Make of youre wifhod no comparysoun;
Hyde ye youre beautes, Ysoude and Eleyne:
My lady cometh, that al this may disteyne.

Thy faire body, lat yt nat appere,

Lavyne; and thou, Lucresse of Rome toun,
And Polixene, that boghten love so dere,
And Cleopatre, with al thy passyoun,
Hyde ye your trouthe of love and your renoun;
And thou, Tisbe, that hast for love swich peyne:
My lady cometh, that al this may disteyne.

(*Legend of Good Women*,

F 249–62)

Boccaccio was to write the *Decameron*, yet he describes how he first met his court patroness and his inspiration, the Countess of Aquino, on Holy Saturday, 30 March 1336, in the church of San Lorenzo at Naples – 'a gracious and fair temple named after him who to become a god suffered himself to be burnt upon a grill'. 'Renaissance' is the most overworked term in cultural history, but at least some of the roots of the Italian Renaissance lay in the Gothic international court culture that immediately preceded it.

The effect of Boccaccio on Chaucer was to be as profound as it was unacknowledged; his influence on the Paris court was exercised through the circle of Gontier Col and through the translations of his works by Laurence Premierfait; Boccaccio is obviously a source for the later Italian Renaissance. But he was formed by the Angevin Court of Naples: he had come there first when he was aged fifteen, he had centred there till he was thirty-seven, he was always to maintain his contacts with it. His contemporary significance has been obscured by the nineteenth-century emphasis on his *Decameron*. By his contemporaries he was most prized for his *De Genealogia Deorum Gentilium* dedicated to Hugh de Lusignan. With this would be classed his *De Claris Mulieribus* dedicated to the Countess of Altavilla, and his stories of illustrious men dedicated to the Seneschal of Naples. It was his early court romances, the *Filocolo*, the *Teseide* and the *Filostrato* that had most influence in the north. He had proved that the new courts could provide a career open to talent. Born in Paris in 1313, probably of a French woman, he had owed his entrée to the Angevin court to the fact that he was the natural son of the Florentine agent of the firm of Bardi, who were then helping to subsidize King Robert. He was buried in 1375 at Certaldo beneath the inscription:

Under this stone lies the ashes and bones of John. His soul rests with God. His life was adorned by the merits of his labour. His study was Poetry his beloved.

And Coluccio Salutati was to write: 'There is no age that will be silent of you.' He had always had a zest for honour: 'We are all actuated by the desire of praise, glory is the peculiar incentive to every excellence' – and perhaps this led him to develop his conception of the poet that he had first learned from Petrarch his 'father and master'.

According to the seventh section of the fourteenth book of his *Genealogy of the Gods* the poet is essentially a learned man. He is not only possessed of a strong and abundant vocabulary but he has mastered the principles of all the liberal arts, holds in his memory the history of nations and is familiar with all seas, rivers and mountains. This is precisely the kind of knowledge that was displayed so publicly by Geoffrey Chaucer and John Gower. With this there went a new and aristocratic ideal of the poet in contrast to an earlier medieval conception of the versifying minstrel. Petrarch had written to Tommaso Calogero: 'Poetry is for delight, not for necessity like cobbling and baking and the vile mechanic arts.' He had written to Francesco Nelli: 'Poetry, that Divine Gift, belongs by necessity to the few; to write verse does not make a poet.' For Boccaccio in the *Genealogy of the Gods*, poets are 'the rarest of men'.

Yet Boccaccio, unlike Petrarch but like Machaut and Deschamps, Chaucer and Gower, was a professional entertainer. This perhaps partly resulted from the exigencies of court life with its perpetual need for evening entertainment. It led him to develop a theory of realist story-telling as part of the function of a poet. For this he claimed the authority of classical comedy: 'Plautus and Terence describe the manners and words of different sorts of men and if these things have not actually taken place they could have taken place.' 'I admit that poets are the apes of nature.' In fact this classical source had probably been reinforced by the North French *fabliau* and by a number of bawdy anecdotes which had not yet reached literary form, but the result was to be the realist European novel.

The romantic novel in western Europe had descended from the Hellenistic romances of the third century A.D. They had a limited cast; the heroine and the hero and at times a shadowy villain and an occasional confidant. They had a limited plot; mounting improbable trials that were the test of constancy in love, or the tension between conflicting loyalties. Their public demanded a happy ending and a moral lesson. It is likely that their appeal lay in the self-identification by members of their audience with hero or with heroine. This is a tradition that has never died, but in the second half of the fourteenth century it was supplemented. The *Canterbury Tales* and the *novelle* of the *Decameron* not only developed a fresh cast and a realist comedy of manners: they frequently denied the happy ending; they were usually amoral. It is this that distinguishes them so sharply from the great mass of medieval didactic literature. In their final form their public must have been found as much among the *haute bourgeoisie* as at the courts, but it is tenable that their techniques first developed in the evening story-tellings in the new international court circle.

(1–6)

Acknowledgements

For permission to use copyright material acknowledgement is made to the following:

For the extract from W. P. Ker, *Form and Style in Poetry*, to Macmillan & Co. Ltd; for the extract from G. L. Kittredge, *Chaucer and his Poetry*, to Harvard University Press; for the extract from Virginia Woolf, *The Common Reader*, to Leonard Woolf, The Hogarth Press Ltd, and Harcourt, Brace & World Inc.; for the extract by J. M. Manly, from the *Proceedings of the British Academy*, to The British Academy; for the extract from Walter Raleigh, *On Writing and Writers*, to Edward Arnold (Publishers) Ltd; for the extract from G. K. Chesterton, *Chaucer*, to Miss D. E. Collins, Faber & Faber Ltd, and Collins-Knowlton-Wing Inc.; for the extract from A. E. Housman, *The Name and Nature of Poetry*. to the Society of Authors and the Estate of A. E. Housman; for the extract from John Livingston Lowes, *Geoffrey Chaucer*, to The Clarendon Press, Oxford; for the extract from Ezra Pound, *ABC of Reading*, to Faber & Faber Ltd and New Directions Publishing Corporation; for the extract from C. S. Lewis, *The Allegory of Love*, to The Clarendon Press, Oxford; for the extract from Ezra Pound, *A Guide to Kulchur*, to Faber & Faber Ltd and New Directions Publishing Corporation; for the extract from Nevill Coghill, *The Poet Chaucer*, to The Clarendon Press, Oxford; for the extract from William Empson, *The Structure of Complex Words*, to Chatto & Windus Ltd and New Directions Publishing Corporation; for the extract from Kemp Malone, *Chapters on Chaucer*, to the author and The Johns Hopkins Press; for the extract from John Speirs, *Chaucer the Maker*, to Faber & Faber Ltd; for the extract from Raymond Preston, *Chaucer*, to the author and Sheed & Ward Ltd; for the extract from W. K. Wimsatt, *The Verbal Icon*, to the University of Kentucky Press; for the extract from J. A. W. Bennett, *The 'Parlement of Foules': An Interpretation*, to The Clarendon Press, Oxford; for the extract from Charles Muscatine, *Chaucer and the French Tradition*, to the University of California Press; for the extract from Erich Auerbach, *The Literary Language and its Public*, translated from German by R. Manheim, to the Bollingen Foundation and Routledge & Kegan Paul Ltd; for the extract from Paull F. Baum, *Chaucer, A Critical Appreciation*, to Duke University Press; for the extract from E. T. Donaldson, *Chaucer's Poetry: An Anthology for the Modern Reader*, to the author and The Ronald Press Co.; for Rosemary Woolf's article to the author and the editors of the *Critical Quarterly*; for the extract from Bertrand H. Bronson, *In Search of Chaucer*, to the University of Toronto Press; for the chapter from J. V. Cunningham, *Tradition and Poetic Structure*, to The Swallow Press Inc.; for the extract from R. E. Kaske's article in *Critical Approaches to Medieval Literature*, ed. D. Bethurum, to Columbia University Press; for the extract from John Stevens, *Music and Poetry in the Early Tudor Court*, to Methuen & Co. Ltd; for R. Neuse's article to the author and the University of Toronto Press; for the extract from Wolfgang Clemen, *Chaucer's*

Early Poetry, to Methuen & Co. Ltd; for the extract from A. C. Spearing, *Criticism and Medieval Poetry*, to the author and Edward Arnold (Publishers) Ltd; for the extract from F. W. Bateson, *A Guide to English Literature*, to Longmans Green & Co. Ltd and Doubleday & Co. Ltd; for the extract from P. G. Ruggiers, *The Art of the Canterbury Tales*, to the author and the University of Wisconsin Press; for the extract from Gervase Mathew, *The Court of Richard II*, to John Murray.

Plates

For Plate 1 to the Librarian and Fellows of Corpus Christi College, Cambridge; for Plate 2 to Glasgow Museums and Art Galleries, Stirling Maxwell Collection, Pollok House; for Plate 3 to The Trustees of the Tate Gallery; for Plate 4 to The Trustees of the Tate Gallery.

Select Bibliography

This bibliography lists only books published since 1900. No references are given to articles in learned journals. I have included all post-1900 books represented in the present anthology, together with some other books of general interest from the same period. For further guidance see, besides the formal bibliographies listed below, Beryl Rowland (ed.), *Companion to Chaucer Studies*, Oxford University Press, 1968.

Editions

W. W. Skeat (ed.), *The Complete Works of Geoffrey Chaucer*, Clarendon Press, 1894, 6 vols.

W. W. Skeat (ed.), *Chaucerian and Other Pieces, Supplement to the Complete Works of Geoffrey Chaucer*, Clarendon Press, 1897.

F. N. Robinson (ed.), *The Complete Works of Geoffrey Chaucer*, Houghton Mifflin and Oxford University Press, 2nd edn, 1957.

A. C. Baugh (ed.), *Chaucer's Major Poetry*, Appleton-Century-Crofts, 1963; Routledge & Kegan Paul, 1964.

E. T. Donaldson (ed.), *Chaucer's Poetry: An Anthology for the Modern Reader*, Ronald Press, 1958.

R. A. Pratt (ed.), *Selections from the Tales of Canterbury and Short Poems*, Riverside Editions and Houghton Mifflin, 1966.

D. S. Brewer (ed.), *The Parlement of Foules*, Nelson and Barnes & Noble, 1960.

A. C. Cawley (ed.), *The Canterbury Tales*, Dent & Dutton, 1958.

R. K. Root (ed.), *The Book of Troilus and Criseyde*, Princeton University Press, 1926.

Bibliographies

Three volumes together provide comprehensive coverage up to 1963:

W. R. Crawford, *Bibliography of Chaucer*, 1954–63, University of Washington Press, 1967.

D. D. Griffith, *Bibliography of Chaucer*, 1908–1953, University of Washington Press, 1955.

E. P. Hammond, *Chaucer: A Bibliographical Manual*, Macmillan, 1908.

Biographical and Critical Studies

Chaucer criticism before 1900:

C. F. E. Spurgeon, *Five Hundred Years of Chaucer Criticism and Allusion, 1357–1900*, Cambridge University Press, 1925, 3 vols.

Chaucer criticism since 1900:

R. Baldwin, *The Unity of the Canterbury Tales*, Rosenkilde & Bagger, 1955.

P. F. Baum, *Chaucer, A Critical Appreciation*, Duke University Press and Cambridge University Press, 1958.

P. F. Baum, *Chaucer's Verse*, Duke University Press and Cambridge University Press, 1961.

J. A. W. Bennett, *Chaucer's Book of Fame: An Exposition of the House of Fame*, Clarendon Press, 1968.

J. A. W. Bennett, *The Parlement of Foules: An Interpretation*, Clarendon Press, 1957.

M. A. Bowden, *A Commentary on the General Prologue to the Canterbury Tales*, Macmillan, 1948.

B. H. Bronson, *In Search of Chaucer*, University of Toronto Press, 1960.

G. K. Chesterton, *Chaucer*, Faber & Faber, 1932.

W. Clemen, *Chaucer's Early Poetry*, trans. C. A. M. Sym, Methuen, 1963; Barnes & Noble, 1964.

N. Coghill, *The Poet Chaucer*, Home University Library, 1949; Oxford University Press, 2nd edn, 1967.

T. W. Craik, *The Comic Tales of Chaucer*, Methuen and Barnes & Noble, 1964.

W. C. Curry, *Chaucer and the Medieval Sciences*, Barnes & Noble and Allen & Unwin, 1960.

R. D. French, *A Chaucer Handbook*, Appleton-Century-Crofts and George Bell, 2nd edn, 1947.

G. L. Kittredge, *Chaucer and his Poetry*, Harvard University Press and Oxford University Press, 1915.

W. W. Lawrence, *Chaucer and the Canterbury Tales*, Columbia University Press and Oxford University Press, 1950.

J. Livingston Lowes, *Geoffrey Chaucer and the Development of his Genius*, Houghton Mifflin, 1934; published in Britain as *Geoffrey Chaucer*, Clarendon Press, 1934.

R. M. Lumiansky, *Of Sondry Folk: The Dramatic Principle in the Canterbury Tales*, University of Texas Press, 1955.

K. Malone, *Chapters on Chaucer*, Johns Hopkins Press and Oxford University Press, 1951.

J. M. Manly, *Chaucer and the Rhetoricians* (Warton Lecture on English Poetry), *Proceedings of the British Academy*, 1926.

S. B. Meech, *Design in Chaucer's Troilus*, Syracuse University Press, 1959.

C. Muscatine, *Chaucer and the French Tradition*, University of California Press and Cambridge University Press, 1957.

R. O. Payne, *The Key of Remembrance: A Study of Chaucer's Poetics*, Yale University Press, 1963.

R. Preston, *Chaucer*, Sheed & Ward, 1952.

D. W. Robertson, *A Preface to Chaucer: Studies in Medieval Perspectives*, Princeton University Press, 1962; Oxford University Press, 1963.

R. K. Root, *The Poetry of Chaucer*, Houghton Mifflin, revised edn, 1922.

P. G. Ruggiers, *The Art of the Canterbury Tales*, University of Wisconsin Press, 1965.

P. Van Dyke Shelly, *The Living Chaucer*, University of Pennsylvania Press, 1940.

J. Speirs, *Chaucer the Maker*, Faber & Faber, 2nd edn, 1960.

J. S. P. Tatlock, *The Mind and Art of Chaucer*, Syracuse University Press, 1950.

Books containing discussions of Chaucer:

E. Auerbach, *Literary Language and its Public in Late Latin Antiquity and in the Middle Ages*, trans. R. Manheim, Pantheon Books and Routledge & Kegan Paul, 1965.

F. W. Bateson, *A Guide to English Literature*, Longmans Green and Aldine, 1965.

D. Bethurum (ed.), *Critical Approaches to Medieval Literature* (Selected Papers from the English Institute 1958–9), Columbia University Press, 1960.

D. S. Brewer (ed.), *Chaucer and Chaucerians: Critical Studies in Middle English Literature*, Nelson and University of Alabama Press, 1966.

J. V. Cunningham, *Tradition and Poetic Structure*, Swallow, 1960.

W. Empson, *The Structure of Complex Words*, Chatto & Windus and New Directions, 1951.

D. Everett, *Essays on Middle English Literature*, ed. P. M. Kean, Clarendon Press, 1955.

A. E. Housman, *The Name and Nature of Poetry* (Leslie Stephen Lecture), Cambridge University Press, 1933.

W. P. Ker, *Form and Style in Poetry*, new edn with introduction by J. Buxton, Macmillan and Russell & Russell, 1966.

C. S. Lewis, *The Allegory of Love*, Clarendon Press, 1936.

G. Mathew, *The Court of Richard II*, J. Murray, 1968.

E. Pound, *ABC of Reading*, Yale University Press, 1934.

E. Pound, *Guide to Kulchur*, Faber & Faber, 1938.

W. A. Raleigh, *On Writing and Writers*, ed. G. Gordon, E. Arnold, 1926.

A. C. Spearing, *Criticism and Medieval Poetry*, E. Arnold and Barnes & Noble, 1964.

J. E. Stevens, *Music and Poetry in the Early Tudor Court*, Methuen, 1961.

W. K. Wimsatt, *The Verbal Icon*, University of Kentucky Press, 1954.

V. Woolf, *The Common Reader* (First Series), V. and L. Woolf, 1925.

Paperback collections of articles from learned journals:

R. J. Schoeck and J. Taylor (eds.), *Chaucer Criticism: I The Canterbury Tales*, University of Notre Dame Press, 1960.

R. J. Schoeck and J. Taylor (eds.), *Chaucer Criticism: II Troilus and Criseyde and the Minor Poems*, University of Notre Dame Press, 1961.

E. C. Wagenknecht (ed.), *Chaucer: Modern Essays in Criticism*, Oxford University Press Inc., 1959.

Biographical:
D. S. Brewer, *Chaucer in his Time*, Nelson, 1963.
M. G. Chute, *Geoffrey Chaucer of England*, Dutton, 1946.
M. M. Crow and C. C. Olson (eds.), *Chaucer Life-Records*, Clarendon Press, 1966.

Index

Extracts included in this anthology are indicated by bold page references.

Absalom (in Bible) 237, 238, 239
Absolon (in *Miller's Tale*) 102, 179, 180, 181, 182, 183, 185, 186, 233–5, 236–67, 238, 239, 252
Achilles (in *Troilus*) 204
Achitophel Character in Dryden's political satire *Absalom and Achitophel* (1681) 167
Addison, Joseph (1672–1719) **60**; 37, 95
Aeneas 26, 27, 47
Aeson Father of Jason, restored to youth by Medea's concoction of herbs 55
Alceste (in *Legend of Good Women*) 226
Alcyone (in *Book of the Duchess*) 225
Alisoun (in *Miller's Tale*) 68, 179, 183–5, 186, 214–15, 233, 235–6, 237, 238, 252
Altavilla, Countess of 288
Amour courtois French phrase (modern) on which English expression 'courtly love' was modelled 276, 281 ◇**Courtly love**
Andreas Andreas Capellanus (*fl.* 1175–80), French author of a treatise on courtly love, *De Amore* (*c.* 1200), trans. J. J. Parry (1959) 152
Anelida (in *Anelida and Arcite*) 107, 110
Anelida and Arcite 105–8, 109, 110, 130, 151
Angela 26, 27–8
Anne, Queen Wife of King Richard II 287
Antenor (in *Troilus*) 158
Antigone (in *Troilus*) 266
Antiqua comoedia The 'Old Comedy' of Greece (e.g. Aristophanes), as against the 'New Comedy' (e.g. Menander) 53
Apelles 57–8 ◇**Darius**
Apollo
  god of the sun 279
  patron of music and the arts 25, 82
Apollodorus (3rd century B.C.) Greek poet of the New Comedy (◇**Antiqua comoedia**), translated by Terence 53
Aquinas, Thomas ◇**Thomas Aquinas**
Aquino, Countess of Maria d'Aquino, natural daughter of King Robert of Naples and supposed original of Boccaccio's 'Fiammetta' 288

Arcite (in *Knight's Tale*) 60, 62, 72, 77, 86, 102, 106, 107, 110, 159–60, 214, 216, 243, 244, 245, 247, 248, 249, 251, 253, 254, 255, 259, 261, 262

Ariosto, Lodovico (1474–1533) Italian poet, author of the romantic epic *Orlando Furioso* (trans. A. Gilbart, 1954) 50

Aristotle 33, 39, 41, 72, 100

Arnold, Matthew (1822–88) 'The Study of Poetry', first published as introduction to T. H. Ward's anthology, *The English Poets* (1880), and included in *Essays in Criticism*, Second Series (1888) 96–101

  as critic of Chaucer 39, 113, 135–6, 188

Artimisia 58 ◊**Mausolus**

Arveragus (in *Franklin's Tale*) 276, 277, 278, 279, 281, 283, 284

Astrophel and Stella Sonnet sequence by Sir Philip Sidney 221

Auden, W. H. (1907–   ) 221

Auerbach, Erich (1892–1957) Romance philologist; *Literary Language and its Public in Late Latin Antiquity and in the Middle Ages*, trans. R. Manheim (1965) from *Literatursprache und Publikum in der lateinischen Spätantike und im Mittelalter* (1958) **186–7**

Augustine, St (354–430) Church Father 129, 172

  allegorical interpreter of Scripture 117

  supposed author of a monastic rule 209

Augustus 64

Aulus Gellius (Auglus) 26, 27

Aureate style 'Gilded', high-sounding Latinate style cultivated by late-medieval poets and followers of Chaucer 35, 144, 150

Aurelius (in *Franklin's Tale*) 278, 279, 280, 281, 282, 284

Bacchus 81

Bacon, Roger (?1214–?94) English philosopher and scientist 176

Bagehot, Walter (1826–77) Writer on economic, political and literary subjects; 'Charles Dickens', first published in *National Review* (Oct. 1858) and included in *Literary Studies* (1879), ed. E. I. Barrington in *Works*, vol. III (1915) **95–6**

  quoted 188

Bardi Lombard firm of bankers 288

Bartholomew Fair Comedy by Ben Jonson 62

Bateson, F. W. 273–5

Baucis and Philemon Old country couple in Ovid's *Metamorphoses*, VIII, trans. Mary M. Innes (1955) 61, 119

Baum, Paull F. 188–9; 260

Beatrice (in *Divine Comedy*) 102

Beatrice (in *Much Ado About Nothing*) 105

Beaumont, Sir Francis (d.1598) Judge and father of Francis Beaumont the dramatist; letter to Speght, as printed in the second edition (1602) of Speght's *Chaucer* 51–4; 37

Beichner, P. E. 238

Belle Dame Sans Merci (Merciless Lady) Poem by Sir Richard Roos included among works of Chaucer by Pynson (1526), Thynne (1532) and Speght (1598); ed. W. W. Skeat, *Chaucerian and Other Pieces* (1897) 53

Bennett, J. A. W. 175–6; 261

Beowulf Old English epic poem 143, 263

Bernard of Cluny (12th century) Monk of Cluny; *De Contemptu Mundi* ('Of Scorning the World'), trans. H. Preble, *The Source of 'Jerusalem the Golden'* (1910) 211, 212

Bernardus Silvestris (12th century) Member of the School of Chartres (◊**Chartres**); *De Mundi Universitate*, poem concerning the creation of the world and of man 175

Béroul (12th century) Norman author of a romance of Tristan 155

Beryn, Tale of (15th century) Pseudo-Canterbury-Tale of unknown authorship, first printed by Urry (◊**Urry**), ed. F. J. Furnivall and W. G. Stone, Chaucer Society (1887) 121, 143

Bestiary Medieval book of beasts with moralizations 166

Bible 89

Black Knight (in *Book of the Duchess*) 148–50, 193, 225, 227

Black Knight ◊**Complaint of the Black Knight**

Black letter Heavy-faced type in Gothic style used in early editions of Chaucer 36

Blague (in *Merry Devil of Edmonton*) 124

Blake, William (1757–1827) *A Descriptive Catalogue of Pictures* (1809), issued on occasion of the exhibition at which Blake's *Canterbury Pilgrims* (Plate 3) was first shown, ed. G. Keynes in *Complete Writings* (1957) 77–83

as critic of Chaucer 38, 113

Blanche ◊**White**

Blanche, Dream of ◊**Book of the Duchess**

Boccaccio, Giovanni (1313–75) Italian writer of vernacular and Latin works in prose and verse. See H. G. Wright, *Boccaccio in England from Chaucer to Tennyson* (1957) 129, 138, 189, 212, 287, 288–9

compared with Chaucer 65, 67, 71–2, 74, 91, 95, 102, 104, 105–8, 110, 141, 154–5, 187, 190–91, 219, 262, 290

De Casibus Virorum Illustrium ('Of the Falls of Famous Men') 288

De Claris Mulieribus ('Of Famous Women') 288

Boccaccio, Giovanni—*continued*

De Genealogia Deorum Gentilium ('Of the Genealogy of the Gentile Gods') 288, 289

Decameron 60–61, 65, 67, 68, 76, 84, 95, 187, 219, 288, 290

Filocolo 288

Filostrato (c. 1335, source of Chaucer's *Troilus*, trans. R. K. Gordon, *The Story of Troilus*, 1934) 110, 190–91, 202, 288

Teseida (*Teseide, Theseid*, c. 1340, source of Chaucer's *Knight's Tale*) 91, 105–8, 154–5, 262, 288

Boccace ⟡ **Boccaccio**

Boece Chaucer's form of Boethius ⟡ **Boethius**

Boethius (c. 480–524) Roman author of *De Consolatione Philosophiae* ('Of the Consolation of Philosophy'), chief source of philosophical material in Chaucer's poetry and translated by him 36, 129, 201, 257, 277–8, 283

Book of Courtesy Anonymous poem printed by Caxton in 1477–8, ed. F. J. Furnivall, Early English Text Society, Extra Series 3 (1868) 44; 35–6

Book of the Duchess 53, 114, 115, 129, 138, 144–5, 147–50, 153, 192–3, 218, 225, 226

Bradwardyn, Bishop Thomas (?1290–1349) English prelate and philosopher, author of *De Causa Dei* 129

Brathwait, Richard (?1588–1673) Poet and north-country squire; *A Comment upon . . . the 'Miller's Tale' and the Wife of Bath* (begun before 1617, published 1665), ed. C. F. E. Spurgeon, Publications of Chaucer Society, Second Series 33 (1901) 55–8

Breton, Nicholas (?1545–?1626) English poet 50

Bronson, Bertrand H. 214–18

Browne, Sir Thomas (1605–82) Doctor, writer of ornate prose (e.g. *Urn-Buriall*) 131

Brutus Legendary founder of Britain 26, 27

Buckhurst, Thomas Lord (1536–1608) Thomas Sackville, Earl of Dorset and Baron Buckhurst, diplomat and author of the Induction to the *Mirror for Magistrates* 50

Burns, Robert 98, 99, 100, 133

Caesar, Julius 152

Calchas (in *Troilus*) 200

Calogero, Tommaso 289

Cambalo (**Camball**, in *Squire's Tale*) 51, 109

Cambyuskan (**Cambuscan**, in *Squire's Tale*) 51, 75, 92–3, 109, 135

Canon (in *Canterbury Tales*) 65

Canon's Yeoman (in *Canterbury Tales*) 156

Canon's Yeoman's Tale 34, 178, 189

Canterbury Tales General references 37, 38, 42–4, 45, 50, 51–3, 65, 66–8, 71, 76, 77, 84–5, 90, 95, 114–15, 116, 119–24, 136, 142–4, 165, 176–8, 187, 190, 227–8, 243–4, 256–8, 264, 287, 290

Canticle of Canticles Song of Songs ('Song of Solomon') 233–9

Carlyle, Thomas (1795–1881) 131

Carpenter ⇨ **Reeve**

Catullus (*c.* 84–*c.* 54 B.C.) Roman lyric, erotic and epigrammatic poet, trans. P. Whigham (1966) 52

Martial's phrase *nimis poeta* ('too much of a poet') wrongly attributed to him by Dryden 63

Caxton, William (?1422–91) First English printer, produced first printed edition of Chaucer, the *Canterbury Tales* of 1478; Proem to second edition of *Canterbury Tales* (1484), ed. W. J. B. Crotch, *Prologues and Epilogues of William Caxton*, Early English Text Society, Original Series 176 (1928) **44–5**; 35, 43

Cethegus, Marcus 54

Ceyx (in *Book of the Duchess*) 225

Charles of Anjou (1226–85) Count of Provence and King of Naples and Sicily 286

Chartres French cathedral town, centre in 12th century of a school of Platonic thinkers and poets 176

Chaucer, Geoffrey (Galfryde), works of

Anelida and Arcite 105–8, 109, 110, 130, 151

Book of the Duchess 53, 114, 115, 129, 138, 144–5, 147–50, 153, 192–3, 218, 225, 226

Canterbury Tales 37, 38, 42–4, 45, 50, 51–3, 65, 66–8, 71, 76, 77, 84–5, 90, 95, 114–15, 116, 119–24, 136, 142–4, 165, 176–8, 187, 190, 227–8, 243–4, 256–8, 264, 287, 290

Canon's Yeoman's Tale 34, 178, 189

Clerk's Tale 39, 52, 60, 102, 104, 128, 129, 132, 276

Cook's Tale 43, 52, 229

Franklin's Tale 37, 128, 129, 189, 276 85

Friar's Tale 120, 156

General Prologue 30; 22, 38, 42, 54, 61, 65, 66, 67, 76, 77–83, 95–6, 98, 116, 119–20, 122, 124, 128, 129, 143, 157, 171, 173–4, 177, 206–14, 216, 218–32, 244, 256–7, 259, 268

Knight's Tale 52, 60, 62, 69, 72, 77, 86, 87, 90–91, 102, 106, 107, 108–9, 110, 125, 134, 136–7, 159–60, 177, 178, 189, 214, 216, 228, 229, 242–63, 287

Man of Law's Tale 19, 22, 39, 49, 52, 86, 105, 177

Chaucer, Geoffrey—*continued*

Melibee 34, 74

Merchant's Tale 52, 67, 177, 178, 218, 233, 238, 277, 278, 283, 285

Miller's Tale 43, 52, 55, 67, 68, 102, 115, 129, 134, 156, 177, 178–86, 189, 196, 214–15, 228, 229, 233–9, 252–3, 261

Monk's Tale 79–80, 102, 130–31, 177, 201

Nun's Priest's Tale 49, 61, 126–7, 129, 132, 136, 166–9, 172, 177, 270

Pardoner's Tale 129, 143, 156–9, 159, 233

Parson's Tale 34, 49

Physician's Tale 132

Prioress's Tale 39, 99, 134–5, 178

Reeve's Tale 43, 52, 67, 115, 129, 156, 177, 178, 180, 229

Shipman's Tale 67, 177

Sir Thopas 22, 55, 74, 105, 116, 134–6

Squire's Tale 34, 51, 52, 75, 89, 92–4, 109–10, 135

Summoner's Tale 43, 67, 120, 129, 156

Wife of Bath's Prologue 55–9, 67, 72, 83, 141, 156, 177, 178, 180, 185, 187, 276, 277

Wife of Bath's Tale 61, 71–2

Complaint of Mars 145–6, 150, 231

Complaint of Venus **31**; 22, 130

Complaint to his Lady 130, 147

Complaint unto Pity 147, 154

Envoy to Scogan 170

Equatorie of the Planetes 175

House of Fame **25**; 21, 23, 75, 123, 138–40, 176, 218, 225–6, 264

Legend of Good Women **28–9**; 21, 47, 110, 130, 160–65, 218, 219, 222, 225, 226, 227, 232, 242, 287–8

Merciles Beaute 151

Parliament of Fowls 105, 146, 151–5, 175–6, 178, 191, 217, 218, 228–9, 241, 261, 264, 269, 274–5

Romance of the Rose (translation) 19, 20, 21, 26, 27, 34, 50, 53, 142, 230–31

Rosemounde 150–51

Treatise on the Astrolabe 48–9, 60, 175

Troilus and Criseyde **25–6**; 20, 23, 29, 33, 37, 50, 51, 53, 60–61, 85–6, 104, 110–11, 116, 117, 123, 129, 144, 152, 158, 175, 178, 190–206, 210, 215, 218, 239, 240–41, 242, 265–73, 287

Truth 214

Poems formerly ascribed to Chaucer:

Belle Dame Sans Merci 53

Complaint of the Black Knight 53

Flower and the Leaf 73
Isle of Ladies 53
Plowman's Tale 34, 64
Chauntecleer (in *Nun's Priest's Tale*) 126, 127, 129, 166–8, 177, 270
Cherubim of Phoenicia Visionary beings in Asiatic myth from which, according to Blake, Greek gods derived 82 ◊**Priam**
Chesterton, G. K. (1874–1936) 134–6; 113
Chiasmus Figure of speech where the order of words in one parallel clause is inverted in the other 172, 274
Chrétien (Chrestien) de Troyes French poet of later 12th century, author of Arthurian romances, trans. W. W. Lomfort, *Arthurian Romances* (1913) 97, 152, 155
Christian of Troyes ◊**Chrétien de Troyes**
Cicero ◊**Tullius**
Cid, Le Tragedy of duty by French dramatist Pierre Corneille (1606–84) 106
Clemen, Wolfgang *Chaucer's Early Poetry*, trans. C. A. M. Sym (1963) from revised edition of *Der junge Chaucer* (1938) 263–5
Clerk of Oxford (in *Canterbury Tales*) 39, 52, 83, 128, 129, 132, 176, 211
Clerk's Tale 39, 52, 60, 102, 104, 128, 129, 132, 276
Clifford, Sir Lewis 27, 28
Clough, Arthur H. Subject of Matthew Arnold's elegy *The Scholar Gipsy* 149
Coghill, Nevill See also his translation of *Canterbury Tales* (1952) 156–9
   quoted 189
Col, Gontier (?1354–1418) Centre of an early group of French humanists 288
Coleridge, S. T. (1772–1834) Comment on Chaucer, in T. M. Raysor (ed.), *Coleridge's Miscellaneous Criticism* (1936) 88; 107, 126, 140
Comparatio 'Comparison', term of medieval rhetoric 177
Complaint Genre of short poem in which a lover complains, attempted by Chaucer most elaborately in *Anelida and Arcite* 130, 218
Complaint of Mars 145–6, 150, 231
Complaint of the Black Knight Poem by Lydgate included among works of Chaucer by Thynne (1532) and Speght (1598), ed. W. W. Skeat, *Chaucerian and Other Pieces* (1897) 53
Complaint of Venus 31; 22, 130
Complaint to his Lady 130, 147
Complaint unto Pity 147, 154
Conceit Ingenious or fanciful notion or expression 61, 62, 68

Concrete universals Term in medieval philosophy meaning individuals which are also classes 244

Constance (in *Man of Law's Tale*) 86, 177

Cook (in *Canterbury Tales*) 43, 52, 66, 82, 90, 176, 210, 229

Cook's Tale 43, 52, 229

Cooper, Elizabeth (*fl.* 1737) Bluestocking widow of auctioneer; *The Muses' Library* (first volume only published, 1737) **73**

Cornhill Magazine 33

Coulton, G. G. 274

Courtly love 20, 33, 36, 115, 142, 147, 148, 151, 152, 153, 186, 188, 190, 199, 229, 245, 252, 254, 259, 272, 277, 278 ◊ **Amour courtois**

Cowley, Abraham (1618–67) 68, 69

Crabbe, George (1754–1832) *Tales* (1812), in *Works*, vol. III (1823) 84–5; 143

Criseyde (in *Troilus*) 85–6, 111, 158, 191, 192–6, 197–205 *passim*, 215, 240, 265–8, 270–73

Cunningham, J. V. 'Convention as Structure: The *Prologue* to the *Canterbury Tales*', first published in *Modern Philology*, vol. 49 (1952), pp. 172–81, included in *Tradition and Poetic Structure* (1960) **218–32** as critic of Chaucer 116

Cupid God of Love 20, 21, 26, 27, 130, 142, 153, 154, 191, 223, 224, 226, 229, 241, 242, 254, 255, 258

Curia Regis King's court 285

Cyples, William 33

D'Aloul Anonymous French fabliau 186

Dante Alighieri (1265–1321) Chaucer borrowed from *Divina Commedia* in *House of Fame* and in later works, e.g. story of Ugolino of Pisa in *Monk's Tale* 39, 50, 96, 97, 100, 105, 106, 107, 129, 137, 152, 189, 282

compared with Chaucer 102–3, 104, 138–9, 141

Divinia Commedia 130, 138–40, 176, 204

Daphne 69, 246

Dares the Phrygian Reputed author of supposedly contemporary account of the fall of Troy, accepted by the Middle Ages as a primary authority 202–3

Darius King of Persia, buried (according to medieval accounts) in a magnificent tomb designed by a Jewish artist, Apelles 57–8, 59

Daun Catoun Dionysius Cato, supposed author of a Latin collection of maxims, the *Disticha*, much studied in medieval schools 129

David, King 238

Davus (in Terence's play *Phormio*) 53

Demande d'amour 'Question of love', problem in love-casuistry, cultivated in medieval courtly circles 244

Demophilus Greek dramatist from whom Plautus derived his comedy *Asinaria* 53

Denham, Sir John (1615–69) Poet, author of *Cooper's Hill*, regarded by Dryden as first master of modern metrical technique ('numbers') 64, 143

Deschamps, Eustache (1346–?1406) French poet, author of treatise on verse, the *Art de Dictier*. Ballade to Chaucer (?1386), edited with translation and commentary by T. A. Jenkins in *Modern Language Notes*, vol. 33 (1918), pp. 268–78 (consult for further details)

　Art de Dictier 22, 289

　Ballade 26–8; 19, 20, 21, 23, 34, 35, 142, 175

Diana (in *Knight's Tale*) 69, 245, 246, 247, 248

Dido 47, 62

Dinadan, Sir Scorner of knightly feats in Malory's *Morte D'Arthur* 152

Diomede (in *Troilus*) 202, 203, 204

Dioneo (in *Decameron*) 72

Diphilus (*c*.355–*c*.288 B.C.) Greek comic dramatist, contemporary of Menander, imitated by Roman dramatists 53

Dit de la gageure Anonymous French fabliau 186

Doctor of Physic (in *Canterbury Tales*) 81, 209

Don Quixote Hero of Cervantes' burlesque on romances of chivalry 74

Donaldson, E. T. See also 'Chaucer the Pilgrim', *PMLA*, vol. 69 (1954), and 'The Ending of Chaucer's *Troilus*', in *Early English and Norse Studies*, ed. A. Brown and P. Foote (1963) 190–206; 260, 261

　as critic of Chaucer 116, 117

Donne, John (?1571–1631) 221

Dorigen (in *Franklin's Tale*) 37, 276–84 *passim*

Douglas, Gavin (?1474–1522) Scottish bishop and poet 35, 36

　translation of *Aeneid* (1513), ed. D. F. C. Coldwell, vol. II, Scottish Text Society, Third Series 25 (1957) 47

Drake, Dr James (1667–1707) Author of an answer to Jerome Collier's *Short View of the Immorality and Profaneness of the English Stage* 65

Dream, Chaucer's ⟡Isle of Ladies

Dream-vision poetry 114, 148, 218, 222–32, 269

Dryden, John (1631–1700) *Fables, Ancient and Modern* (1700) contains versions of three of Chaucer's Tales (Knight's, Nun's Priest's, Wife of Bath's), together with 'The Character of a Good Parson' from

Dryden, John—*continued*
  the *General Prologue* and *The Flower and the Leaf*; Preface, ed. with
  notes by W. P. Ker, *Essays of John Dryden* (1900) **60–73**; 133, 189
  The Cock and the Fox 166–8
  as critic of Chaucer 33, 34, 36–7, 38, 39, 73–4, 98, 113, 114, 119,
    138, 155
  Palamon and Arcite 136–7
Du Clerc cui fu repus Anonymous French fabliau 186
Duck (in *Parliament of Fowls*) 151, 152, 153
Dunbar, William (*c.* 1460–?1521) One of the 'Scottish Chaucerians' 35
  The Golden Targe (1503), in *Poems*, ed. W. M. Mackenzie (1932) **45–6**
Durazzo, Duchy of 286
Dyer, Sir Edward (d. 1607) Courtier, poet and friend of Sidney 50

Eagle (in *House of Fame*) 21, 140, 226
Eagles (in *Parliament of Fowls*) 151
Edward III 49, 64, 133
Edward VII 285
Effictio Term of medieval rhetoric, 'external description of a person'
  (as against *notatio*, 'description of inner qualities') 185, 235, 237
Egeus (in *Knight's Tale*) 248–9, 259
Eliot, T. S. (1888–1965) 189
Elizabeth I 33, 50, 78, 100
Emily (*Emilia*, in *Knight's Tale*) 62, 86, 90–91, 136, 243, 245, 247, 248,
    250, 251, 255, 259, 261, 262
Empson, William 159–60; 116
Ennius (239–169 B.C.) 'Father of Roman poetry', author of an epic
  Annals which influenced Virgil 54, 61, 64
Entelechy Self-realization 179
Envoy Short section at the end of a poem, often containing a dedica-
  tion 22
Envoy to Scogan 170
Equatorie of the Planetes 175
Equivocal rhyme 22
Erigena, Johannes Scotus (9th century) Philosopher and theologian
  141
Esculapius Roman god of healing 81
Exegesis, patristic Interpretation of Scripture practised by Church
  Fathers such as Augustine and Gregory 117, 233
Exemplum (pl. *exempla*) Story used by a preacher or didactic writer
  to illustrate a point 158, 167, 187

Fabliaux French poems (mostly 13th-century), short stories of sex and trickery, imitated by Chaucer in tales of Miller, Reeve, Shipman, Merchant and Summoner 115, 179, 180, 186, 238, 289

Fairfax, Edward (d. 1635) English poet, follower of Spenser and translator of Tasso 64

Falstaff, Sir John 124

Fergusson, Robert (1750–74) Scottish poet 133

Fescennine licence Freedom allowed Romans in *versus fescennini*, ribald wedding-songs 152

Fiametta 72 ◊ **Aquino, Countess of**

Ficino, Marsilio (1433–99) Italian Platonist 141

Fielding, Henry (1707–54) 156–67

Fiorentino di mercato vecchio The Florentine speech of the old market-place (one of the oldest districts of Florence) 287

Flaubert, Gustave (1821–80) 138

Flemer 'Putter-to-flight' (*Canterbury Tales*, II 460) 152

Flower and the Leaf, The Anonymous 15th-century poem printed first among works of Chaucer by Speght (1598), generally accepted as Chaucer's (see *Legend of Good Women, Prol.*, F 72) and praised as his by Dryden, Keats and Hazlitt; ed. D. A. Pearsall (1962) 73

Four levels of meaning, the The four kinds of meaning recognized in Scripture by medieval interpreters: literal (or historical), moral (or tropological), allegorical and anagogical 188

Francesca (in *Divine Comedy*) 102

Franco-Veneto Italianized form of French used by Venetian poets in Middle Ages 141

Franklin (in *Canterbury Tales*) 81, 82, 90, 128, 129, 210, 278, 279, 284

Franklin's Tale 37, 128, 129, 189, 276–85

Frederick II (1194–1250) King of Sicily and Holy Roman Emperor 286

French Academy 132

French, R. D. 219

Freud, Sigmund 271–2

Friar (in *Canterbury Tales*) 43, 65, 78, 79, 81, 120, 156–7, 176, 208–9

Friar's Tale 120, 156

Froissart, Jean (1337–after 1404) French contemporary of Chaucer, poet and chronicler 141, 152, 240

Ganymede 140

Garden of Eden 211, 283–4

Gascoigne, George (?1539–77) Poet and dramatist 50

Gaston de Foix 240

Gaufred de Vinsauf ◊ **Geoffrey of Vinsauf**

General Prologue to Canterbury Tales 30; 22, 38, 42, 54 61, 65, 66, 67, 76, 77–83, 95–6, 98, 116, 119–20, 122, 124, 128, 129, 143, 157, 171, 173–4, 177, 206–14, 216, 218–32, 244, 256–57, 259, 268

Geoffrey of Monmouth 27

Geoffrey of Vinsauf (Galfridus Vinosalvensis, Gaufred de Vinsauf) (d. ?1249) English rhetorician and author of an art of poetry, *Poetria Nova*, which Chaucer knew 127, 130, 168, 274

Geta (in Terence's play *Phormio*) 53

Giraldi, Giovan Battista (known as *Cintio*) (1504–73) Italian author of *Ecatommiti*, a collection of stories in imitation of Boccaccio's *Decameron* 95

Godfrey Gobelive (character in *Pastime of Pleasure*) 152 ⟡ **Hawes**

Golden Age 211

Goldsmith, Oliver 95

Goose (in *Parliament of Fowls*) 146, 151, 152, 153

Gower, John (d. 1408) Friend of Chaucer, author of poems in French, Latin and English. Allusion to Chaucer (found only in first version of poem) in *Confessio Amantis*, ed. G. C. Macaulay, Early English Text Society, Extra Series 81–2 (1900–1901). See J. H. Fisher, *John Gower: Moral Philosopher and Friend of Chaucer* (New York, 1964; London, 1965) 30–31; 33, 49, 50, 63, 74, 98, 133, 142, 151, 152, 176, 222, 224–5, 227, 240, 274, 289

as critic of Chaucer 19, 20, 21, 142

Granson (Graunson) ⟡ **Oton de Granson**

Grazzini, Antonio (1503–84) Italian author of *Le Cene*, a collection of stories in imitation of Boccaccio's *Decameron* 95

Greville, Sir Fulke (1554–1628) Statesman and poet 50

Griselda (Grisilde, in *Clerk's Tale*) 60, 102, 104

Grizild ⟡ **Griselda**

Guildsmen (in *Canterbury Tales*) 78, 81, 82–3, 209, 230

Guillaume de Lorris (13th century) French author of first part of the *Romance of the Rose* 138, 147, 148, 152, 155 ⟡ **Romance of the Rose**

Guillaume de Machaut (?1300–1377) French musician and author of lyrics and longer works in courtly allegorical style (e.g. *Jugement dou Roy de Navarre*) which influenced Deschamps, Froissart and Chaucer 140, 148, 151, 289

Guillaume de Poictiers (1071–1126) Earliest known Provençal troubadour 141

Hallam, Arthur Subject of Tennyson's elegy *In Memoriam* 149

Hamlet 120

Hardying, John (1378–?1465) Author of a verse *Chronicle* 49, 50

Harold, King 274

Harrington, Sir John (1561–1612) Poet and translator of Ariosto 64

Hart, W. M. 278, 281

Harvey, Gabriel (?1545–?1630) Poet, controversialist and friend of Spenser; marginal notes in his copy of Periegetes' *Survey*, ed. G. C. Moore Smith in *Gabriel Harvey's Marginalia* (Stratford-upon-Avon, 1913) 48–9; 21

notes in his copy of Speght's *Chaucer* (Moore Smith, pp. 225–34) 34

Hawes, Stephen (1474–1523) Author of *Pastime of Pleasure* 152, 240

Hazlitt, William (1778–1830) *Lectures on the English Poets* (1818), ed. A. R. Waller and A. Glover in *Works*, vol. v (1902) 85–8

as critic of Chaucer 38, 114

Helen of Troy (in *Troilus*) 199

Hellenistic romances Romantic prose narratives composed in Greek around 3rd century A.D., e.g. *Daphnis and Chloe* 289

Henry II 65

Henry IV 64, 274

Henry VIII 33, 48, 49, 59

Herbert, George 283

Hercules Classical hero, according to Blake, type both of benevolent labour on behalf of others (Chaucer's Plowman) and of brute strength (Chaucer's Miller) 82 ◊**Spectrous shadow**

Hermogenes 54

Hernani Tragedy by Victor Hugo (1802–85) 106

Hilton, Walter English prose writer, author of mystical treatise *The Ladder of Perfection* 274

Hippolyta (in *Knight's Tale*) 110, 250

Hoccleve, Thomas (c.1368–c.1430) Londoner, civil servant and poetic disciple of Chaucer; *Regement of Princes* (1412), ed. F. J. Furnivall, Early English Text Society, Extra Series 72 (1897) 41–2

as critic of Chaucer 33, 35, 36, 143

Homer (?8th century B.C.) 26, 39, 53, 62, 63, 72, 95, 100, 111, 137, 154, 189, 204, 245, 260–61, 287

Homoeoteleuton Rhetorical figure, use of a series of words with the same or similar endings 170, 172, 174

Hopkins, Gerard Manley (1844–89) 221

Horace (65–8 B.C.) Roman poet, author of odes, satires, epistles and an *Ars Poetica*, trans. T. S. Dorsch, *Classical Literary Criticism* (1965) 34, 52, 53, 54, 60, 63, 64, 70, 212–13 ◊**Multa renascentur**

Host (in *Canterbury Tales*) 22, 38, 44, 74, 80, 81, 95, 120–24 *passim*, 128, 129, 132, 135, 158–9, 177, 223, 227, 228

House of Fame 25; 21, 23, 75, 123, 138–40, 176, 218, 225–6, 264

Housman, A. E. (1859–1936) **136–7**

Hrimm hramm ruff Ezra Pound's version of Chaucer's version of what alliterative verse sounded like (*Canterbury Tales*, x 43) 141

Hudibras Satirical poem by Samuel Butler (1612–80) 128

Hugelin of Pisa (in *Monk's Tale*) 132–3

Hugh de Lusignan 288

Huizinga, J. 260

author of a study of play, *Homo Ludens* 257

Humanism The neo-classicism of Renaissance men-of-letters 187

Humours Four bodily fluids (blood, choler, melancholy and phlegm) thought to determine a person's bodily and mental constitution 269

Hunt, James Henry Leigh (1784–1859)

Imagination and Fancy (1844) 89

Stories in Verse (1855) 90–94

Wit and Humour (1846) 90

as critic of Chaucer 38, 39

Hurd, Richard (1720–1808) Bishop and lover of 'fine fabling'; *Letters on Chivalry and Romance* (1762) **74–5**

as critic of Chaucer 38

Iago 120, 157

In Memoriam (Tennyson's) 189

Inner Temple One of the Inns of Court 130

Isaiah 137

Isle of Ladies (Chaucer's Dream) Anonymous poem printed first among Chaucer's works by Speght (1598) and admired by Ruskin; ed. W. W. Skeat, *Chaucerian and other Pieces* (Oxford, 1897) 53

January (in *Merchant's Tale*) 238, 277, 283

Jean de Meun (13th century) French author of second part of the *Romance of the Rose* 50, 115, 150, 155, 175–6 ⟡ **Romance of the Rose**

Jeffrey, Francis, Lord Jeffrey (1773–1850) Scottish critic and jurist, one of the founders and first editor of *Edinburgh Review* **88–9**

Jerome, St (340–420) Church Father and anti-feminist writer 280

Jeu *Jeu parti*, genre of poetry in which a question is proposed and debated 284

Jingle Arrangement of words to produce pleasing or striking sounds 61

John (the Carpenter in *Miller's Tale*) 179, 180, 181–2, 186, 253

John of Gaunt (1340–99) Son of Edward III and father of Henry IV, patron of Chaucer (whose sister-in-law he married) and of Wycliffe 64, 151

311 Index

Johnson, Samuel (1709–84) **73–4**; 98
Jonson, Ben 189
Jupiter (in *Knight's Tale*) 248, 249, 252, 259
Juvenal (A.D. *c.* 50–*c.* 130) Roman satiric poet 209, 212, 213

Kaske, R. E. 'Patristic Exegesis: The Defence', in *Critical Approaches to Medieval Literature*, Selected Papers from the English Institute 1958–9, ed. D. Bethurum (1960) **233–9**; 117
Keats, John (1795–1821) 98, 100, 131
  Isabella, or The Pot of Basil, a pathetic tale based on Boccaccio's *Decameron* 102
Ker, W. P. (1855–1923) British scholar, Professor of English at London University; *Essays on Medieval Literature* (1905); 'Chaucer and the Renaissance', one of the Clark Lectures delivered at Cambridge in 1912, published posthumously in *Form and Style in Poetry*, ed. R. W. Chambers (London, 1929, new edn, 1966) **104–11**; 37, 113
King, Edward Subject of Milton's elegy *Lycidas* 149
King Lear 92
Kingis Quair 'The King's Book', Chaucerian poem of 15th century, often ascribed to King James I of Scotland 34
Kittredge, George L. (1860–1941) *Chaucer and his Poetry* (Cambridge, Mass., 1915), based on lectures delivered in 1914 **119–24**
  as critic of Chaucer 114–15, 116, 220, 232
Knight (in *Canterbury Tales*) 52, 77–8, 79, 84, 119, 121, 123, 124, 134, 165, 170, 177, 228, 242 62 *passim*
Knight's Tale 52, 60, 62, 69, 72, 77, 86, 87, 90–91, 102, 106, 107, 108–9, 110, 125, 134, 136–7, 159–60, 177, 178, 189, 214, 216, 228, 229, 242–63, 287

Landor, Walter Savage (1775–1864) Poet and prose writer; wrote *Imaginary Conversations* (see especially, 'Chaucer, Boccaccio and Petrarca'); letter of refusal to R. H. Horne, who had asked him to contribute to a volume of modernizations of Chaucer (which appeared in 1841 with contributions by Wordsworth, Leigh Hunt, etc.), recorded in *Letters of E. B. Browning Addressed to R. H. Horne*, ed. S. R. Townshend Mayer (1877) **89**
Langland, William (14th century) English poet, author of *Piers Plowman*, a religious dream-allegory with satire in it 49, 204, 210, 211, 212
Langue d'oc Provençal, language of Southern France in Middle Ages (oc = oui) 96

Langue d'oïl Language of Northern France in Middle Ages (oïl = oui) 96

Latini, Brunetto (?1220–?95) Italian writer, friend of Dante, author of an encyclopedia *Li Livres dou Tresor* (*Treasure*) 97

Laureate poet
  Chaucer as 45
  Skelton as 49
  Dryden as 72

Lawrence, W. W. 220, 232

Lawyer ◊Man of Law

Leavis, F. R. 116

Legend of Good Women 28–9; 21, 47, 110, 130, 160–65, 218, 219, 222, 225, 226, 227, 232, 242, 287–8

Leicester, Third Earl of (1619–98) Eldest brother of Algernon Sidney, friend of Dryden 68, 69

Lewis Probably Lewis Chaucer, the 'lyte Lowys my sone' to whom Chaucer addressed his *Treatise on the Astrolabe* 49

Lewis, C. S. (1898–1963) English writer, Anglican controversialist, teacher of English at Oxford and Cambridge **142–55**
  as critic of Chaucer 33, 115

Linneus, Carolus (1707–78) Swedish botanist and father of modern systematic botany 77

Lollius Non-existent author of Latin version of story of *Troilus* to which Chaucer refers (*Troilus*, I 394, and see *House of Fame*, 1468) 50, 191

Lorenzo de' Medici (1449–92) 'The Magnificent', ruler of Florence, author of *L'Altercazione*, an imaginary conversation in which the Platonic philosophy of Ficino is expounded 141

Lounsbury, T. R. (1838–1915) **103**

Love, God of ◊Cupid

Lowell, James Russell (1819–91) American poet, essayist and diplomat; 'Chaucer', first published in *North American Review* (July, 1870) and included in *My Study Windows* (Boston, 1871) **94–5**

Lowes, John Livingston (1867–1945) **138–40**; 148, 151, 219

Lucan (A.D. 39–65) Latin poet, author of *Pharasalia*, an epic on the civil war of Caesar and Pompey 26, 62, 287

Lucilius (c.180–c.102 B.C.) Latin satirist imitated by Horace 64

Lucina The moon 42, 279

Lucretius (94–55 B.C.) Roman poet and philosopher, author of *De Rerum Natura* 64

Lycidas (Milton's) 149

Lydgate, John (?1370–?1450) Monk of Bury St Edmunds and poetic

follower of Chaucer; *Siege of Thebes*, a pseudo-Canterbury-Tale (1420–22), ed. A. Erdmann, Early English Text Society, Extra Series 108 (1911) **42–4**; 34, 36, 48, 49, 50, 63, 74, 145, 147, 240, 275
as imitator of Chaucer 35, 142–3

Macbeth 80, 91–2, 120
Mackintosh, Sir James 88
Maecenas (d. 8 B.C.) Friend of Roman emperor Augustus and patron of Horace and Virgil 64
Magician (in *Franklin's Tale*) 281, 282, 284
Malatesta The Italian family of Rimini, prominent in later Middle Ages 141
Mallarmé, Stéphane (1842–98) 275
Malone, Kemp 160–65; 208
Malory, Sir Thomas (d. 1471) 152
Man in Black (in *Book of the Duchess*) ◊**Black Knight**
Man of Law (in *Canterbury Tales*) 19, 22, 39, 52, 81, 210, 213
Man of Law's Tale 19, 22, 39, 49, 52, 86, 105, 177
Manciple (in *Canterbury Tales*) 78, 82, 123, 209
Manilius (*fl.* 1st century A.D.) Roman author of *Astronomica*, didactic poem on astrology written under Augustus and Tiberius 60
Manly, J. M. (1865–1940) **126–30**
as critic of Chaucer 115
Marcus Cethegus 54
'Marriage Group' 177
Mars
  (in *Complaint of Mars*) 150
  (in *Knight's Tale*) 246, 247, 248, 259
Martial (A.D. *c.* 40–*c.* 104) Latin poet best known for twelve books of Epigrams 62 ◊**Catullus**
Martini, Simone (?1283–1344) Leading Italian painter of the Sienese school 286, 287
Marvell, Andrew (1621–78) 221
Masefield, John (1878–1967) English poet laureate and author of narrative poems 143
Mathew, Gervase 285–90
Matilda (in *Divine Comedy*) 102
Matthieu de Vendôme (later 12th century) French rhetorician 274
Mausolus Satrap of Cana; his magnificent tomb ('Mausoleum'), built by his sister and widow Artemisia, was one of the Seven Wonders of the ancient world, alluded to by Pope's Wife of Bath following Brathwait 58, 59

Medici, Lorenzo de' ◊**Lorenzo de' Medici**

Melibee 34, 74

Menander (*c.* 342–*c.* 290 B.C.) Greek comic dramatist of the New Comedy, imitated by Plautus and Terence 53

Merchant (in *Canterbury Tales*) 52, 67, 83, 90, 121, 177

Merchant's Tale 52, 67, 177, 178, 218, 233, 238, 277, 278, 283, 285

Merciless Lady ◊**Belle Dame Sans Merci**

Merry Devil of Edmonton Anonymous English comedy (*c.* 1603) 124

Merry Wives of Windsor, The 124

Merton ◊**Walter de Merton**

Midsummer Night's Dream, A 152

Milbourne, Luke (1649–1720) Poet and clergyman, remembered for his attack on Dryden's translation (1697) of Virgil, to which Dryden replied in the Preface to *Fables* 69

Miller (in *Canterbury Tales*) 43, 52, 66, 67, 82, 84, 102, 115, 119, 121, 129, 134, 156, 176, 177, 179, 183, 185, 186, 211, 228, 229, 252–3

Miller, R. P. 233

Miller's Tale 43, 52, 55, 67, 68, 102, 115, 129, 134, 156, 177, 178–86, 189, 196, 214–15, 228, 229, 233–9, 252–3, 261

Milton, John (1608–74) 34, 39, 98, 107, 143, 144, 275
lines on Chaucer in *Il Penseroso* 75, 92
quoted 109

Moira Fate (Greek) 247

Monk
(in *Canterbury Tales*) 38, 65, 78–9, 79–80, 123, 177, 208–9, 210, 228, 230, 262
(in *Shipman's Tale*) 160

Monk's Tale 79–80, 102, 130–31, 177, 201

Montaigne (1533–92) French author, whose highly personal and informal Essays were among Dryden's favourite books 36, 61

Morris, William (1834–96) English poet and artist, author of narrative poems in a Chaucerian manner, designer and publisher of Kelmscott Chaucer 143

Mortimer 64

Mozart, Wolfgang 153

Multa renascentur . . . et norma loquendi 'Many terms that have fallen out of use shall be born again, and those shall fall that are now in repute, if Usage so will it, in whose hands lies the judgement, the right and the rule of speech', from Horace's *Ars Poetica*, quoted by Dryden 70

Muscatine, Charles 176–86
  as critic of Chaucer 115–16, 117
Mystery plays Medieval plays based on Bible stories 181, 213

Naevolus (in Juvenal) 209
Napier's History of the Peninsular War 108
Naples, Seneschal of 288
Narcissus Beautiful youth described by Ovid (*Metamorphoses*, III) 62
  well of, in *Romance of Rose* 149, 223–4
Narrator, Chaucer the
  in *Canterbury Tales* (the pilgrim) 55, 79, 83, 116, 123, 135, 206–11,
    214, 227
  in dream poems (the dreamer) 116, 150, 227, 241–2, 264
  in *Troilus* 116, 191–2, 194–5, 200, 201, 202, 203, 241–2
Nature (in *Parliament of Fowls*) 175, 217, 229
Nelli, Francesco 289
Neuse, R. 242–63
Newton, Sir Isaac 77
Nicholas (in *Miller's Tale*) 102, 177, 179, 180, 182, 186, 252–3, 261
Noe (Noah) 181, 238
Novelle ◇**Novels**
Novels Short stories, either in prose (Boccaccio's *novelle*) or in verse
  (Chaucer's *Canterbury Tales*) 67, 71, 77, 290
Nun's Priest (in *Canterbury Tales*) 78, 166–7, 169, 177
Nun's Priest's Tale 49, 61, 126–7, 129, 132, 136, 166–9, 172, 177, 270

Occupatio Term of medieval rhetoric 260
  defined 275
Ockham, William (d. ?1349) English scholastic philosopher 176
Octavian (in *Book of the Duchess*) 225
Old Saxon friends Lovers of older English 70
Orwell, George (1903–50) 169
Oton (Otes) **de Granson** (c. 1345–97) Knight of Savoy, courtly poet
  from three of whose ballades Chaucer derived his *Complaint of
  Venus* 22, 31, 130
Ovid (43 B.C.–A.D. ?17) 21, 26, 27, 37, 69, 72, 104, 189, 213, 287
  'book of the Roman feasts' (*Fasti*), trans. J. G. Frazer (1929) 60
  compared with Chaucer 60–62, 68, 119
  Metamorphoses, trans. Mary M. Innes (1955) 139
  poems of love (*Amores, De Arte Amandi*, etc.) 33, 51
Owl and the Nightingale Early Middle English debate poem (c. 1200)
  151

Oxford, Edward de Vere, Earl of (1550–1604) Poet and courtier 50

Paget, Henry, Second Baron Paget (d. 1568) 50
Paideia Teaching (Greek) 259
Palaeologoi Greek Byzantine family 286
Palamon (in *Knight's Tale*) 60, 62, 72, 77, 86, 87, 106, 107, 110, 214, 243, 244, 247, 248, 250, 251, 253, 254, 255, 259, 261, 263
Palinode Place in a work where the author retracts something he has formerly said 151, 152
Pandarus (in *Troilus*) 111, 152, 193, 194, 196–8, 199, 200, 201, 202, 240–41, 265, 269
Pandras(us) 26, 27
Papageno Comic character in Mozart's *The Magic Flute* 152
Pardoner (in *Canterbury Tales*) 43, 78, 80, 81, 119, 120, 121, 156–9, 159, 211
Pardoner's Tale 129, 143, 156–9, 159, 233
Parliament of Fowls 105, 146, 151–5, 175–6, 178, 191, 217, 218, 228–9, 241, 261, 264, 269, 274–5
Parson (in *Canterbury Tales*) 65, 66, 81, 84, 208
Parson's Tale 34, 49
Peasant's Revolt Revolt of English peasantry in 1381, referred to in *Nun's Priest's Tale* (VII 3393–6) 165, 168
Pendennis (novel by Thackeray) 111
Persius (A.D. 34–62) Roman author of a book of satires 60, 129
Pertelote (in *Nun's Priest's Tale*) 126, 129, 270
Petrarch (1304–74) 50, 96, 129, 138, 221, 287, 289
  Canzoniere, sequence of songs (*canzoni*) and sonnets imitated by Wyatt, Surrey, etc. 104–5
  His Latin version of Boccaccio's story of Griselda, cited by Chaucer's Clerk as his source 60, 104, 129
Philemon (*c.* 361–262 B.C.) Greek comic dramatist and rival of Menander 53
Philemon ◊Baucis
Phillips, Edward (1630–?96) Writer, nephew and pupil of Milton; *Theatrum Poetarum* (1675), a catalogue of poets; selections ed. J. E. Springarn in *Critical Essays of the Seventeenth Century* (Oxford, 1908), vol. II 59
Phormio (in Terence's play of that name) 53
Physician's Tale 132
Piers Plowman ◊Langland
Piers Plowman, tale of ◊Plowman's Tale
Plato 30, 67

Plautus (d. 184 B.C.) Roman comic dramatist, imitator of Greek New Comedy 52, 53, 289

Plowman (in *Canterbury Tales*) 81, 82, 165, 256

Plowman's Tale Pseudo-Canterbury-Tale of unknown authorship, strongly anti-clerical, first printed with Chaucer's works by Thynne (1542), accepted by Speght (1598) and generally thereafter (e.g. by Dryden) until Tyrwhitt's edition (1775); ed. W. W. Skeat, *Chaucerian and Other Pieces* (Oxford, 1897) 34, 64

Poet Laureate ◇Laureate poet

Pope, Alexander (1688–1744) Pope's conversation is recorded in Joseph Spence's *Observations, Ancedotes, and Characters of Books and Men*, ed. J. M. Osborn (Oxford, 1966) **73**

Wife of Bath her Prologue (1714) **58–9**; 37

his rhyming technique compared with Chaucer's 170–74

Temple of Fame (1715), a version of Chaucer's *House of Fame* 75

Porta, Giambattista della (1535–1615) Italian physiognomist 66

Pound, Ezra (1885–) **141–2, 155**; 221

Premierfait, Laurence (1388–1420) French humanist, friend of Col, translator of Cicero and Boccaccio 288

Preston, Raymond 166–9

Priam King of Troy. The gods of Priam, lofty myths of Asia, were degraded (according to Blake) into abstract deities by the Trojans and Greeks 82, 177, 199 ◇**Cherubim of Phoenicia**

Priapus God of fertility 152, 154

Prioress (in *Canterbury Tales*) 39, 66, 78, 83, 84, 121, 123, 134

Prioress's Tale 39, 99, 134–5, 178

Provençal Properly language of Provence, in southern part of what is now France, but used loosely by Dryden of Old French 71, 73

Puttenham, George (?1530–90) *Art of English Poesy* (published anonymously, 1589), ed G. Gregory Smith in *Elizabethan Critical Essays* (Oxford, 1904) vol. II **49–50**

as critic of Chaucer 33

Quodlibet Form of musical joke, in which two incongruous tunes are combined 166

Raleigh, Sir Walter (?1552–1618) Poet and favourite of Elizabeth I 33, 50

Raleigh, Sir Walter A. (1861–1922) **131–4**

Ramsay, Allan (1686–1758) Scottish poet 133

Reeve (in *Canterbury Tales*) 43, 66, 67, 82, 102, 115, 123, 129, 156, 176, 177, 229

Reeve's Tale 43, 52, 67, 115, 129, 156, 177, 178, 180, 229

Reynard Fox hero of medieval French beast-epic, *Roman de Renard* 166

Richard I 127

Richard II 33, 49, 64, 242

Richard Feverel (novel by George Meredith) 111

Richards, I. A. 116

Riding rhyme 50

Rioters (in *Pardoner's Tale*) 157, 158

Robert of Anjou (1275–1343) Angevin King of Naples, father of Maria d'Aquino (supposed mistress of Boccaccio) 72, 286–7, 288

Robertson, D. W. 117, 233

Robinson, F. N. 161, 219, 222–3, 260

Robyn (in *Miller's Tale*) 179, 180

Rochester, John Wilmot, Lord (1647–80) Poet and companion of Charles II 63

Romance of the Rose (13th century) French allegory of love, started by Guillaume de Lorris and finished by Jean de Meun 19, 20, 21, 26, 27, 50, 115, 142, 146, 147, 148–9, 152, 153, 154, 155, 176, 222, 223–4, 225, 226, 230, 231, 232

Middle English translation (the first part thought to be Chaucer's) 19, 20, 21, 26, 27, 34, 50, 53, 142, 230–31

Romances, Middle English 22, 74, 105, 133, 134, 263

Rosemounde 150–51

Rosiphelee (in Gower's *Confessio Amantis*) 225, 227

Ruggiers, P. G. 276–85

Ruskin, John (1819–1900) 94

Russell (the fox in *Nun's Priest's Tale*) 126, 166, 270

Saint Simon, Duc de (1675–1755) French soldier and author of Memoirs of the courts of Louis XIV and XV 286

Salutati, Coluccio (1331–1406) Early Italian humanist 289

San Severini 286

Saturn (in *Knight's Tale*) 248, 249, 259

Scholar ▷Clerk of Oxford

Scogan, Henry (?1361–1407) Recipient of Chaucer's *Envoy to Scogan* and author of a Moral Ballade in which Chaucer is referred to 151

Scotus Erigena, Johannes (9th century) Philosopher and theologian 141

Scudéry, Magdeleine de (1607–1701) French poet, novelist and lady of fashion, not known to have translated Chaucer 71

Second Nun (in *Canterbury Tales*) 78

Seneca the Younger (?4 B.C.–65 A.D.) Roman statesman, tragedian and author of ethical treatises (e.g. *De Ira*) frequently cited by Chaucer 26, 27, 34

Sergeant of the Law ◊**Man of Law**

Seven Arts The seven liberal arts which provided a syllabus of medieval education: Grammar, Rhetoric and Logic; Arithmetic, Geometry, Music and Astronomy 130

Shakespeare 39, 80, 88, 89, 92, 98, 100, 141, 165–6, 192, 221

Shelley 126

Shipman (in *Canterbury Tales*) 67, 82, 156

Shipman's Tale 67, 177

Sidney, Sir Philip (1554–86) *Apology for Poetry* (written about 1581, published 1595), ed. G. Gregory Smith in *Elizabethan Critical Essays* (Oxford, 1904), vol. 1 **51**; 33, 50
  Astrophel and Stella 221

Sigismonda Heroine of one of Boccaccio's *Decameron* tales, translated by Dryden in *Fables* 72

Silenus A satyr, lover of fun and drink 81, 152

Sir Gawain and the Green Knight Anonymous Arthurian romance of later 14th century 241, 267

Sir Thopas 22, 55, 74, 105, 116, 134–6

Skelton, John (?1460–1529) Poet and tutor of Henry VIII, laureated at Oxford and Cambridge; *Phillip Sparrow* (before 1509), ed. P. Henderson in *Complete Poems* (1959) **46**; 35, 49, 211, 240

Skinner, Stephen (1623–67) English philologist who, in *Etymologicon Linguae Anglicanae*, blamed Chaucer for adulterating the language with foreign words 74

Socrates 26, 27, 33, 175

Solomon 238

Song of Songs ◊**Canticle of Canticles**

Sources and Analogues of Chaucer's Canterbury Tales ed. W. F. Bryan and G. Dempster 220

Southey, Robert (1774–1843) 96

Spearing, A. C. 265–73

Spectrous shadow The lower part of divided man, according to Blake's system, in which the whole man (here Hercules) divides into four: the Humanity (here the Plowman), the Emanation, the Spectre and the Shadow (here the Miller) 82

Speght, Thomas (*fl.* 1600) Schoolmaster whose edition of Chaucer, first published in 1598, had no rival until the appearance of Urry's in 1721; *The Works of our Ancient and Learned English Poet Geoffrey Chaucer* (1598, 2nd edn 1602, another edn 1687) **54–5**; 34, 36, 51, 53, 63

Speirs, John 165–6

Spenser, Edmund (1552–99) *Faerie Queene* (2nd part, 1596) 51; 64, 98, 111, 114, 131, 152, 261
  compared with Chaucer, 85, 89, 143, 176
  as critic of Chaucer, 21, 34, 36, 75

Squire (in *Canterbury Tales*) 52, 75, 77, 78, 81–2, 135, 210, 216, 230, 259

Squire of Dames Cynical servant of ladies in Spenser's *Faerie Queene* 152

Squire's Tale 34, 51, 52, 75, 89, 92–4, 109–10, 135

Statius (*c*. A.D. 45–96) Latin poet, author of the epic *Thebais* which provides the background to the *Knight's Tale* 26, 105, 261, 287

Statius Caecilius (d. 168 B.C.) Roman comic dramatist 53

Stefano da Verona (?1374–1438) Late Gothic Italian painter 287

Stendhal (1783–1842) 286

Stesichorus 54

Stevens, John 239–42

Summoner (in *Canterbury Tales*) 43, 67, 78, 80, 84, 120, 128, 156–7, 176, 210

Summoner's Tale 43, 67, 120, 129, 156

Surigo, Stephen 'Laureate poet' from Milan, author in the 1470s of a much-quoted Latin epitaph hung by Chaucer's tomb in Westminster Abbey 33, 36

Surrey, Countess of 240

Surrey, Henry Howard, Earl of (?1517–47) Soldier and poet, translator of *Aeneid* and author of amorous poems 33, 49, 239

Swift, Jonathan (1667–1745) 169, 262
  A Modest Proposal 157, 158

Swinburne, A. C. (1837–1909) 'Short Notes on English Poets', first published in *Fortnightly Review* (1880) and included in *Miscellanies* (1886) 101–3; 38, 39

Tacitus (*c*. A.D. 55–after 115) Roman orator and historian 63

Tamino Hero of Mozart's opera *The Magic Flute* 152

Tartar King ◊**Cambyuskan**

Tatlock, J. S. P. 282

Terence (?195–159 B.C.) Roman comic dramatist, successor to Plautus and imitator of Greek New Comedy 52, 53, 289

Thackeray, William Makepeace (1811–63) 95

Theomachia Battle of the Gods 247

Theophrastus (d. 287 B.C.) Greek philosopher and pupil of Aristotle, author of the *Characters*, a collection of thirty short portraits of typical characters 76

Theseid ⟡**Boccaccio**

Theseus (in *Knight's Tale*) 110, 242–62 *passim*

Theseus (in *Midsummer Night's Dream*, see Act v Scene 1) 84

Thomas à Becket, St 65, 84, 121, 122

Thomas Aquinas, St (?1225–74) Scholastic philosopher and follower of Aristotle 176

Thynne, William (d. 1546) Member of household of Henry VIII commissioned by him to search libraries and monasteries for copies of Chaucer's work; *Works of Geoffrey Chaucer*, ed. Thynne (the first attempt at a collected edition, published in 1532) 33, 48

Tibullus (?48–19 B.C.) Roman poet, author of elegies on love and country life 52

Tiddy, R. J. 166

Tillyard, E. M. W. 179

Tragic Comedians (novel by Meredith) 111

Trajan (A.D. 53–117) Pagan Roman Emperor who appears in the heaven of the just in *Paradiso*, xx, and claims to have been saved by his 'truth' in *Piers Plowman*, B xi 204

Treatise on the Astrolabe 48–9, 60, 175

Trinity Manuscript Containing Milton's proposals for future poems 107

Troilus (in *Troilus*) 29, 111, 144, 191–8 *passim*, 198–202, 203, 204, 205, 210, 215, 265, 266, 268, 270, 271, 272

Troilus and Criseyde 25–6; 20, 23, 29, 33, 37, 50, 51, 53, 60–61, 85–6, 104, 110–11, 116, 117, 123, 129, 144, 152, 158, 175, 178, 190–206, 210, 215, 218, 239, 240 41, 242, 265–73, 287

Troubadours Medieval lyric poets who wrote in the language of Provence, langue d'oc 96, 141

Truth 214

Tuke, Sir Brian (d. 1545) Gentleman of antiquarian interests, with William Thynne in Henry VIII's household; Preface for Thynne's edition of Chaucer written 'then being tarrying for the tide at Greenwich' 48; 33–4, 36

Tullius Marcus Tullius Cicero (106–43 B.C.), Roman statesman and orator 41, 128

Turbervile, George (?1540–1610) English poet and author of treatises on falconry and hunting 50

Ugolino (in *Divine Comedy*) 102

Ulyssean art Art of navigation as practised by Ulysses on his journey back from Troy 82

Underwood, D. 242, 243, 250, 260

Unjust Steward, Parable of 157

Urry, John (1666–1715) Author of an edition (published posthumously in 1721) of Chaucer, the first since Speght 36

Usk, Thomas (d. 1388) London writer, influenced by Chaucer and by Langland; *The Testament of Love* (*c.*1387); ed. W. W. Skeat, *Chaucerian and Other Pieces* (Oxford, 1897) **29**; 152
  as critic of Chaucer 19, 20, 21, 142, 175

Vanity Fair (novel by Thackeray) 111

Vekke Hag, name of the cynical old woman in the Middle English translation of the *Romance of the Rose* (in French, 'La Vieille') 152

Venus 20, 29, 30, 33, 127, 142, 145, 168, 175, 224, 226
  in *Knight's Tale* 246, 247, 248

Villon, François (b. 1431) French poet of humble family and irregular life, author of *La Belle Heaulmière* ('The Fair Armouress') 101, 103, 189

Vincent of Beauvais Author of the chief encyclopedia of the 13th century, *Speculum Maius* 176

Virgil (70–19 B.C.) *Priapus*, three *Priapea* or poems to Priapus, phallic god of fertility, included in *Appendix Vergiliana*, a set of shorter poems ascribed to Virgil 26, 41, 53, 60, 62, 63, 64, 101, 104, 124, 143, 189, 287
  Aeneid 47, 72, 105, 204, 226
  Priapus 51

Virginia (in *Physician's Tale*) 132

Volgare illustre 'The noble vernacular' 287

Vulcan (in *House of Fame*) 226

Vulgate That Latin version of the Bible (made by St Jerome) most widely used in Middle Ages and since 234

Waller, Edmund (1606–87) Poet regarded by Dryden as an early master of modern metrical technique ('numbers') 64, 143

Walter de Merton (d. 1277) Founder of Merton College, the most notable college in 14th-century Oxford 175

Ward, T. H. 113

Warton, Joseph (1722–1800) Poet and literary critic, elder brother of Thomas; *Essay on the Genius and Writings of Pope* (4th edn, 2 vols., 1782) **76–7**
  as critic of Chaucer 38

Warton, Thomas (1728–90) Younger brother of Joseph, literary historian, poet laureate and precursor of Romanticism; *The History of English Poetry* (3 vols., 1774–81) **75–6**
  as critic of Chaucer 38

Watts-Dunton, Theodore 176

Webb, H. J. 252, 260, 261

Webbe, William (*fl.* 1568–91) Elizabethan critic, author of a *Discourse of English Poetry* (1586) 34

White (Blanche, in *Book of the Duchess*) 149, 192–3

Wife of Bath (in *Canterbury Tales*) 66, 67, 83, 84, 102, 119, 121, 141, 156, 176, 177, 185, 187, 256, 262, 277

Wife of Bath's Prologue 55–9, 67, 72, 83, 141, 156, 177, 178, 180, 185, 187, 276, 277

Wife of Bath's Tale 61, 71–2

Wimsatt, W. K. 169–74

Wolfram of Eschenbach (12th century) German poet, author of lyric, epic and romance (*Parzival*) 97

Woolf, Rosemary 206–14

Woolf, Virginia (1882–1941) 125–6

Wordsworth, William (1770–1850) The modernization of *Prioress's Tale* composed, together with other versions of Chaucer, in 1801 and published in 1820 99, 126, 143

Wyatt, Sir Thomas (?1503–42) Poet and courtier, best known for love lyrics and sonnets 33, 49

Wycliffe, John (d. 1384) Religious reformer who attacked the worldliness of the medieval church 64, 274

Yeoman (in *Canterbury Tales*) 77, 78, 173, 174

Zephirus Personification of the West Wind (*Canterbury Tales*, 1 5) 216

Penguin Critical Anthologies

Published simultaneously with Geoffrey Chaucer

Andrew Marvell Edited by John Carey

Part One Contemporaneous Criticism, Neglect and Revival

Introduction. John Milton, Samuel Parker, William Lisle Bowles, Mark Pattison, Hartley Coleridge, Edgar Allan Poe, Edward FitzGerald, Goldwin Smith, Alfred Lord Tennyson, Alice Meynell, T. S. Eliot.

Part Two Modern Views

Introduction. The Setting: Christopher Hill, F. W. Bateson, Patrick Cruttwell, J. B. Leishman, Susan Shrapnel. *General Estimates:* William Empson, Joseph H. Summers, Robert Ellrodt, J. B. Broadbent, S. L. Goldberg, Yvor Winters. *An Horation Ode:* Cleanth Books, Douglas Bush. *To his Coy Mistress:* John Crowe Ransom, J. V. Cunningham, Barbara Herrnstein Smith, René Wellek and Austin Warren, Harold E. Toliver, R. S. Crane. *The Garden:* William Empson, John McChesney, Don A. Keister, Frank Kermode, Pierre Legouis. *The Nymph Complaining for the Death of Her Fawn:* E. S. LeComte, Karina Williamson. *Upon Appleton House:* Maren-Sofie Røstvig, Robin Grove, Harold E. Toliver, Kitty Scoular. *The Gallery:* Winifred Nowottny. *Mourning:* Winifred Nowottny. *The Satires:* George De F. Lord.

John Carey is a Fellow of St John's College and Lecturer in English at the University of Oxford. He has edited Milton's poems (with Alistair Fowler, 1968) and James Hogg's *Confessions of a Justified Sinner* (1969), and has published a critical book on Milton (1969).

Walt Whitman Edited by Francis Murphy

Part One Contemporaneous Criticism

Introduction. Ralph Waldo Emerson, Walt Whitman, Edward Everett Hale, Henry David Thoreau, William Howitt, Henry James, William Dean Howells, Matthew Arnold, John Burroughs, Algernon Charles Swinburne, Gerard Manley Hopkins, George Santayana, Edward Dowden.

Part Two The Developing Debate

Introduction. Henry James, John Jay Chapman, George Santayana, William James, G. K. Chesterton, Paul Elmer More, Bliss Perry, Ezra Pound, Basil de Selincourt, D. H. Lawrence, T. S. Eliot, Amy Lowell, Constance Rourke, Frederick Schyberg, D. Mirsky.

Part Three Modern Views

Introduction. Newton Arvin, F. O. Matthiessen, Lionel Trilling, Yvor Winters, Randall Jarrell, Charles Feidelson Jr, William Carlos Williams, Richard Chase, Malcolm Cowley, Leslie Fielder, Roy Harvey Pearce, Roger Asselineau, Gay Wilson Allen, Martin Green, Denis Donoghue, R. W. B. Lewis, Louis Simpson.

Francis Murphy, the editor of this exceptionally full collection of writing on and by Whitman, has also edited an anthology of *Major American Poets* (1967) and volumes of essays on *Poetry: Form and Structure* (1964) and *Edwin Arlington Robinson* (1969). He is Associate Professor of English at Smith College, Massachusetts.

John Webster Edited by G. K. and S. K. Hunter

Part One Contemporaneous Criticism

Introduction. John Webster, Henry Fitzjeffrey, Orazio Busino, Thomas Middleton, William Rowley, John Ford, Abraham Wright, Samuel Sheppard, Samuel Pepys, Lewis Theobald, Philip Frowde.

Part Two The Developing Debate

Introduction. Charles Lamb, George Darley, R. H. Horne, Charles Kingsley, George Daniel, A. C. Swinburne, John Addington Symonds, William Archer, William Poel, Rupert Brooke, T. S. Eliot.

Part Three Modern Views

Introduction. T. S. Eliot, W. A. Edwards, U. Ellis-Fermor, James Smith, M. C. Bradbrook, Edmund Wilson, David Cecil, Ian Jack, Gabriele Baldini, Travis Bogard, Hereward T. Price, Inga-Stina Ekeblad, R. W. Dent, J. R. Brown, G. K. Hunter, Harold Jenkins, James L. Calderwood, Clifford Leech, Elizabeth Brennan, William Empson, A. W. Allison.

This volume on Webster is the first survey and anthology of Webster criticism to be published, and the account of stage and other adaptations draws on new material. G. K. Hunter is Professor of English at the University of Warwick; Mrs S. K. Hunter is Lecturer in English at Coventry College of Education.

Edmund Spenser Edited by Paul J. Alpers

Part One Contemporaneous Criticism

Introduction. E. K., Edmund Spenser, Gabriel Harvey, Sir Philip Sidney, William Webbe, Sir Walter Raleigh, Joseph Hall, Everard Guilpin, Edmund Bolton, Robert Salter, Henry Reynolds, Ben Jonson, Sir Kenelm Digby, John Milton, Sir William Davenant.

Part Two Neoclassical and Romantic Criticism

Introduction. Thomas Rymer, John Dryden, Joseph Addison, Alexander Pope, Matthew Prior, John Hughes, Joseph Spence, Samuel Johnson, Thomas Warton, Joseph Warton, Richard Hurd, S. T. Coleridge, William Wordsworth, William Hazlitt, John Keats, Charles Lamb, Sir Walter Scott, John Ruskin, James Russell Lowell, Edward Dowden, Walter Raleigh, W. B. Yeats.

Part Three Modern Views

Introduction. William Empson, C. S. Lewis, D. A. Traversi, G. Wilson Knight, Hallet Smith, C. S. Lewis, Yvor Winters, Alastair Fowler, Harry Berger Jr, Frank Kermode, Northrop Frye, Rosemond Tuve, Martha Craig, Paul J. Alpers, Roger Sale.

Paul J. Alpers, the editor of this comprehensive anthology of Spenser criticism, has also edited *Elizabethan Poetry: Modern Essays in Criticism* (1967) and is the author of *The Poetry of 'The Faerie Queene'* (1967). He is Associate Professor of English in the University of California at Berkeley.